Ambidextrous Leadership

Julia Duwe

Ambidextrous Leadership

How leaders unlock innovation through
ambidexterity

 Springer

Julia Duwe
Stuttgart, Baden-Württemberg
Germany

ISBN 978-3-662-64034-0   ISBN 978-3-662-64032-6   (eBook)
https://doi.org/10.1007/978-3-662-64032-6

This book is a translation of the original German edition „Beidhändige Führung" by Duwe, Julia, published by Springer-Verlag GmbH, DE in 2018. The translation was done with the help of artificial intelligence (machine translation by the service DeepL.com). A subsequent human revision was done primarily in terms of content, so that the book will read stylistically differently from a conventional translation. Springer Nature works continuously to further the development of tools for the production of books and on the related technologies to support the authors.

This Springer imprint is published by the registered company Springer-Verlag GmbH, DE, part of Springer Nature.
The registered company address is: Heidelberger Platz 3, 14197 Berlin, Germany

Foreword to the Second Edition

A culture of leadership is needed - now more than ever
—By Dr. Eberhard Veit

Since the publication of the book *Ambidextrous Leadership* in December 2017, the business world has been changing rapidly. Industrial companies are transforming toward data-driven service providers. Traditional markets are giving way to global ecosystems. Technologies are changing entire industries and domains. And yet, or precisely for this reason, the concept of ambidexterity is more relevant than ever.

Both strategically and in terms of leadership, companies today find themselves as never before in a constant *tug-of-war* between a known world and an uncertain future. We have to expect serious events like the global Corona Crisis in 2020 to repeat themselves at any time. Stability is no longer guaranteed. We must prepare ourselves for this world.

As a strong believer in the idea of ambidextrous leadership, I want to stretch the concept of ambidexterity far beyond its original meaning. Beyond the trade-off between exploration and exploitation I plead in favor of a *multi-handed* corporate leadership that confronts contradictions at all levels. It is a management that identifies the opportunities in precisely these contradictions and that actively shapes the future by means of these opportunities.

Let me coin the term "four-dimensional ambidexterity" for this. The four dimensions of ambidexterity are the transformation-environment factor (TEF), the political-environment factor (PEF), the event-environment factor (EEF), and finally the leadership-environment factor (LEF).

Behind the TEF we find the three T's: technology, technical engineering, and transformation. The PEF e.g. is characterized by the keywords local, regional, and global, including political currents and trends, whereas the EEF is often shaped by environmental factors such as special events, hypes, or crises with regard to health and the political situation. Always present, but also dependent on culture and economics, however, is the LEF with leadership, culture, people, as well as the organization with regard to governance, decision-making processes, and committees.

For all four dimensions, both a horizontal and a vertical shift of the megatrends is to be expected. While horizontally a reaction by the STRATEGY of the company becomes necessary, vertically a reaction by the TACTICS applies, and this within the company. These are "both/and" areas of tension to which we as management and corporate leadership must react decisively.

Technology, Technical Engineering, Transformation (TEF)

For the strategy dimension of technology, technical engineering, and transformation in industry, it is most important to improve the old and the tried and tested while building the new digital and data-driven world (horizontally). The vertical axis, however, describes the tactics of existing business models and customer relationships of companies challenged by new digital business models and new customer relationships. Digital here means *direct, on-site, real time* with the customer. The opportunities created by data-driven business models are immeasurable. But companies must prepare for this in terms of strategy and tactics systematically and at great speed.

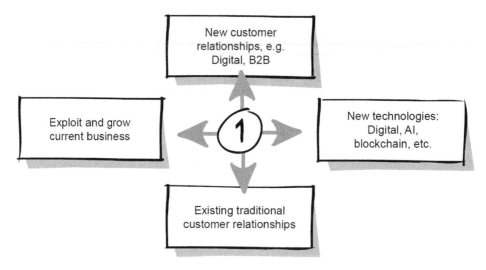

Ambidexterity dimension No. 1: Transformation-environment factor (TEF)

Local, Regional, and Global (PEF)

In strategic terms (horizontally) with regard to the political-environment factors "local, regional, and global," including the political currents and trends of recent years, companies and entire industries must manage the tensions between the regions USA and China with the *sandwich position* of Europe. Concerning the vertical tactics axis, the global versus the local business strategy and corporate resilience within the value creation must be balanced carefully by the management.

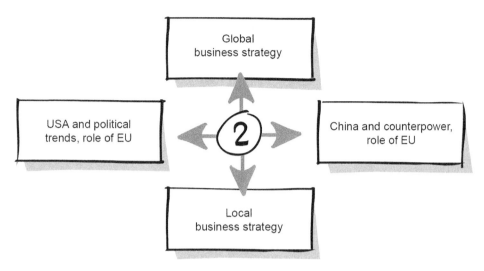

Ambidexterity dimension No. 2: Political-environment factor (PEF)

Event-Environment Factor (EEF)

With regard to the environmental factors "hypes, health crises, and the political situation," ambidexterity is also required to balance tensions. So on the one hand it is necessary to find the strategic balance between reactive and proactive action when trends and game changers from outside affect the company. And at the same time, in the case of multinational companies, the question of the autonomy of the local entities is decisive in regard to such influences.

A suitable example for this is the reaction of a global company to the corona crisis (cf. Chap. 6), which developed from a local to a global issue. The poles of possible tactics (vertical dimension) in response to the crisis range, on the one hand, from the headquarters ignoring the local problem to, on the other hand, excessive intervention by the headquarters. In times of crisis, it is particularly important to balance whether autonomous action by local entities or strong steering from the head office makes sense. It is therefore all the more important to master the vertical field of tension between a "controlled autonomy" and a loosely "guided autonomy" as best as possible.

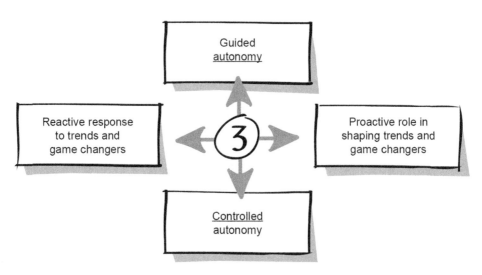

Ambidexterity dimension No. 3: Event-environment factor (EEF)

Leadership, People, and Organization (LEF)

Tools of ambidextrous leadership in organization, people, governance, decision-making, and committees are the factors of organizational operations and processes that need to be urgently dealt with. From strict hierarchy up to agile working environments, every approach needs to be considered. In the horizontal strategy dimension of this four-quadrant, it is necessary to determine to what extent control and leadership are necessary and how far freedom and self-organization are required to achieve the best and most successful results.

Also, the vertical tactics dimension, which describes a realignment of responsibilities and decision-making guidelines, is to be adjusted. It is precisely the question of tactics and thus the corporate hierarchy that is one of the essential factors for the future, for it is increasingly being observed how important well-organized "steering and control" in fact is in order to act quickly and make clear decisions in companies. What new role will shareholders and supervisory boards play in the future and according to which rules will these bodies act?

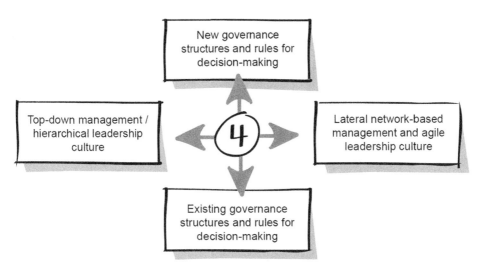

Ambidexterity dimension No. 4: Leadership-environment factor (LEF)

The four ambidextrous dimensions of technology (TEF), politics (PEF), events (EEF), and leadership and people (LEF) are an approach to illustrate the complexity of corporate management in the years and decades to come. If we manage to move from a rigid view of the world to an utmost flexibility in dealing with contradictions, we will have a good chance to master the leap into the future successfully, both strategically and tactically, and walk through the finish line as winners.

This leap begins within the organization. From the global perspective, I would therefore like to invite you to dive into the micro level of the company and familiarize yourself with the basics of ambidextrous thinking and acting. A new culture of leadership is needed—now more than ever. Three years after the first publication of "*Ambidextrous Leadership*", I therefore recommend this book to you once again.

Göppingen, Germany   Eberhard Veit
June 2020

Foreword to the First Edition

What Industry 4.0 means for leaders: From agile sprints to ambidextrous leadership
—By Dr. Eberhard Veit

Many years ago, when I was a CEO at Festo, I was able to observe the speed with which people accepted the effects of digitalization in their private lives. At that time, I met consumers who enthusiastically embraced the latest technologies and services. And at the same time, it was all the more frustrating to observe how reluctant industry was to embrace the newly available digital technologies. I kept asking myself at that time again and again, "We all have smartphones. Companies like eBay and Amazon are spawning entirely new business models. But why doesn't this change make its way into industry?" As a consequence, I fundamentally changed my leadership style and from then on practiced something we now call "ambidextrous leadership." In addition to the evolutionary development of the core business, I systematically created space for the future digital business.

Today, it is critical to success and of central importance for organizations in both private and public sectors to accept and embrace new technologies in order to remain competitive. In Germany, the *Plattform Industrie 4.0* initiated by the federal government ensures a close exchange between government and industry representatives with the goal of strengthening the global competitiveness of Germany's as well as Europe's industry. As part of my role in Germany's supervisory board for the *Plattform Industrie 4.0*, I advocate and actively support not only an "evolutionary revolution" in regard to technology, but also the radical transformation of leadership in organizations. This change must begin in supervisory and executive boards and extend throughout the entire organization. I have a clear vision of the kind of leadership required to successfully navigate the digital transformation.

In order to motivate people to fully embrace a digital culture and to also meet the expectations of customers for the future, as Chairman of the *Plattform Industrie 4.0* initiative, I have to follow the four C's of transformation myself: "Culture, Content, taking a Chance, starting the Change." It is about creating a new culture, about communicating the right content, about the courage and willingness to take risks, and about actively shaping the change. It is not only the management that needs to be part of a bold, long-term vision of digitalization but the entire organization. Each individual must therefore support ambidextrous leadership so that we can successfully transform today's business while looking far into the future.

Involving the Whole Company

My formula for digital transformation is **"SPRINT"**:

- **S**pirit/Speed
- **P**articipation
- **R**eliance
- **I**nspiration
- **N**eed
- **T**rust

The digital world will inevitably permeate the entire enterprise. It will change the way a company operates at all levels. CEOs must therefore unite the entire organization under the banner of urgency. They must not only embody the **spirit** and exemplify the **speed** that change requires, but also create a culture of open communication and active **participation**. They must encourage the entire company to act in unison and learn to fully accept and **rely** on the new digital systems as well. The role of the CEO is to **inspire** people throughout the organization to align their thinking and actions with new digital processes and methods, to understand how the new tools will be used, and to recognize the **need** for transformation. Finally, the process of change requires the people's **trust** in the new technologies and practices.

On the basis of these principles, I was able to guide Festo through the digital transformation process. They also form my recommendations for the Industry 4.0. They furthermore contain five key elements, which I summarize under the term **"AGILE,"** which is my second formula:

1. **A**rchitecture
2. **G**eneral business models
3. **I**nnovation
4. **L**earning
5. **E**ducation

1. **Architecture:** Flexible, architecture-based products and components work together collaboratively in a network and can be integrated intuitively.
2. **General business models:** New business models result from new ways of organizing manufacturing as well as from cross-company networks and effective collaboration.
3. **Innovation:** European companies must produce better and more innovative products and services, as they generally develop and produce their products at a much higher cost: we can and must do better by at least as much as we are more expensive.

4. **Learning:** We need an attitude of lifelong learning and a willingness to continuously acquire new skills.
5. **Education:** We need a clear commitment to invest in people's knowledge, to develop their skills through state-of-the-art training programs, and to continuously invest in re- and upskilling.

Hiring and Promoting Talent

If we want to become fit for digitalization, do we have to bring completely new skills and people on board? I think not. But I recommend a mix of new talents and experienced long-term employees, because success will be largely based on training and educating people. I deliberately emphasize that technological change alone will not be enough to transform industry. It is the people in the organizations that need to be continuously trained and educated—an area that is far too often overlooked.

Last year, Germany spent EUR 12.4 billion euros (2016) on new technologies, but only 1.2 billion euros were invested in training and education to prepare people for the digital age. We urgently need to speed up in this field. We need to get people in organizations on the right track and at the same time support universities and training institutions. I am convinced that 50% of our success will be technology, but 50% will be leadership, training, and lifelong learning.

I therefore believe that supervisory boards in particular will play a crucial role in the transformation of the industry. Management must orchestrate the entire transformation along the four C's. The people in supervisory boards, on the other hand, must focus on the strategies and risks and on putting the right people in place. Therefore, they too need to be prepared for digitalization and Industry 4.0 so that they really understand what boards and executives are reporting. In turn, supervisory boards must also trust and rely on company managements. And that requires a real cultural change!

I do not favor frantically clinging to outdated management models or traditional organizational structures. We rather need to change now and renew the way how industry operates. And we need to do it quickly. There is no more time now for numerous static business plans.

As we are moving into a new era of confidence in the digital industry, I want to strongly emphasize that agile, ambidextrous leadership will be the key driver for the success of digitalization and the fourth industrial revolution. After all, companies will only be successful in the long run if their leaders take the change and focus intensively on the leap into digital future against the backdrop of today's core business.

I wish you many new insights while reading this inspiring book.

Göppingen, Germany   Eberhard Veit
June 2017

Acknowledgments

Since the publication of the dissertation *Ambidexterity, Leadership and Communication* in 2016, the communication-based model of ambidextrous leadership has been constantly evolved. It was by the end of 2016 that the idea to publish a practice-oriented book on ambidextrous leadership was born. The intention was to create a solid scientific basis to explain the topical field-tested tools for the daily life of an ambidextrous company and to share the experiences with other leaders. In 2020, the book moreover included an interview study on ambidextrous leadership during the time of the COVID-19 crisis.

Ambidextrous Leadership is a handbook for leaders and a report of experiences from daily professional life. Being deeply involved in the digital transformation while working on this book, I was able to meet various people and I found myself in unique situations that you only can experience during times of transformation or exceptional crisis. These are empirical insights from a professional balancing act between today's corporate world with all its tensions and a constantly emerging digital, data-driven future. I would like to thank all those colleagues who were directly or indirectly involved in driving the two worlds forward for sharing their experiences with me.

Furthermore, I would like to give my thanks to all those who kept reading the manuscript again and again during its development for their helpful advice and discussions. In particular, I would like to thank the editor at Springer Verlag, **Christine Sheppard,** for her comprehensive and encouraging support.

I am especially indebted to the author of the foreword, Dr. Eberhard Veit, to the interview partners of the first edition, and to the six new interview partners of the second edition of this book.

In the course of my professional life, I have been lucky to meet these people in different places in the environment of industry and research. They struck me as people who are deeply involved in processes of change. They actively encourage change in their environment and are constantly busy with the question of how people can be led in today's VUCA world with its constant new challenges and crises into an exciting future worth living. For this reason, they were selected for this project and the interviews were incorporated into the book *Ambidextrous Leadership* enthusiastically.

In alphabetical order, I would like to thank in detail: Prof. Dr. Manfred Aigner, director of the Institute of Combustion Technology at the German Aerospace Center (DLR) in Stuttgart; Dennis van Beers, managing director Cluster Benelux of the automation solutions provider FESTO in Delft; Prof. Dr. Wilhelm Bauer, managing director of the Fraunhofer Institute for Industrial Engineering IAO in Stuttgart and technology representative of the State of Baden-Württemberg; Thomas Fischer, chairman of the supervisory board of MANN+HUMMEL; Prof. Dr. Ronald Gleich, professor of management practice and control at the Frankfurt School of Finance & Management in Frankfurt am Main; Dr. Constanze Holzwarth, psychologist and top management consultant; Anne Elisabeth Krüger, innovation researcher and expert for user-driven innovation and user experience at the Fraunhofer Institute for Industrial Engineering IAO in Stuttgart; Andreas Leinfelder, vice president of business development at Bosch Power Tools GmbH; Prof. Dr. Hans Müller-Steinhagen, former rector of the Technical University of Dresden; Prof. Dr. Volker Nestle, chairman of the board of Hahn-Schickard-Gesellschaft für angewandte Forschung; Karin Pahl, owner of PAHL Resilienz-Förderung in Bremen; Wiltrud Pekarek, member of the management board of HALLESCHE Krankenversicherung aG; Gregor Pillen, chairman of the management board of IBM Deutschland GmbH; Frank Riemensperger, chairman of the management board of Accenture Deutschland; and Dr. Eberhard Veit, owner of 4.0-veIT GmbH.

Contents

About the Author

Julia Duwe has been working as a leader in the research and development environment of high-tech companies and research organizations, including FESTO, TRUMPF, and the German Aerospace Center (DLR) for many years. In her daily professional life she deals with the transformation of businesses, respective product architectures, and organizations toward the digital, data-driven world and accompanies teams in multidisciplinary, cross-company high-tech ecosystems.

Julia Duwe studied communication, business administration, and American studies at the Johannes Gutenberg University Mainz and the University of Bergen in Norway. From 2013 to 2016, she completed her PhD at the European Business School (EBS) Wiesbaden on the role of leadership communication in ambidextrous technology companies.

As an expert in digital leadership, ecosystem management, and organizational ambidexterity as well as an author and blogger, she focuses on the question how companies drive their core business forward while simultaneously opening up new business fields in a digital platform economy. In 2019, she was accepted into the thought leader community of Handelsblatt and the Boston Consulting Group (BCG) for the area of "Digital and Analytics." Since 2020, Julia Duwe has been a member of the University Council of the Technische Universität Dresden.

The author's website: www.ambidextrie.de

Introduction: The Trade-Off

Abstract

Evolution or revolution? Today companies all over the world face an unprecedented trade-off between today's core business and future business opportunities. They must improve their products and services dramatically to remain competitive in global markets and fierce price wars. At the same time, against the background of digitalization and artificial intelligence, they must shape the future with radically new ideas to keep the organization viable for a long time. While evolution pays the salaries, revolution must guarantee future success. And both worlds must also increasingly stand completely unpredictable crises.

Moving constantly in diametrically opposed worlds is a balancing act that requires utmost flexibility and adaptability from organizations and the people who work in them. Corporate success today requires that you master *both*: evolution and revolution. Leadership today means orchestrating both present and future and driving *both worlds* in a similar manner.

1.1 Evolution or Revolution?

How can firms navigate the digital transformation successfully? How can companies manage the change? Which ways, methods, structures are best to make the leap into the future? If you ask managers these questions, you will rarely hear agreement. We know for sure that there is no way to avoid digitization, but at the same time a recipe for a successful transformation doesn't exist. Yet the demands on organizations in a digital environment grow exponentially. According to analysts, the number of networked Internet of Things (IoT-) devices will increase to 125 billion by 2030, with an average annual growth rate of

© Springer-Verlag GmbH Germany, part of Springer Nature 2022
J. Duwe, *Ambidextrous Leadership*,
https://doi.org/10.1007/978-3-662-64032-6_1

12%. Global data traffic is expected to increase from today's 20–25% annual growth to an average of 50% growth per year within the next 15 years [1].

On the long run only those companies will successfully master the way into the digital, data-driven world that actively shape their future and that assert themselves in a new, digital and competitive ecosystem. The efforts here range from hesitant to absolutely consequent acting: "From 2025 on, every Bosch product will contain artificial intelligence or has been developed or produced with its help," declares industrial company BOSCH before the start of the Consumer Electronics Show CES 2020 in Las Vegas [2]. But the demands on companies are more diverse than ever. AI and the IoT confront each sector and each industry with special and unique challenges.

If a company already operates on the side of the Internet, it needs to enter into partnerships with the hardware world, e.g. to move just as elegantly in the smart factory environment of the Industry 4.0 at the field level of intelligent hardware components as at the level of data-based factory control. If an organization is one of the 'thing makers' in the IoT, its strategy is to increasingly expand its IT, software, and data competencies. The aim is to develop networked hardware products into intelligent systems that provide the customer with the best service at all times on the basis of data. These data-driven systems accompany the customer's process around the clock with sensors, read every wish from his lips and adapt independently and with constant new services to the user's changing needs.

How to Succeed in Making the Leap into the Future
But how do product and service providers make this leap into the future? How can the transformation from an automobile manufacturer to a provider of mobility as a service succeed? And how does a manufacturer of components for automation technology become a provider of productivity on demand for the smart factory? How do machine tools become digitally networked data factories? How do filters in combustion engines become intelligent everyday helpers for people in a globalized world? How can we leap into the future even though our current business successfully pays our salaries?

Harvard Business School professor Clayton M. Christensen pointed out the conflict of very successful companies already in 1997 in his much-quoted work "The Innovator's Dilemma". While these firms gain rich profits from today's business, they are at the same time in danger of missing the moment to jump into the future. Especially in times of growth and profitability, however, it is important to invest in new technologies and business models at an early stage—and *even more when* the new solutions completely call the current business into question [3].

In order not to miss the introduction of future solutions despite intense competitive pressure in the core business and *precisely to avoid* falling into the dilemma depicted in Fig. 1.1, companies must orchestrate both worlds in equal measure: present and future. "On the one hand, we need to further develop our structures, products and processes, but, on the other hand, we also need completely new technologies, products and solutions," Ansgar Kriwet, Chief Sales Officer at Festo AG, explained the tension and the ambidextrous strategy of the automation company at the Hannover Messe 2017 [4]. *Evolution*, which

Fig. 1.1   Too busy to innovate? (source: Own illustration inspired by R. van den Bergh [5])

means continuous development and improvement of the automation components for mechanical and plant engineering and global mass markets here goes hand in hand with *revolution*, the leap into the world of intelligent automation solutions for the Industry 4.0.

Companies with Dual Strategies

"From car manufacturer to a company with a dual strategy", headlined the Sueddeutsche Zeitung on the occasion of the 100th birthday of the German automotive company BMW in March 2016 [6]. The newspaper explained the term "disruption" as follows: "One technology replaces another; disruptions happen—maybe even total breaks with the past" [6]. In many companies it is currently visible how two completely opposing worlds collide, how e.g. the combustion engine not only competes with alternative driving concepts, but right away with new and data-based solutions for future mobility. And here a simple approach will help to resolve this conflict. In the transition period, companies will need *both worlds*, because there is no revolution without evolution: "At some point, the BMW Group has to make the big leap," says Tony Douglas, BMW's digital man. "When it comes, we have to organize it in such a way that evolution pays for the revolution" [6].

No matter if automation solutions for the Industry 4.0 or mobility services of the future—these are only selected examples that show that industry is undergoing radical change. And in the course of the digital transformation, however, companies are not only confronted with *technological* change. Already in 2013, the German Academy of Engineering Sciences "Acatech" called for a *"socio-technical* approach" in its recommendations for action for Industry 4.0 [7]. In order to constantly produce new smart products and services for customers worldwide, new forms of collaboration must also be designed. Thus the focus is therefore on the core processes of firms. In these processes, such as research and development, it is essential to always come up with new solutions that secure the companies' leap into the future and inspire the customers.

Mass Personalization

Because what do customers want? On the one hand, industry must be able to serve global mass markets in order to meet the demand for products of soon to be eight billion people (as of May 2020) worldwide [8]. On the other hand, the demands on manufacturing companies to respond to customer wishes in an increasingly targeted manner and to deliver individualized solutions are increasing. "Digitally transformed organizations perform much better in offering their customers a highly personalized service and even hyper-personalize their value propositions," explains management consultant company Accenture [9]. A cross-institute study by the German Fraunhofer-Gesellschaft sees huge market potential for companies in this area. In the study "Mass Personalization", the authors recommend a consistent "Business to User" (B2U) approach and show how personalized products and services are increasingly changing value creation processes in companies [10].

Future business models for personalized products and services could no longer be traditionally categorized as B2B and B2C, but will instead follow the logic of the *B2U*. In the world described, user needs will always continue to change. Products will be defined "as the sum of their services throughout the life cycle". The real added value only arises through their connectivity. In this world, companies consistently put the user at the center. They develop a comprehensive understanding of the users' needs and desires, and they involve the user in the innovation process [10].

And apart from this: Just because a product has been launched on the market, it is far from being finished. Entire ecosystems are now emerging around the product, in which communities use digital services to further individualize and customize the original solution. The customer is continuously involved in this development process. That is a paradigm shift in R+D that must be mastered today and in the future: It is not only value creation *within* companies that will develop into "changeable, flexible networked value creation systems", but more and more *cross-company* cooperation will be needed to meet the customer's requirements [10]. Thus, it is no longer technological innovations alone that save companies a place in the market. It is rather the way in which they cooperate, and act in networks and communities and their ability to take a leading role in value creation ecosystems that extend far beyond corporate boundaries (Chap. 3).

Commoditization

But back to the present. Next to the world of digital ecosystems, industrial companies continue to manage the core business at full speed. Here the markets are globalized and saturated, the technologies fully developed. And while products are becoming commodities, prices sinking to rock-bottom levels and companies continue to struggle with their costs, the strategy is primarily to be better than the competitor. In order to be able to—on the long run—shape the future at all, companies must first master the present (Chap. 4). Customer wishes must be fulfilled, the company must be in the black and sales growth must be achieved. Only those who operate successfully here and now will have sufficient resources to finance the great leap into the future.

So here we are in the ambidextrous organization. Whether globalization, commoditization, digitization, constant shorter life cycles of products, intensified price competition or disruptive technologies—in a highly dynamic market and technology environment it is essential to have the right response to *all* external influences (Fig. 1.2). The fact that external influences recently also include completely unpredictable crises will be explored in detail in Chap. 6.

1.2 In the Digital Transformation, Ambidexterity Is a Key Leadership Skill

In the ambidextrous organization, executives are challenged everyday to drive the present business forward in a highly efficient manner while simultaneously venturing into new, unknown territory. Leaps in innovation are designed to secure the company's future, while optimizing today's business ensures that salaries are paid and customer needs are met immediately.

This is where the book *Ambidextrous Leadership* comes in. As ambidexterity is the key competence for globally operating industrial companies, it prepares leaders for new tasks in the course of digitalization. In the course of the transformation, contradictory innovation approaches are more and more required. Evolution *and* revolution are the two worlds in which leaders must move today.

However, it is precisely in the environment of the *revolution* that often shows the deficits of leaders: "Managers put the brakes on digital transformation" was the headline of the industry magazine Scope in January 2017 [11]. The *German Mittelstand News* notes "knowledge gaps among managers" [12]. The online portal CIO reads: "Executives are oversleeping digitalization" [13]. So what can we do to counteract this trend?

Digital Competence Through Ambidextrous Leadership

This book argues that digital competence does not emerge when managers are retrained into data, software and IT experts; nor does it emerge when successful companies throw their structures and modes of operation overboard, abstain from hierarchies altogether, and fully adopt a start-up culture. Digital competence can emerge at its best when leaders detach themselves from the model of the all-knowing superior and instead continuously learn and develop their networking and communication skills.

With increasingly complex demands on products and services, with an unstoppable merging of hardware, software and services into a single solution offering, the concept of the omniscient boss is outdated. Instead, the market requires completely new leadership skills that are just as critical to success as the detailed knowledge of a technical discipline.

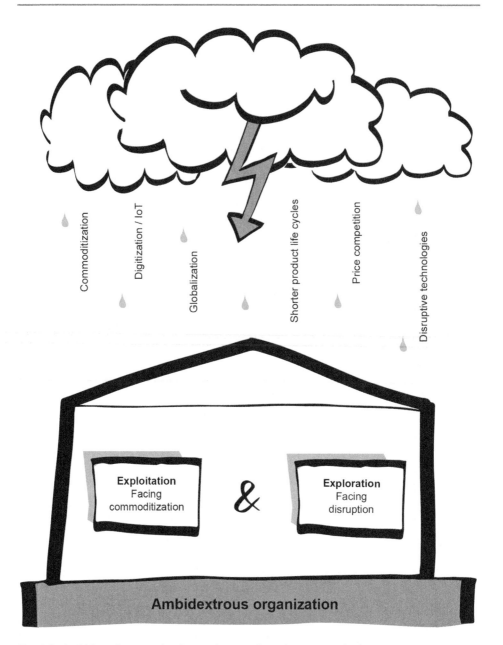

Fig. 1.2 Ambidexterity: opposing innovation paradigms in one organization

In addition to the knowledge of complex control algorithms, networking software, data analytics or IT infrastructures, the development of business models and the establishment of internal and external ecosystems keep playing an increasingly important role. Networking disciplines and the introduction and mastering of collaborative innovation cultures with flat hierarchies are only a few skills that are mandatory for leaders in this environment. And this marks the beginning of a fundamental change of views in the grasp of leadership.

The central leadership competence that applies in both evolutionary and revolutionary environments and combines both worlds is ambidexterity [14, 15]. "Ambidexterity" means the ability to use both hands equally well [16]. Transferred to companies, it describes that on the one hand current product programs have to be optimized and trimmed for adequate cost efficiency (exploitation), while in addition to this new product categories and solution spaces (exploration) emerge [17]. In ambidextrous organizations, price competition *and* technological leaps, radical cost reduction programs *and* investments in R&D, tradition *and* future are orchestrated simultaneously (Fig. 1.2).

Exploration and Exploitation

Ambidexterity researchers Michael Tushman, Wendy Smith and Andy Binns attribute a central role in this field to senior leaders, board members and general managers [18]. In their Harvard Business Review article, "The Ambidextrous CEO" the authors elaborate on three leadership principles that enable ambidexterity [18]. From corporate leaders they require

1. The involvement of the senior leadership team in a forward-looking strategic direction,
2. The explicit withstanding of tensions between innovation units and core business in top management as well as
3. Embracing the inconsistency that arises from maintaining opposing strategic approaches.

According to the authors it helps companies grow, when the leadership teams welcome the tension between the old and the new and when they not only stand a state of constant conflict at the top, but bring it about and balance it consciously [18]. Examples for this are found in industry numerously. Companies increasingly describe the need to be successful in the present while anticipating the future at the same time: Also the car manufacturer Porsche relies on the combination of tradition and innovation in its Strategy 2025: "We combine tradition with the future" declares CEO Oliver Blume on the occasion of the brand's 70th birthday [19].

But how exactly does leadership work when companies are committed to two strategic directions both at a time? How can leaders implement *ambidexterity* in their daily work? And how is it possible to move and to promote and support teams in *both* worlds? A central answer to these questions given in the book is the daily communication of leaders. It shows how they can influence simultaneous exploitation and exploration through their communicative actions and thus drive both worlds and combine them profitably (Fig. 1.3).

Fig. 1.3 Ambidexterity is a new leadership competence

1.3   Overview of Chapters

1.3.1   Objective and Solution Approach

Ambidextrous Leadership is a book for leaders who want to get their organization ready for the world of data and AI. Whether in mechanical and plant engineering, IT, the automotive industry, chemicals and pharmaceuticals, food industry or the energy sector—it addresses across industries and sectors all those companies that want to develop real competitive advantages in global markets by innovative strength. The book addresses leaders in all areas of business and innovation:

1. Leaders who are involved in the creation and commercialization of products and services with their teams and tasks in the areas of research, development, production, sales, marketing, logistics;
2. Leaders who design new processes, methods and procedures in process-oriented areas such as quality, controlling, strategy and planning or process development;
3. Leaders who implement new methods and ways of working and thereby change the corporate culture of organizations sustainably;
4. Leaders who, in an environment of crisis, are looking for new courses of action in order to lead people and organizations through the crisis and into the future in a stable and also flexible and versatile manner (Excursus Chap. 6).

Ambidextrous Leadership was also written for a broad audience of people working in the business and economic environment of digital products and services. It addresses executives as well as scientists, lecturers, students and consultants with a focus on innovation, management and communication for the digital transformation.

The Solution Approach

The solution approach of this book is called *ambidexterity through communication.* The book answers the question of how ambidexterity can be implemented in professional life and how leadership approaches can be easily combined with forward-looking new approaches. It shows precise ways and means how leaders succeed in driving the present business forward and at the same time keeping a permanent eye on the future direction of the company. Numerous practical examples and precise implementation tips for everyday management illustrate how the trade-off can be turned into an elegant balancing act with the help of simple communication tools.

Besides the daily experiences of the author herself, *Ambidextrous Leadership* is based on statements by leaders from German industrial companies who have already become familiar with the challenges in the field of Industry 4.0 and digitalization from their own daily work. As part of a research study [20], managers in the high technology sector were surveyed between 2013 and 2017 about which behavioral patterns they use every day to achieve specific goals in terms of exploration or exploitation. In particular, the study examined the communication behavior of senior leaders operating in the context of exploitation, exploration, and as well in both worlds simultaneously. The results of the study showed that their communicative behavior varied according to the innovation context—exploration or exploitation—and ranged from strictly hierarchically organized communication management to the orchestration of open networks. The results of the study were summarized in a communication-based model of ambidextrous leadership and form the basis of this book.

The Objective

Complementary to the German research study *Ambidexterity, Leadership and Communication* [20] published in 2016, which is an intensive dialogue with science, *Ambidextrous Leadership* is primarily a practical book for everyday leadership in the environment of digitalization and AI. The results of the research, which have meanwhile been tested several times, and the experience gained by the communication-based ambidextrous leadership approach have been updated and prepared for the reader in a leadership handbook.

As long as organizational ambidexterity and ambidextrous leadership still seem to be an exceptional topic in the executive floors of institutions and corporations and as long as ambidextrous leaders are still isolated cases, the leap into digital future will hardly succeed. A long-term sustainability of organizations will only unfold if today's understanding of leadership undergoes a fundamental change, if evolution is used to enable revolution and if leaders move on familiar terrain in both worlds. *Ambidextrous Leadership* provides helpful tools that leaders need not to retard digitization, but to use it as an opportunity and drive it forward.

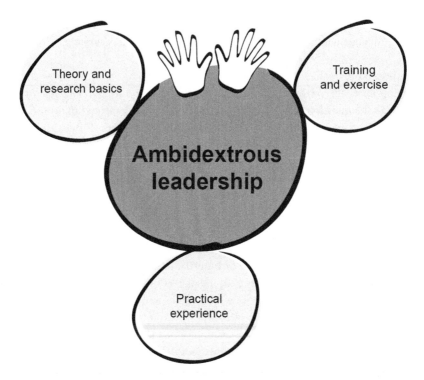

Fig. 1.4 The three perspectives of this book: theory, practice, training

The book was written from three different perspectives (Fig. 1.4):

1. Theory and research basics
2. Training and exercise
3. Practical experience

1. **Theory and research basics:** *Ambidextrous Leadership* has a sound scientific basis. It is built on the scientific research on ambidexterity and includes the aspect of leadership communication. The content is scientifically substantiated by empirical case studies [20].
2. **Training and exercise:** *Ambidextrous Leadership* integrates a training and learning perspective derived from the ambidextrous training that accompanies the book. The solution approach described here is based on the learning content of the training. For this reason, the book repeatedly includes definitions, explanatory illustrations and contains helpful references to further reading. It also offers its readers precise starting points for direct and simple implementation in daily management.

3. **Practical experience:** *Ambidextrous Leadership* builds on numerous practical empirical values and the expert interviews with managers from various industries and organizations were conducted exclusively for this book.

The Interviews

With Prof. Dr. **Wilhelm Bauer**, Managing Director of the **Fraunhofer** Institute for Industrial Engineering IAO (**Fraunhofer**-Institut für Arbeitswirtschaft und Organisation IAO), Stuttgart ("Balancing act in management practice", Chap. 2) and Prof. Dr. **Manfred Aigner**, Managing Director of the Institute for Combustion Technology (Institut für Verbrennungstechnik) at the **German Aerospace Center** (**Deutsches Zentrum für Luft- und Raumfahrt,** DLR) in Stuttgart ("Efficiency through hierarchy", Chap. 4), two representatives of non-university research institutes report on the significance of ambidexterity for economy and on its application in everyday research practice.

The perspective of a German university of excellence is added by Prof. Dr. **Hans Müller-Steinhagen**, former rector of the **Technische Universität Dresden**, and his view on the topic of vision and future viability ("The art of finding the right balance", Chap. 5).

The importance of ambidextrous leadership and communication in the field of innovation and entrepreneurship is explained by Prof. Dr. **Ronald Gleich**, Professor of Management Practice & Control at the **Frankfurt School of Finance & Management** in Frankfurt am Main ("A Culture of entrepreneurship is more important than ever", Chap. 6).

Anne Elisabeth Krueger, expert for user driven innovation and user experience at the **Fraunhofer** Institute for Industrial Engineering IAO ("Fostering creative self-confidence", Chap. 3) and **Andreas Leinfelder**, Vice President Business Development at **Bosch Power Tools** ("New role for managers", Chap. 3) explore the approach of design thinking and explain the significance of design thinking for everyday innovation of industrial companies from the perspective of science and practice.

Practical insights for ambidextrous leaders are given by Prof. Dr. **Volker Nestle**, Chairman of the Board of **Hahn-Schickard Society** for Applied Research (**Hahn-Schickard-Gesellschaft** für angewandte Forschung) and Head of Product Development LifeTech of the technology company FESTO ("Ambidexterity is everyday business", Chap. 5) as well as by the Managing Director Cluster Benelux of **FESTO** in Delft, **Dennis van Beers** ("It is a self-directed team", Chap. 5).

In the 2nd edition six interviews on leadership and crisis management on the occasion of the COVID-19 crisis are added (see Chap. 6):

The interview "Now is the time to be visible" with Dr. **Constanze Holzwarth,** psychologist and **top management consultant**, illuminates the level of the individual manager in the environment of the crisis. The interview "We now need double ambidexterity" with **Wiltrud Pekarek**, Member of the Board of Management of **HALLESCHE** Krankenversicherung aG, provides an insight into the upper management level of a system-relevant private health insurer. The discussion "It's all about empowerment" with **Thomas Fischer**, Chairman of the Supervisory Board of **MANN+HUMMEL**, underlines the importance of empathetic, meaningful leadership in times of crisis and answers the question of how leaders achieve ambidexterity in such periods. In the interview "Resilience is inherent in each of us" **Karin Pahl**, owner of **PAHL Resilienz-Förderung** in Bremen, explains how leaders become resilient and arm themselves for times of crisis. Next we meet **Frank Riemensperger**, CEO of **Accenture** Germany, who in "Reboot into the new, changed world" describes the view of an international management consultancy and its clients. In the interview "It is peaceful coexistence" with **Gregor Pillen**, Chairman of the Management Board of **IBM** Germany, we gain insight into the leadership and crisis management of a global IT company.

Last, but not least, Dr. **Eberhard Veit** summarizes the importance of ambidextrous leadership in the preface to the second edition of this book: "The concept of ambidexterity is more relevant than ever. Both strategically and in leadership, companies today find themselves as never before in a constant tug-of-war between a known world and an uncertain future. We have to expect serious events like the global Corona Crisis in 2020 to repeat themselves in 2020 at any time. Stability is no longer guaranteed. We must prepare ourselves for this world" (Preface to the second edition).

The findings of ambidextrous leadership collected exclusively for this book were supplemented by additional practical voices and case studies through intensive research in the media. They deliver precious suggestions for everyday leadership, in which it is important to *inspire* people in companies, set free their creative potential and to get them prepared for the leap into the future.

1.3.2   Structure of the Book

Ambidextrous Leadership is divided into two parts, a theoretical part (this chapter and Chap. 2) that introduces the topic and presents the solution approach of this book, and a practical part (Chaps. 3–6) to communicate the tools for implementation.

In order to adequately present the motivation of this book, **this chapter** begins with an introduction to the context in which leaders move on a daily basis. It discusses the challenges of organizations in the environment of digitalization, presents the tension between evolution and revolution by presenting cases of companies and introduces ambidexterity as an approach for the digital transformation.

In **Chap. 2**, the central approach of the book, namely communication-based ambidextrous leadership, is explained in detail. First, the scientific concept of organizational ambidexterity is introduced and then followed by the explanation why ambidexterity is at its core a capability of leaders and can only be carried into the organization by them. Finally, based on the key findings of the underlying research study, we learn how leaders can achieve ambidexterity through their daily communication. In doing so, today's widespread understanding of the role of leadership, according to which leaders largely move within hierarchical organizational structures, is not fundamentally called into question, but rather expanded to include a second approach (the second hand) and thus adapted to the challenges of digitalization.

The picture that emerges in the first two chapters makes the tension organizations are facing visible. Leaders are forced to operate in diametrically opposed worlds and sometimes to make highly contradictory decisions in order to orchestrate today *and* tomorrow. The *second part* of the book builds on this frame of reference. Based on the approach presented, Chaps. 3–6 show courses of action for everyday leadership.

Chapter 3 explores the communicative actions of managers in the environment of exploration. It focuses on the future and offers patterns of action that lead to unknown, as yet undefined solution spaces. It describes that, in order to reach unknown territory, the polyphony and interconnectedness of participants in an organization must have priority. Communication in this field is meant to facilitate the individual interactions and to encourage various ideas. In case the exact solution is not yet defined, communication opens up a space of interaction in which collective knowledge can emerge. Subsequently, Chap. 3 will introduce you to a style of ecosystem-based leadership for this purpose. You will learn how leaders can build and nurture internal ecosystems and open the door to unknown, as yet undefined solution spaces. The more a value proposition in the field of digitalization and Industry 4.0 is determined by autonomous, communicating units and their networking, the more precisely these human capabilities must be activated in teams along the innovation process. It is absolutely important to bring about diverse individual interactions, create meeting spaces and use the results of the exchange that take place here to gain competitive advantages. Communication-centered action frameworks such as agile working and methods enhancing creativity such as design thinking will support leaders here in shaping a future-oriented organizational mindset.

For all their future orientation, however, companies must also be successful here and now. **Chapter 4** therefore deals with the communicative actions of managers in the environment of exploitation, the advancement of existing business and the incremental further development of existing solutions. It describes how information dissemination and communication cascades can best be planned and organized to advance the present business. It explains how to distribute information to target audiences, synchronize knowledge levels and bring members of an organization to a common denominator. To achieve unanimity and efficiency in the implementation of strategic goals, formal, out-planned top-down communication is a prerequisite. It manifests itself, for example, in the form of official project communication with its committee structures and regular coordination or also as official employee information via the intranet or events.

Finally, **Chap. 5** denominates the balancing act that leaders engage in when they move in both worlds. It defines the course of action needed to strike a balance between exploitation and exploration in the organization and to advance both simultaneously. This form of communication is especially necessary with senior leaders who can make and reinforce the decision that an organization is moving in both worlds. Board members, managing directors or heads of large divisions here have the task to communicate a convincing vision of the future and to repeatedly emphasize the need to commit to the future already today. Because only when a vision for the future is communicated clearly an organization can align itself accordingly and move in both worlds.

The objective of Chaps. 3–5 is to provide the reader with precise tools that can be used quickly and easily in the organizational environment. In addition to numerous real-world examples, the interviews in each chapter provide accompanying voices from leaders in industry and academia. Each of the three Chaps. 3–5 includes the following elements:

- The application area: introduction to the innovation context
- The course of action for leadership
- The interview: voices of practitioners
- Conclusion
- Recommended reading / sources.

Chapter 6 is the result of an interview study on the question of how people and companies can go through crises in a strengthened way. The chapter was supplemented in the 2nd edition of *Ambidextrous Leadership* on the occasion of the COVID 19 crisis. The additional chapter on leadership and crisis management documents the exceptional situation in six interviews with persons from the German corporate landscape. While the world in spring 2020 looks spellbound at the Corona pandemic and the consequences of the shutdown of public life, the experts shared their leadership experiences and insights on successful crisis management with *Ambidextrous Leadership* during the weeks of the first lockdown in Germany. Their conclusion: In a crisis, "double ambidexterity" increases organizational resilience.

The task of the concluding **Chap. 7** is to combine the individual components of Chaps. 3–6 into an overall picture. This is because it is evident in practice that the innovation contexts (exploration, exploitation) rarely occur in their pure form. Thus, even in the environment of radical innovations there is justification for targeted, well-planned communication cascades to convey information. In the same way, continuous improvement of the existing product range may require a revolutionary new approach to the design of development processes. The 'pure form' of exploitation or exploration is rarely to be encountered. It is only important for the reader to know the basic natures of communication and to be able to use them depending on the context. In addition, for the quick reader with little time, Chap. 7 summarizes the most important statements of the book again and explains how what has been learned today can be put into practice tomorrow.

The Chapters at a Glance (Fig. 1.5)
Chapter 1—Introduction: The Trade-Off: Why is ambidexterity so important? What does it have to do with digitalization? Who is affected and how do we respond? Are organizations stretchable, flexible and adaptable? Or are they rigid entities with fixed structures?

Chapter 2—Success Through Ambidextrous Communication: What is ambidexterity? When does it occur? How does the concept relate to leadership? How can I orchestrate the two worlds of exploitation and exploration through communication?

Chapter 3—Breaking New Ground is dedicated to an explorative environment of action for leaders in which it is necessary to bring forth new solutions. How can existing

Fig. 1.5 Overview of the chapters

value chains be transformed into self-organizing value creation ecosystems? How do internal ecosystems emerge and how can managers use them? How do you create a working environment that promotes creativity? How do new solutions emerge through the exchange of different disciplines?

Chapter 4—Improving Your Current Business presents communication basics, courses of action and tools for the daily life of leaders in the environment of exploitation, existing business and increasing efficiency. How can information be distributed quickly and efficiently? How do I achieve a common denominator in the organization?

Chapter 5—Connecting the Two Worlds places both approaches—exploration and exploitation—on the introduction of ambidexterity and teaches communication approaches that promote ambidexterity. How can leaders give both strategic orientations a 'raison d'être'? How can both worlds be balanced and orchestrated? What role does communicating a strong vision play?

Chapter 6—Ambidextrous Leadership in Times of Crisis documents the exceptional situation of the COVID 19 pandemic in 2020 in six interviews with persons from the German corporate landscape. As an excursus into practice, the chapter provides, in addition to the personal experiences of the interview partners, precise insight and options for action for leadership work in the environment of crises.

Chapter 7—How to Take Action eventually elaborates the essences of this book and offers an outlook on the concrete use of what has been learned in everyday leadership. How can we simply start implementing it? And how do we conserve the 'beginner's mind' that is so valuable for innovation?

References

1. IHS Markit (2020): The Internet of Things: revolutionizing the competitive landscape. Online: https://cdn.ihs.com/www/pdf/IoT_ebook.pdf [Accessed: 17.05.2020].
2. "Bosch strebt Technologieführerschaft bei Künstlicher Intelligenz an", in: Industry of Things vom 07.01.2020. Online: https://www.industry-of-things.de/bosch-strebt-technologiefuehrerschaft-bei-kuenstlicher-intelligenz-an-a-894049/ [Accessed: 21.05.2020].
3. Christensen, C.M. (2011): The Innovator's Dilemma: Warum etablierte Unternehmen den Wettbewerb um bahnbrechende Innovationen verlieren. 2nd revised edition. München: Franz Vahlen.
4. Pressemitteilung der Festo AG & Co. KG (2017): "Digitalisierung: Evolution oder Revolution?", Februar 9, 2017. Esslingen. Online: https://www.festo.com/net/de_de/SupportPortal/Details/419179/PressArticle.aspx?&KeepThis=true& [Accessed: 24.05.2020].
5. Van den Bergh, Rens (2014): Too Busy to Innovate. Online: https://twitter.com/Rensvandenbergh/status/460747654083801088 [Accessed: 12.08.2017].
6. "Vom Autobauer zum Spagatkonzern", in: Süddeutsche Zeitung vom 7.3.2016. Online: http://www.sueddeutsche.de/wirtschaft/jahre-bmw-und-jetzt-1.2881380-3 [Accessed: 24.05.2020].
7. Acatech. (2013): Umsetzungsempfehlungen für das Zukunftsprojekt Industrie 4.0: Abschlussbericht des Arbeitskreises Industrie 4.0. Frankfurt a. M. Online: https://www.bmbf.de/bmbf/shareddocs/downloads/files/umsetzungsempfehlungen_industrie4_0.pdf [Accessed: 24.05.2020].
8. Countrymeters (2020): Population of the world and countries. Online: https://countrymeters.info/en [Accessed: 17.05.2020].
9. Riemensperger, Frank; Falk, Svenja (2019): Titelverteidiger. Wie die deutsche Industrie ihre Spitzenposition auch im digitalen Zeitalter sichert. München: Redline, p. 156.
10. Bauer, Wilhelm; Leistner, Phlipp; Schenke-Layland, Katja; Oehr, Christian; Bauernhansel, Thomas; Morszeck, Thomas H. (2016): Mass Personalization. Mit personalisierten Produkten zum "Business to User" (B2U). Stuttgart: Fraunhofer Gesellschaft: Stuttgart. Online: https://www.stuttgart.fraunhofer.de/de/studie_b2u.html [Accessed: 24.05.2020].
11. "Führungskräfte bremsen digitale Transformation aus", in: Scope Online, January 18, 2017. Online: https://www.scope-online.de/smart-industry/industrie-4-0%2D%2Dfuehrungskraefte-bremsen-digitale-transformation-aus.htm [Accessed: 24.05.2020].
12. "Wissenslücken der Führungskräfte bremsen Digitalisierung", in: Deutsche Mittelstands Nachrichten, January 30, 2017. Online: http://www.deutsche-mittelstands-nachrichten.de/2017/01/87226/ [Accessed: 24.05.2020].
13. "Deutsche Führungskräfte verschlafen die Digitalisierung", in: CIO Online, October 27, 2015. Online: https://www.cio.de/a/deutsche-fuehrungskraefte-verschlafen-die-digitalisierung,3249055 [Accessed: 24.05.2020].
14. O'Reilly, C. A. & Tushman, M. (2013): Organizational Ambidexterity: Past, Present, and Future. Academy of Management Perspectives, 27 (4), p. 324–338.

15. O'Reilly, C. A. & Tushman, M. L. (2004): The Ambidextrous Organization. Harvard Business Review, 82 (4), p. 74–81.

16. Birkinshaw, J. & Gupta, K. (2013): Clarifying the Distinctive Contribution of Ambidexterity to the Field of Organization Studies. Academy of Management Perspectives, 27 (4), p. 287–298.

17. O'Reilly, C. A. & Tushman, M. L. (2008): Ambidexterity as a Dynamic Capability: Resolving the Innovator's Dilemma. Research in Organizational Behavior, 28, p. 185–206.

18. Tushman, Michael M., Smith, Wendy K., Binns, Andy (2011): The Ambidextrous CEO. In: Harvard Business Review, June 2011, 89 (6), p. 74–80.

19. Porsche AG (2018): Wir verbinden unsere Tradition mit der Zukunft. Interview mit dem Porsche-Vorstandsvorsitzenden Oliver Blume anlässlich 70 Jahre Porsche Sportwagen. Online: https://presskit.porsche.de/anniversaries/de/70-years-porsche-sports-cars/topic/category/porsche-bleibt-porsche/items/de-wir-verbinden-unsere-tradition-mit-der-zukunft-334.html [Accessed: 24.05.2020].

20. Duwe Julia (2016): Ambidextrie, Führung und Kommunikation. Interne Kommunikation im Innovationsmanagement ambidextrer Technologieunternehmen. Wiesbaden: Springer Gabler.

Success Through Ambidextrous Communication

Abstract

What is ambidexterity? Why do we need it in companies? How does the concept change today's understanding of leadership? How can I as a manager implement the ambidextrous leadership style?

This chapter introduces the scientific concept of organizational ambidexterity and presents the ambidextrous communication model for leaders. It explains why ambidexterity is at its core a leadership skill and how you can bring ambidexterity into the organization through your daily communication.

The currently widespread understanding of the role of leadership, according to which managers largely move within hierarchical organizational structures, is subjected to a rethinking process in this chapter. A complementary approach, the 'second hand', is needed to make leadership fit for the challenges of the digital transformation.

The second hand is based on an understanding that sees leadership as detached from an assigned authority and as the result of a complex process of social interaction. If the interaction between people in the company moves into the focus of leadership, communication and exchange between individuals also take on a whole new significance. The central solution approach of this book takes this shift in meaning into account. It places communication at the center of daily leadership work.

© Springer-Verlag GmbH Germany, part of Springer Nature 2022
J. Duwe, *Ambidextrous Leadership*,
https://doi.org/10.1007/978-3-662-64032-6_2

2.1   Ambidexterity in Orchestrating Innovation

2.1.1   Key Competence for the Digital Transformation

2.1.1.1 What Happens in the Digital Transformation?

What exactly happens in companies during the digital transformation? What is the best way to understand the transformation process? It is clear that we want to achieve the 'digital goal', because the benefits of the new solutions can be seen in countless areas of everyday digital life. Whether in the form of e-commerce, apps or online services, digital solutions offer enhanced performance, transparency in every situation, round-the-clock and on-demand support services, and increased flexibility many times over.

If we really want to achieve this added value and use it profitably for the future, new skills, technologies, IT infrastructures and, above all, new data-driven business models are urgently needed. There is no doubt about that. In their book "Business Model Generation", Alexander Osterwalder and Yves Pigneur define a business model as the basic principle by which "an organization creates, delivers and captures value" [1]. The Business Model Canvas, which Osterwalder developed with Pigneur as part of his dissertation, describes all the elements necessary to create value and profitably market an offering: a company's key resources and activities, the necessary partnerships, the cost structure, the value proposition, the relationships with the customer, the customer segments, the (sales) channels, and the revenue streams of a company or business unit. In practice, working with the canvas serves as an ideal starting point and pragmatic instrument for questioning, revising or completely redeveloping a business model "from the perspective of value creation, customers and cost structure" [1].

Outdated Processes...

However, when people in organizations start questioning existing business models and launch completely new solutions, the existing proven processes and methods suddenly fall short. They are left alone. It is sobering to see that an existing corporate process simply blocks a new business model, that a successful organization simply does not support an innovation project. In most traditional companies, the processes, structures, methods—the entire mindset—are consistently geared to today's technologies and their successful products. Profits are saturated, processes are specialized, people and teams are well-rehearsed. Here, we know what to do by heart. The solutions are known; the know-how is available in abundance. The product portfolio is optimized under high pressure.

Danger: Loss of Market Share

However, the 100% focus on existing technologies leads to a loss of market share in the medium to long term (Fig. 2.1). At the same time, when we notice that the existing mechanisms for innovation do not work anymore, this leads, in the worst case, to a standstill and apathy among innovators. To escape the gridlock, a run on start-ups or the rapid spin-off of innovation units, incubators and innovation hubs can be observed in many

Performance

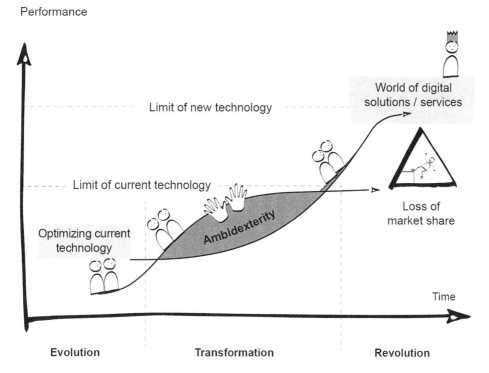

Fig. 2.1 Ambidexterity is a key competence for digital transformation (source: Own illustration based on Gabler Wirtschaftslexikon [2])

places. Whether this is more of a conflict-induced panic act or actually a promising path, and what ultimately matters for the spin-off to work, is discussed in greater depth in Chap. 5.

In any case, one thing is certain: Waiting in the familiar state, i.e. remaining in the comfort zone (which continues to evolve calmly), is just as little a solution as frantically fleeing from the present and glorifying a revolutionary future. Instead, what is needed is an intensive examination of the period of transition, a process of digital transformation that in some cases may last over years (colored orange in Fig. 2.1). This orange period of transition, the phase of ambidexterity, arises (Fig. 2.1) by the intersection of two *technology S-curves*.

▷   **Technology S-Curve** Innovation research uses S-curves to describe the development stages or the degree of maturity of technologies [2]. Many technologies run through an S-shaped curve during their lifetime, the life cycle, in relation to their performance increase or their degree of maturity and the research and development efforts made. The phase of the emergence of a new technology with an initially flat start-up, for example due to a lack of experience, routines and processes or a lack of understanding of the technology, is followed by the phase of the growth of the technology with an accelerated increase in performance, for example due to a better understanding of the technology and experience gained, and the phase of establishment as a recognized technology. Finally, the curve leads to a phase of maturity with decreasing performance increase of the technology towards the end of its lifetime, when the technology has reached its performance limit or is displaced by other technologies [3].

Figure 2.1 illustrates the specific case of technological discontinuity or sudden technological change. It shows a development in which a known, proven technology is still in the phase of performance enhancement, while at the same time the life cycle of a completely new technology begins, which has the potential to substitute previous solutions [4].

Phase of Ambidexterity
New market participants naturally opt directly for the new technology during this period and thus gain their first competitive advantages. For companies that have existed successfully in the market for decades, the same phase is a crucial test. They are confronted with the decision to either extend the life of the proven technology through evolutionary further development or to make a determined leap to the new technology [4]—or to do both. It is therefore crucial to look very consciously at the period of transition, the phase of ambidexterity, which should *not be underestimated,* and to intensively prepare the time of the jump onto the revolutionary technology path into the world of digital services and solutions.

2.1.1.2 Mental Model for the Digital Transformation
We therefore need to deal with the period of change in order to reach the future. If, for example, the core business of a supplier in the automotive industry is based on the combustion engine, it is necessary to analyze and evaluate in detail what new opportunities will be opened up by electromobility, digital mobility services, or entirely new markets and business models outside the mobility sector. Or let us take mechanical and plant engineering: In the medium to long term, companies will replace their current hardware products and on-site services with smart components and networked systems, including new digital services for Industry 4.0.

If you really take the challenge seriously as an organization, it quickly becomes clear how extremely distant the worlds are from each other and what it means to bring forth new digital business fields. A simple jump from one cliff to the next will not succeed here under any circumstances.

Rather, change will be a year-long, cross-technology, constant transformation process, and current solutions will have to carry us into the future until future solutions that are unprofitable today become a company's new cash cow.

As recently as 2017, Daimler CEO Dieter Zetsche spoke on *Deutschlandfunk* radio about the timeframe for the transition from the combustion engine to electromobility [5]:

There is no point in sitting and waiting to see whether costs will eventually fall, because they will only fall if we get to grips with these vehicles, both in development and in production, optimize the processes, the materials used, etc., in order to finally reach that point in time when—and this is what we call the tipping point—both the customer benefits and the costs, and therefore also the prices, become comparable to those of combustion engines.

But just one term later, it is clear: "Cars are becoming smartphones on wheels." The new Daimler boss Ola Kaellenius declares: "In order to remain competitive, we have to master the software". Even with electric drives, manufacturers can hardly differentiate themselves anymore. They are working on their own operating system [6].

The example of the automotive industry illustrates that the period of replacing an existing technology with substitute technologies and completely new business models (Fig. 2.1) can extend over a long period of time and, at the same time, is always taking new directions—reason enough, therefore, to prepare for the crossing (Chap. 5) and to have sufficient material and innovative strength on board to master the lasting transformation process.

The technology S-curve model used here was therefore supplemented in Fig. 2.1 to include the people that companies urgently need for change. After all, the challenge will be to get the existing members of an organization excited about a continuously changing image of the future and to set up the teams for new business areas in the medium to long term: "If we want to become fit for digitization, do we have to bring completely new skills and people on board? I think not," explains Eberhard Veit, who is an expert on Industry 4.0 in Germany, in the preface of this book. "I recommend a mix of new talent and experienced long-term employees. Because success will be largely based on training and educating people," says Veit. It is therefore important to take the people in organizations with us, and this task lies primarily and first and foremost with the *leaders of companies.*

Viable Solution Approach

For the digital transformation process and its effects on all areas of companies and, above all, for the people who work in them, the concept of organizational ambidexterity offers the only *truly* viable solution approach. It not only provides managers with a tailor-made thought model that maps the acid test of the present and the digital future, but also with a foundation that has been empirically researched from many perspectives, as well as strategic options for action for everyday corporate life [7].

The application of the solution approach presented in this book, i.e. the daily practice of ambidexterity through communication, does *not require* companies to carry out multi-million-dollar consulting projects or restructurings. Instead, it starts specifically at the level of action of the individual manager. Because the transformation process must begin with the people and the corporate culture and not at an abstract level of the organization. This time of transition should not be "sat out" or even skipped. It is up to the managers to consciously shape it.

▶ **Ambidexterity** describes the ability to use both hands equally well [8]. Applied to the context of organizations, management researchers Michael L. Tushman and Charles O'Reilly [9] define organizational ambidexterity as the ability of organizations to pursue radical and incremental innovation simultaneously. At the core of the concept is the parallel orchestration and balancing of exploration, the opening up of new technological territory, new business models and new markets, and exploitation, the expansion and evolutionary further development of the existing business.

Organizational ambidexterity thus describes the competence of organizations to create completely new solution spaces on the one hand, while at the same time optimizing their existing product programs and trimming them for cost efficiency. Ambidextrously managed organizations create the space for technological leaps and completely new solutions, while successfully holding their own with their existing products in price competition and saturated markets: "We will continue to focus on our core business as before and at the same time build capacity to innovate," explains Heinz-Jürgen Prokop, Managing Director of the Machine Tool Division of the laser technology company TRUMPF, in an interview with the German magazine *Maschinenmarkt*. The goal is to "create space for innovation and future topics and to play a significant role in shaping the digital transformation in mechanical engineering" [10].

Ambidextrous companies intensively drive their core business forward and, in this way, create the financial scope to invest in research and development for the future. They exploit and explore at the same time and count both incremental as well as radical innovations among their central fields of action. Their secret lies in celebrating and leveraging the best of the past while simultaneously tapping into new areas of innovation and business.

▶ **Radical and Incremental Innovation** According to Harvard innovation researchers Rebecca Henderson and Kim Clark, incremental innovation describes the minor change or further development of existing solutions [11]. Incremental innovation draws from a firm's existing knowledge and aims to create a strong position for existing firms in an existing, saturated market (exploitation). In terms of product innovation, it involves minor adaptations of existing products. Established technologies are exploited, existing competencies are expanded. In markets, incremental innovation contributes to consolidation.

▶ Radical innovation breaks through this continuous process. It marks existing competencies as obsolete and instead builds on new knowledge and new technologies. It increases customer benefits and enables completely new applications compared to previous solutions. It also helps new companies to enter markets and can fundamentally challenge existing industries (exploration) [12].

The path of exploration, the departure into the unknown, with the goal of bringing forth something revolutionary new, is often diametrically opposed to the requirement of optimizing the existing top-selling business. It is an area of tension that is examined from numerous perspectives in the research field of organizational ambidexterity [13]. Companies try to meet this tension with different approaches. From the temporal, spatial or structural separation of exploration and exploitation to situational context management, different approaches can be found, which are explained in more detail in the following section.

2.1.2 Forms of Organizational Ambidexterity

For the first time, the 'acid test' between exploitation and exploration was explicitly mentioned by the American researcher of organizational design Robert Duncan in 1976 [14]: Organizations had to be able to drive strategic change and at the same time trim current activities for efficiency. In 1991, organizational theorist James G. March introduces the notion of the "exploration / exploitation trade-off" for this conflict of goals between the present and the future [15]. He underlines the extent to which the two approaches of exploration and exploitation diverge and interfere with each other.

▶ **The Exploration / Exploitation Trade-Off** Already in 1991, Stanford professor James March [15] emphasized the necessity of balancing exploration and exploitation in companies. Firms should neither fall into stagnation nor be caught in cost-intensive experiments. Maintaining an appropriate balance between exploration and exploitation, he argues, is the primary success factor for a corporate system to survive and grow. March underlines the challenge that both strategies compete with each other: "Both exploration and exploitation are essential for organizations, but they compete for scarce resources." He describes that exploration of new alternatives reduces the speed of improving existing alternatives. At the same time, improving existing competencies would make experimenting with new ones less attractive. March refers to this as "exploration/exploitation trade-off."

The different approaches of corporate management for exploration and exploitation are also highlighted by the ambidexterity researchers Charles O'Reilly and Michael Tushman in their much-cited Harvard Business Review article on ambidextrous organizations [16]: While the exploitation approach pursues incremental improvement of products, reduction of costs, maximum profit and highest productivity and is based on continuity (Fig. 2.2), the exploration approach focuses on radical innovation, growth, entrepreneurship, and

Fig. 2.2 Exploitation builds on continuity

breaking new ground (Fig. 2.3). Exploitation is all about efficiency, low risk and quality. Exploration is all about risk-taking, flexibility and a willingness to experiment. The researchers also observe completely contrasting leadership styles in both worlds: from authoritarian top-down approaches in the exploitation environment to flat hierarchies and a visionary leadership style in the exploration environment.

In the scientific literature on ambidexterity, three focal approaches crystallize with regard to the different manifestations of organizational ambidexterity: sequential, structural and contextual ambidexterity [17]. These are three different strategies that organizations develop to manage the "trade-off" between activities of exploration and activities of exploitation. The neuroscientist Nancy Andreasen adds a remarkable fourth type: the 'intellectual ambidexterity' of the individual (see Table 2.1).

1. Sequential ambidexterity
   As an early proponent of sequential ambidexterity, Robert Duncan [14] divides the process of innovation into a phase of initiation and a phase of implementation. To resolve the tension between exploration and exploitation organizations temporally separate both activities from each other. This type of ambidexterity usually takes a back seat in current discussions regarding the digital transformation, as it does not address the demand of highly dynamic environments of digital businesses in which everything must take place simultaneously.
2. Structural ambidexterity
   Ambidexterity research further distinguishes between the contextual and structural form of ambidexterity [18]. Structural ambidexterity refers to the establishment and maintenance of dual structures within the company, for example separate organizational units for exploitation (e.g. business units) and exploration (research and development, innovation hubs).

Fig. 2.3 Exploration = opening up new territory

3. Contextual ambidexterity

   Contextual ambidexterity, on the other hand, occurs when exploitation and exploration are not strictly separated in sequence or structure, but both activities occur simultaneously within an organization or management context. Contextual ambidexterity is generally needed when a company's current and future business must be balanced within an organizational unit. It appears at the latest when reintegration processes take place and previously separated innovative ideas are to be brought to market with the help of existing structures.

   While structural ambidexterity usually requires leaders to make an either/or decision (Do I move in one world *or* the other?), the concept of contextual ambidexterity is about

Table 2.1 Forms of ambidexterity in the company

Type	Feature
1. Sequential ambidexterity	Temporal separation of exploration and exploitation
2. Structural ambidexterity	Structural separation of exploration and exploitation
3. Contextual ambidexterity	Contextual balance of exploration and exploitation
4. Intellectual ambidexterity	Cross-over talent of individuals

a "both/and" question (How can both worlds be orchestrated *simultaneously?*). This state of contextual ambidexterity requires leaders to be continuously aware of the context in which they operate and to find a way to deal with conflicting demands and balance the tensions [19]. In the environment of the digital transformation, in which existing products compete with new digital solution spaces, contextual ambidexterity becomes one of the central requirements that leaders must meet in everyday business.

4. Intellectual ambidexterity

The American neuroscientist and professor of Renaissance literature Nancy Andreasen takes ambidexterity even a step further and brings an additional type of ambidexterity into play.

She explains ambidexterity not only as a result of the external context, but as a 'cross-over ability' of individuals. In her research on highly creative people, Andreasen coined the term "intellectual ambidexterity" for this. She uses it to describe people who, in addition to their field of expertise, also have a pronounced talent in completely unrelated fields, produce cross-disciplinary abilities and are able to establish connections between the fields [20].

With a doctorate in literature and a fascination for art and culture, and at the same time a world-renowned brain researcher and neuroscientist, Andreasen herself is an example of the type of intellectual ambidexterity. In an interview with the American National Public Radio (NPR), she explains her own creativity and her success as a neuroscientist in particular with the decision to change her field of action and, with this change, also to have empowered herself to think in an interdisciplinary way: "I am I guess somebody who's intellectually ambidextrous, good at two different fields" [21].

Applied to companies, Andreasen recommends in an interview with the German business magazine *brand eins* to foster creativity in new fields by breaking down silos, crossing disciplinary boundaries and by consciously promoting diversity and curiosity among people [22].

Ambidexterity as a Dynamic Capability

However, even if an intrinsic mental ambidexterity cannot be assumed in individuals, an ambidextrous context brought about by external factors is challenge enough in the daily work environment. Despite the contradictions that ambidexterity brings for companies, it is precisely this contextual cross-over competence that is indispensable for managers in order to master the digital transformation and to be able to survive in global markets in the long term.

O'Reilly and Tushman [23] therefore describe ambidexterity as a crucial dynamic capability of organizations. For the scientists, flexibly adapting to change and actively bringing about change is one of *the central capabilities* of sustainable companies. Ambidextrous firms are able to move simultaneously in mature and emerging markets. They make efficient use of their existing, proven capabilities and processes and at the same time make the leap into the future.

Comparable to the ever-impressive cross-over ability of a basketball player, who switches the ball from one hand to the other almost unnoticed in order to pass the opponent [24], these companies manage to simply pass the competition through their ambidextrous ability. However, in the following conversation with Wilhelm Bauer, the Stuttgart-based Fraunhofer expert on future working environments, it becomes apparent that this requires a radical rethink of current management practices.

"Balancing Act in Management Practice"

Interview with Prof. Dr. Wilhelm Bauer, Managing Director of the Fraunhofer Institute for Industrial Engineering IAO (Fraunhofer-Institut für Arbeitswirtschaft und Organisation IAO), Stuttgart and Technology Officer of the State of Baden-Württemberg.

What does organizational ambidexterity mean to you? What do you think is important in companies?

Ambidexterity is an exciting topic in organizational development. It covers all areas of a company that are subject to different market requirements in terms of reaction speed, innovative capacity and market access. Wherever innovation, experimentation and immediate market access are required, agile network structures make sense—whereas in production, for instance, the focus is rather on other principles and values such as quality assurance, safety and cost efficiency. Both areas are important, but they need different working principles, management concepts, and ultimately also different people.

In 2012, you were honored by the federal state of Baden-Württemberg as a "Maker of Tomorrow". What do you think is important in shaping the future and what role does ambidexterity play in this?

In my opinion, ambidexterity is a central requirement for organizations and leaders. It is a balancing act in daily management practice, but one that is characterized, above all, by the equal appreciation and recognition of both poles: the tradition and the future. By all means, leaders should avoid to create an atmosphere of important and less important company divisions and respective groups of employees. Instead, they need to examine carefully if the different systems and approaches can be balanced and managed in an integrated manner or whether spin-offs, start-ups or similar separate units for innovation should be considered.

Ambidextrous leadership is part of Fraunhofer's leadership guidelines. What can leaders contribute through an ambidextrous leadership approach? What can they achieve as a result?

(continued)

By adopting ambidextrous leadership, managers can ensure that the organization's existing resources are used to best effect. In balancing the worlds, leaders respect the diversity of employees and job profiles, but they also meet the organizational need to be capable of innovation and change, which is extremely important for Fraunhofer. We also integrate employees with various professional backgrounds, from different areas of work and in different phases of their lives. This helps us to maintain and expand our leading position in innovation in alignment with our mission.

Thank you very much Professor Bauer for the interview!

Wilhelm Bauer emphasizes how important the careful orchestration of both areas—exploration and exploitation—is for companies and that both approaches follow different principles and values. Leading the two worlds means to equally recognize and appreciate both poles. At the same time, leaders must help to position the organization for the future and make it as effective as possible in the period of transition. Against this background, Bauer describes ambidexterity as a central organizational leadership skill that requires basic rules, concepts and people who act accordingly. So let us dive deeper into the ambidextrous leadership approach in the next sections.

Summary: Ambidexterity Is a Key Competence

The period of digital transformation in manufacturing companies is often determined by optimizing the existing hardware-oriented core business while simultaneously opening up new digital solution spaces. The essence of transformation was explained here as the overlapping of two S-curves describing the degree of maturity of a technology. It is based on the replacement of an existing technology with its substitute technology—a transformation that can last for years. The current solutions must carry us into the future until the future solutions, which are unprofitable today, become the new cash cow of a company. For this reason, an intensive examination of the transition period is necessary.

The concept of organizational ambidexterity is a helpful thought model providing a theoretical explanation and at the same time practical options for action in everyday corporate life. The concept provides solution approaches that help navigate the exploration/exploitation trade-off. It is a wide variety of forms of ambidexterity that appear in organizations: beginning with the temporal sequence of exploration and exploitation, the structural separation in different organizational units, up to the contextual and intellectual ambidexterity, when the boundaries between the two worlds blur in everyday corporate life.

In this book, we are primarily concerned with the *contextual* cross-over competence. We focus on the associated requirement for managers to constantly adapt to exploration or exploitation depending on the situation and environment and to counter both approaches with appropriate strategies for action. ◄

2.2 Ambidexterity Is a Leadership Task

2.2.1 Leadership in a Hybrid World

Just like Fraunhofer expert Wilhelm Bauer, the ambidexterity researchers O'Reilly and Tushman anchor the ability to exercise organizational ambidexterity in the management practice of companies. For the experts, ambidexterity is a capability of leaders and a leadership task. In their view, ambidexterity is a specific competence that is expressed in the willingness of leaders to learn, in their ability to constantly reconfigure existing resources and strengths of the organization and thus to adapt to changing conditions [23]. In the following sections, we will dive deeper into this and answer the question of how *exactly* managers can shape an environment that promotes ambidexterity and why communication, of all things, plays a central role in this.

For a more precise determination of the situation, Fig. 2.4 zooms in the period of the intersection of two technology S-curves, referred to here as the 'hybrid world'. While a well-known, proven technology is still in the phase of performance enhancement and growth, the life cycle of a new technology begins. It has the potential to replace existing solutions in the medium to long term. As this period of overlapping may extend over several years or even decades, it is not enough for managers to decide for *one* world *or* the other and focus on *either* the existing *or* the future business. Rather, they need specific patterns of action for the transformation period that establish a balance and equilibrium between the existing *and* the new business. This period requires ambidexterity.

Principles for CEOs and Senior Managers
For Michael Tushman, Wendy Smith and Andy Binns, ambidexterity is the very responsibility of the CEO and his entire senior management team: "They don't leave the battle to their middle managers" [25]. At the very top, an overarching identity must be developed, tensions must be held, and contradictions must be actively embraced, according to the bottom line of the recommended Harvard Business Review article "The Ambidextrous

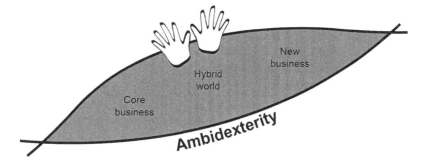

Fig. 2.4 The hybrid world of ambidexterity

CEO" [25]. The article describes the repeatedly observed tendency of managers, when they are under pressure of day-to-day business and especially in difficult times, to opt for short-term profit with the core business, even though they see the need to develop new markets and business areas. Often, the CEO is the only remaining friend of innovation—an approach doomed to failure.

For this reason, the ambidexterity experts strongly recommend that senior managers engage in an ambidextrous approach and develop a leadership style that balances both worlds. Building on a study among twelve management teams from different companies, they propose three principles for ambidextrous leadership [25]:

Already in the development of an overarching identity for a company, the upper management must be involved (1). This identity must create space for contradictory fields of action of a company. The decision-making in favor of innovation projects should not take place at lower levels, but at the very top with the CEO and her management circle to ensure that innovation is not displaced by established routines and processes (2).

Finally, companies should apply adequate performance standards for both innovation and core businesses, and not evaluate them according to the same criteria and performance indicators (3). This of course would always be disadvantageous for activities to explore new territory compared to the established business. In times of scarce resources, this requires flexibility in decision-making and allocation of resources, as well as a willingness to move resources between businesses. This requires senior teams to "abandon feudal battles and engage in forward-looking debate about the tensions at the heart of the business" [25].

Three Areas of Transformation

In addition to the three principles for the CEO and his/her senior management team, leaders at all levels of the organization need further approaches to practice ambidexterity.

To be able to balance the increasing tensions in companies caused by the digital transformation, it is important to better understand the different areas where the transformation process takes place.

Transformation is not only taking place on the *technology side*. The *business model* of technology- and product-centric organizations is also changing as software and data conquers the world and data-based services become increasingly important for the customer [26]. Finally, organizational processes, people's ways of working and thinking also have to be transformed when firms want to bring about new digital business models. If the objective is to establish and expand a new promising business within an existing company, the necessary activities and fields of action must be considered at three different levels or areas (Table 2.2).

From technology and competence management to integrate new knowledge and skills in the organization (1), the transformation of the current transaction-based business model towards relationship-based business models (2), to the organizational change in the ways of thinking and working, in the mindset of the people and in the culture of an organization (3): Holistic innovation management considers these three areas and, above all, does not

Table 2.2 Three areas of the digital transformation

Field of change	Field of tension	Field of action
1. Technology	Existing vs. new digital technologies	Technology and competence management towards digital data-driven technologies
2. Business model	Existing vs. new digital business models	Shift from transaction-based, technology- and product-centric business model to relationship-based, service-oriented digital business model
3. Organization and corporate culture	Existing vs. new processes, procedures, methods	Practicing ambidextrous leadership; introducing ecosystem management, agile ways of working, agile project management, design thinking

neglect the area of organization and corporate culture. Because if managers want to change and shape the first two areas, they urgently need ambidextrous leadership skills and a mindset in the organization that enables them to build a new world alongside the existing business.

Let us consider the following case for illustration: In a hardware company in the business-to-consumer environment, there is an idea for a revolutionary new, intelligent solution for a specific market need: To bring the new technology to the market, our company, which has grown successfully over decades with simple mechanical products, is now aware of a change on the technology side (1). The existing hardware and production-oriented development processes and competencies must be adapted and changed. Software and data-driven skills and procedures must be included in the development process and teams. So far so good. The leadership team knows that the technological change will be severe. However, if they now assume that today's product-centric transaction-based business model will fit the future offering just as well, the company will probably miss an important opportunity. Only if the management understands the nature of software-based services and the chances that emerge from an adequate data-driven product architecture, it will be able to tap the full potential of the innovation. If the firm sticks to today's standards, routines and organizational structures coming from a hardware-driven world to develop the new digital solution, elements of the new technology with a huge potential for increasing customer value will be missed. In the worst case, old processes and encrusted structures will lead to a once brilliant idea turning into an innovation that is only half as successful. But our hardware company is aware of this danger and therefore addresses a second area of transformation: The transformation of its business model (2). As the development period proceeds, it becomes increasingly apparent that the new solution will affect more than just research and development activities. After a careful analysis of the opportunities and potentials of the new technology, business opportunities are developed that affect the processes of the entire company: Beginning with new price models and licensing concepts, to digital sales processes and infrastructures behind, up to iterative customer-centric agile development methods. It becomes clear that the new digital business will require numerous activities, sub-steps, competencies and procedures that did not exist in the existing world of the company's core business. Step by step and in constant dialogue and evaluation with the R+D teams new activities are implemented to establish an adequate digital business model. But this intervention now affects a third area in the hardware company: the organizational structures, ways of working, and above all the leadership culture (3).

In the middle of the orange field (Fig. 2.4), the hybrid world, it is necessary to sound out very precisely which competencies, resources and processes are needed. Operating in the hybrid world means fundamentally questioning the existing world: which is technologies + business models + the mindset, processes and organization of a company. This third, often neglected level of culture, organization, and leadership is the most important and overarching area of the digital transformation. Because culture and organization can empower or completely prevent new business models and technologies from growing successful.

For this reason, the book *Ambidextrous Leadership* focuses on the level of the organizational culture, which can be shaped and designed through leadership and communication. In order to raise the principles and fields of action for ambidextrous leadership in top and senior management for everyday practice, Chaps. 3–5 present concrete communication-based options for action that help to actually implement ambidextrous leadership in day-to-day business.

For the reader with little time, there is the option of jumping straight into the practical chapters at this point. Or you can dive further into the theory and take a look at current leadership theories that underlie the concept of ambidextrous leadership.

2.2.2 Leadership as a Result of Social Interaction

2.2.2.1 Transactional and Transformational Leadership

Charisma, authority, control, power, moderation, coaching, empowerment... in science and corporate practice, leadership appears in countless different natures. Theories and management manuals revolve around the question of what constitutes successful leadership. Why do employees follow a person? Which leadership approaches lead to economic success in which environment? How must the hierarchy-centered world of companies change? What kind of leadership is needed when companies find themselves in the digital transformation?

In order to gain a basic understanding of the approaches and roles, we first follow the organizational researchers Rainhart Lang and Irma Rybnikova. They distinguish between management techniques for the "classical, Taylorist-Fordist production regime", which, according to the authors, "has been at least partially replaced by post-Fordist regimes and structures" [27]. While the former established itself over decades in the mass production environment and pursued a centralist and authority- and hierarchy-dominated understanding of management, management styles in the second half of the twentieth century increasingly included the role and influence of employees. Thus, a variety of new concepts and leadership theories emerged that increasingly moved away from a manager-centric view to consider leadership in the overall context of the organization.

In the meantime, leadership no longer means merely being granted an assigned authority in a functional way [28]. Leadership is increasingly independent from a specific function or official authority in the company. It emerges flexibly and dynamically and based on specific competences of people.

This distinction between a hierarchy-centric management style by a top-down installed boss and a motivating, people-centric style of leadership that enables change and transformation can be found, e.g., in the "full range of leadership" approach of the American leadership experts Bruce Avolio and Bernard Bass [29]. As early as the 1990s, the scholars introduced the distinction between *transactional* and *transformational* leadership, which is still widely cited today, and integrated both into a holistic model. Transactional leadership is based on the hierarchy-oriented principle of directing and ordering tasks and motivates employees through external incentives, such as salary or promotion, to perform well. It corrects or sanctions poor performance.

Transformational leadership, on the other hand, relies on people's intrinsic motivation and on empowering employees to change. In contrast to the "closing nature" of transactional leadership, which aims first and foremost at carrying out instructions, transformational leadership presupposes an opening behavior of the leader. In this environment creativity and new ideas can emerge. In their book "Developing Potential Across a Full Range of Leadership", Bass and Avolio present case studies of transactional and transformational leadership [29].

Example: Transactional and Transformational Leadership at Fraunhofer

The combination of a *transformational* and a *transactional* leadership approach forms the basis of the German Fraunhofer-Gesellschaft's leadership model: In order to enable "excellent applied research", managers must balance "contradictory requirements" in everyday life: "On the one hand, managers must grant their employees the greatest possible creative freedom in which creativity and innovation can emerge. On the other hand, they must ensure that the creative ideas also turn into products and results" [30]. In order to master this balancing act for the field of applied research, Fraunhofer explicitly refers to an "ambidextrous leadership approach", which moves between opening, transformational leadership behavior and closing leadership behavior. The corporate psychologists Rosing, Frese and Bausch emphasize that innovation is only made possible by the interplay of transactional and transformational approaches and an opening and closing leadership behavior [31]. ◄

2.2.2.2 Blurring Boundaries Between Leading and Being Led

We will not delve deeper into the multitude of leadership theories and concepts at this point, but rather try to find the essence for everyday leadership. What is really important for my everyday leadership as an ambidextrous leader? What do I need to know in order to successfully navigate through the digital transformation? In everyday practice, it turns out that two insights are helpful:

- First, the distinction just described between *closing* and *opening* leadership behaviors by managers and
- Second, the separation of leadership from a predefined position or authority of a manager.

A rigid understanding of leadership no longer matches with the situation of companies that have to survive in highly dynamic markets and technology environments of the digitalization. Instead, managers must continually adapt their behavior in an innovation-driven environment depending on the innovation context and, first and foremost, give up their personal, emotional attachment to an assigned management function to do so. Instead, the complex process of social interaction between individuals inside and outside an organization, and thus an opening approach, is moving into the focus of leadership. As organizational researcher Ingo Winkler sums up, "Leadership is the result of the various interactions between members of an existing group, it is thus hardly predictable" [28]. The understanding of the organization based on fixed predefined management structures changes depending on the context.

This book agrees with this approach. The awareness that leadership is determined by social interaction processes—and thus by communication and exchange between the members of an organization—and *not* by predetermined authorities and offices, must become more important, especially in the explorative environment of the digital transformation:

In the interaction process, communication describes on the one hand the transmission of information between persons (closing behavior). On the other hand, it describes the process of constructing reality (opening behavior). In the process of communication between people, new knowledge and new ideas as well as new connections within (and outside) a company emerge. Thus, new realities (innovation, ecosystems, networks) can appear and grow.

For leaders in the digital world, it is precisely this bimodal nature of communication (opening and closing) that holds huge potential for a new ambidextrous leadership style. The American organizational researchers and leadership experts Gail Fairhurst and Stacey Connaughton [32] also describe this leadership style as a "communication-centered view of leadership", which both ensures the exchange of information and contains a sensemaking element.

In a consistent communication-centered approach to leadership, the predefined under-standing of the roles of leader and co-worker dissolves. This is because leadership continuously unfolds anew in the communicative interaction of people. People acting as leaders shape realities and at the same time are themselves shaped by the reality that they cocreate. This is an uncertain, elusive but highly flexible, mobile understanding of the role. "Who becomes a leader thus appears to be less a function of position in the hierarchy than a function of the ability to manage or resolve key oppositions or tensions" [32].

Anthony Giddens' Theory of Structuration
The understanding of leadership described here can be traced back to the theory of structuration developed by Anthony Giddens in 1984 [33]. The theory explains the tension that exists between the individual actions of the members in a system, e.g. a company, and the prevailing structures of the system. It places the two in a close relationship. Giddens uses the process of structuration to explain how a system produces and constantly reproduces itself through the interaction of its members. He describes the reciprocal effect between the actions of the individual and the system in which he or she operates. In doing so, he assigns the individual a role that is not externally controlled but an active part as an independently acting knowledgeable person and shaper in a continuously changing system.

However, the path towards this understanding of leadership is just as serious a transformation process as the change on the technology and business model side. This is because the leadership role, which arises from the interactions in the team of knowledgeable persons and designers, must also be actively seized by the team, as the following example from everyday practice illustrates. Particularly in the digital transformation, when teams enter new territory, they will repeatedly come to crossroads where the well-known 'decision-makers' are missing and decisions have to be made by a responsible team.

Case Study: Power Vacuum

For the development of a new IT infrastructure for the distribution and use of completely new software offerings of a traditional hardware company in the business-to-consumer environment, members from different company divisions and disciplines come together in an agile design thinking team (Sect. 3.3.3). In the initial development of the first prototypes of the software-based infrastructure, the team—coordinated by a project manager appointed by the team—picks up speed and produces an MVP—a minimum viable product—in a very short time. The presentation of the first prototype at the company's most important consumer trade fair becomes a success.

When it comes to the final clarification and completion of the required infrastructure shortly before the market launch and to making decisions with company-wide consequences, the team suddenly calls for decision-makers. "Where are the people who make the final decisions here?" some participants ask. The initial speed of the agile cross-functional team gives way the demand for a leader with power and decision-making authority. This happens at the moment when decisions suddenly have company-wide significance. The question arises, "Who is actually calling the shots here?"

While this question remains unanswered, since *there are no* authorities for decisions of this kind in the company, the team is suddenly faced with a power vacuum (unknown from the existing business). The management that the team now expects from above is absent. No one is making the decision from the outside. And even more importantly, if there were assigned authorities, they probably would not know the right answer for a highly dynamic, interdisciplinary, continuously changing market. After all, it is the interdisciplinary team that has developed the highest level of expertise in this field. The

team has been working on the solution for months and has built up the most comprehensive knowledge. This is why the direction must be set by the team.

However, using the gained scope of responsibility in all consistency and on the basis
of their competence is also a transformation process for the team itself.

While they have been used to the final management decisions made "from above",
they now have to take on the leadership role themselves. They must dare to take the leap
and, after examining all the available options, courageously decide on what they see as
the best way forward. ◄

What does this mean for you now, if you are a manager or project leader in such an
environment of uncertainty? When solutions come less and less *from above* and instead
social interaction—and thus communication and exchange between individuals—become
the key to finding solutions? Then, in any case, it is worth taking a look at the nature and
importance of communication. It can become an important vehicle for actually practicing
ambidexterity in everyday leadership and firmly implementing it in your daily (!) actions. If
you are present as a project leader in the explorative situation described above, you can
play your role and encourage the team to make the decision confidently on the basis of the
existing competence.

Summary: Detach from the Predefined Managerial Role

For experts in ambidextrous research, ambidexterity is a leadership capability and a
leadership task. In the hybrid world of transition, it is not enough for managers to choose
between exploration *and* exploitation and to be experts in either the existing or the future
business. For the transformation period, they need specific patterns of action that create
a balance between existing and new business areas. At the very top of the company, a
comprehensive identity for the organization must be developed, the tensions must be
endured, and the contradictions at all levels—technology, business model, and organization and culture—must be actively confronted.

To explain the concept of ambidextrous leadership, this section distinguished
between a transactional, hierarchy-oriented, directive management approach and a
transformational, motivational and transformational leadership style. In addition to
this distinction, another insight was captured as a building block for ambidextrous
leadership: the detachment of the leadership task from a predefined position or authority
of the manager.

In the digital transformation, leadership no longer means exercising an office func-
tionally. Instead, leadership is independent of a specific function in the company. It
arises flexibly and dynamically based on specific relevant competences in the interaction
of the team members. Communication between individuals thus moves to the center of
the decision-making processes. Leaders can promote this process through their communicative actions. In a consistent communication-centric understanding of leadership,
they consequently detach themselves from a predefined managerial role. Instead leadership unfolds in the communicative interaction within the team. ◄

2.3   Ambidextrous Leadership Through Communication

2.3.1   Three Fields of Action for Communication in Companies

As early as 1961, the well-known American social researcher Rensis Likert [34] emphasized the role of communication in the company: it was essential for the functioning of an organization and was widely seen as one of the most important management processes. However, if we really want to understand the importance and role of communication in the company, we must first consider the different fields of action.

Different Views of Communication in Companies
As an interdisciplinary field of research, corporate communication deals with diverse aspects of internal and external communication of organizations. It is analyzed in management research, organizational research, communication sciences as well as in marketing research and thus has numerous different definitions. Especially in the literature of communication and marketing science, communication in the company is often described as a discipline that aims at a homogeneous image and reputation of a company, i.e. it unites all communicative activities of a company under one banner. Corporate communication serves to coordinate, orchestrate and align all individual interests of the stakeholders. It helps in implementing a corporate strategy and supports the achievement of corporate goals.

While this approach primarily focuses on the 'common denominator' and a homogenous external appearance of the firm, the discipline of organizational studies primarily looks at the *internal* communication processes and structures of an organization. Organizational researchers often emphasize the importance of the *heterogeneity* of voices and opinions that exist within an organization.

Fields of Action
In order to finally bring clarity to the discipline of communication in the company and to clearly position this book, we draw on the perspective of the German communication scientist Ansgar Zerfass [35]. He divides the communication of companies into three fields of action that are aligned with the corporate strategy:

- Market communication (external),
- Public relations (external) and
- Internal communication.

Accordingly, communication in the company deals on the one hand with the shaping of market-oriented and socio-political external relationships of a firm. On the other hand, it is concerned with the control of internal communication processes within the company.

Market communication, the subject of marketing research, encompasses "all communicative actions of organizational members (managers, communication professionals) and their agents (e.g. consultancies) with which transactional and competitive relationships are being shaped" [35]. In this context, it is primarily concerned with the "exchange process" [36] or the relationships with stakeholders in the market.

Public relations is also directed at external reference groups: it is oriented "in a broader sense to communication relationships with reference groups in the social and political context" [37]. It is the task of public relations to "enforce the corporate strategy in the fields of action of politics, education, science, etc. and to implement corresponding contradictions and social requirements into the organizational decision-making system", explains communications professor Ansgar Zerfass [35]. In addition to direct customer and market communication, public relations is another important field of action in the external presentation of a company. It shapes the public image of an organization in terms of goal achievement and maintains the dialogue with the relevant stakeholders of a company.

Internal communication, on the other hand, describes all internal communication processes that take place between the members of a company, e.g. between different departments, hierarchical levels or individuals. It considers the internal players of the organization against the background of the common goal achievement and value creation [35]. It ranges from everyday communication between internal participants to internal communication in exceptional cases. In this context, internal participants are, on the one hand, constitutional persons "for whom one can assume the principle of direct communication between the participants", and, on the other hand, all other organizational members, e.g. employees, whose performance processes have to be structured and controlled within the constitutional framework [35].

We will take a closer look at the structuring and control of the performance process through internal communication later on. In this book, market communication and public relations take a back seat. Instead, *internal communication of leaders will* move into the center of attention. The aim is to understand what role the communicative actions of individuals play in their role as members of a profit-oriented organization and how leaders can use communication profitably. Especially in the environment of the digital transformation, the role of leaders is increasingly changing: "The more communication takes place via networks and the less controllable it becomes, the more important leadership through communication becomes," emphasizes communication scientist Claudia Mast [38].

"Leadership through communication" is based on two essential natures of communication in an ambidextrous environment: communication as *transmission* and communication as *reality construction*. Understanding these two natures of communication is of utmost importance in practice in order to lead successfully in the environment of digitalization. The two natures are presented in the following section.

2.3.2 Two Natures of Communication: Transmission and Reality Construction

There are two fundamentally different natures of communication that form the basis of ambidextrous leadership [7]. This is also described by organizational researchers as the 'bimodal nature' of communication [39]. This bimodal nature includes

1. Communication for the transmission of information and
2. Communication to construct reality.

This bimodal understanding thus describes, beyond the mere transmission of information, a *constitutive* character of communication that creates organizational reality. We address both *in detail* in this section. After all, knowing that these two dimensions exist and consciously using both dimensions will be extremely helpful in the day-to-day business of the digital transformation. Once understood and tested, you will soon no longer want to do without.

2.3.2.1 Communication Is Transmission

When we speak of the *transmission of information* in the following paragraph, we will refer to the specific form of communication between the members of an organization, when content is exchanged and messages are conveyed. This takes place, e.g. when a boss informs the team in a meeting about the latest news from the company management, or when the managing director presents the new corporate strategy in a video message to the employees. This type of communication is about the *distribution* of information. It represents a *closing* behavior (described above), which leaves as few questions as possible unanswered (Sect. 2.2). It presupposes that the information to be distributed, i.e. the content of a message, is available before the communication activities start. When the company management announces the new corporate strategy for the next couple of years, the contents of the strategy have been worked out in advance and the communication documents for it have been prepared. You have put the letter into the envelope. You have sealed the envelope. Now it is time to send it out. It is a matter of delivering news, distributing it, transmitting it—mostly from the top down to the employees. The letter itself will not be changed anymore. The content is fixed. In the case of presenting a corporate strategy, all recipients receive the same letter, the same message, to ensure that there is a common understanding in the organization.

This type of communication, shown on the left in Fig. 2.5, serves to *distribute* information as efficiently as possible and aims at a uniform understanding among the recipients. It is based on a rather hierarchical organizational environment and on the linear sender-receiver model of the mathematician Claude Shannon [40]. In 1948, Shannon had developed the communication model, which is still known and used today, to describe the exchange of information between two systems in the field of communications engineering.

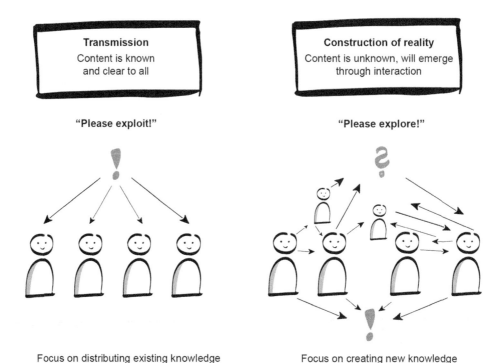

Fig. 2.5 Two natures of communication

The linear model describes a central transmitter that has information to be transmitted and transmits it to a receiver using a transmission channel [40].

In the organizational context, this process of information transfer usually is a one-way communication from the upper levels of the hierarchy to the employees. This approach is focused on the transmission and exchange of information and aims to elicit appropriate goal-directed behavior from the recipients, e.g. a team or all employees. You will find courses of action in Chap. 4.

It is undisputed that the top-down transmission of information to the employees is a core pillar for the effective operations of companies and thus belongs to the basics of corporate management. However, if managers understand communication exclusively as the process of transmission and exchange of messages, they waste an important potential of communication. It is precisely the countless communicative interactions that take place in companies every day that can change information. Through this kind of communication completely new organizational realities emerge. The possible effects of the diversity and heterogeneity of voices and opinions within an organization can be the very most important prerequisite for breaking new ground. So let us look at the second nature, the often still blind spot of internal communication, shown in Fig. 2.5 on the right.

2.3.2.2 Communication Is Reality Construction

In its *second nature,* communication is "a joint activity, within which both speakers and addressees co-produce, moment-by-moment, an understanding of their social relationship and joint understanding", communication scholars describe the constituent essence of organizational communication [41]. In recent years, this view has been shaped in particular by a North American school of organizational scholars. According to the Canadian communication scholars James Taylor and Elizabeth van Every [39] "a bimodal theory of information as both transmission and generation of knowledge throws an entirely new light on the genesis of organization.". The representatives of the "Montréal School of Organizational Communication" refer to Anthony Giddens' theory of structuration [33] (Sect. 2.2). They describe communication between organizational members as the fundamental mode of action for organizations to come into being at all. "A situation is talked into existence and the basis is laid for action to deal with it." [39]. Organizational reality only emerges when the members of an organization interact with each other and thereby produce circumstances including people, objects, institutions, history and their own temporal and spatial location [39]. Organizations therefore only exist through communication.

Communication Is the Negotiation of Reality

In this *constitutive* understanding of communication, reality is thus negotiated by the individual players in the first place. The result is open (Sect. 2.2). The starting point for this view is the work of the renowned organizational psychologist Karl Weick. According to Weick, organization is to be defined as a social process of organizing. Organizing itself is "first and foremost based on agreements about what is reality and what is illusion" [42]. Weick describes organization as an "interpretive system" [43]. In this system, communication plays a central role in forming and maintaining organizations.

Organization emerges through the continuous assignment of meanings (organizational sensemaking) by organizational members in mutual exchange. The process of organizing itself is to be located in the actions and conversations that appear with regard to an *assumed* organization [44]. In Weick's understanding, events and organizations thus only become real through the interactive exchange of members of an organization. Situations, organizations and environments would only exist through communication [44]. Reality becomes a matter of negotiation.

Taylor and van Every [39] put this idea at the center of their communication theory. For them, communication is an interactive process, in which organizational members decode the meaning of situations in mutual exchange. The negotiation, interpretation and assignment of collective meaning, referred to in organizational theory as "sensemaking", takes place in interactive conversation. Communication is thus freed from its exclusively passive mediating function. It acquires an active reality-creating character.

2.3.2.3 What It Means for Leaders in the Innovation Environment

Back to the digital transformation: What does this insight mean for the digital transformation? What does the knowledge of the two natures of communication mean for companies that want to earn money with new digital solutions in addition to existing product programs? If we assume that, next to the realm of information transfer, a second communication space opens up in which new knowledge (innovation) is created through the communicative interactions of people, then we can use this as an effective instrument for innovation management (Fig. 2.4).

The Problem

The problem is, that in everyday corporate life the first nature of communication, the top-down transmission of content, is seen as the official and only way of communication. However, the second nature of communication that creates new reality lives a shadow existence. It happens informally instead of being institutionalized at the center of innovation. In some places, it is even prevented by a strictly hierarchical and centralized environment. What may work for the efficient rollout of a strategy and the mere improvement of existing products in the existing business is often counter-productive when it comes to building the new digital business. Instead of new ideas, you only get the old wine...

This will only change, when organizations institutionalize the second nature of communication and actively use it to generate new knowledge. Institutionalization has increasingly (but hesitantly) taken place in recent years through the introduction of design thinking or agile working methods in companies. Such frameworks for action consciously use the reality-creating and emergent dimension of communication. They put networking and communicative interaction at the center of collective action for innovation (see Chaps. 3 and 4).

If managers consciously incorporate this second nature of communication into their management work and choose between the different action patterns of both natures (see Chaps. 3 and 5) depending on the situation and context, they can better navigate through the ambidextrous organization *themselves.* But above all, they actively shape the time and space in which incremental developments coexist with radical innovation projects and thus create an ambidextrous culture in the company. The role that the two natures of communication can play for the emergence of innovation is shown in Fig. 2.6, based on Zerfass's representations of the bimodal nature of innovation communication [45].

The two fundamentally opposing communication models in the field of innovation management, "communication as transmission" and the model of "communication as reality construction", which is close to the North American school of organizational communication (see Sect. 2.3), focus on different aspects of innovation. In the former understanding, what we call innovation is an already existing result. It is "qualitatively novel products or processes that are characterized as new by a firm (or its managers)" [45]. It is an already created *artifact.* In this context communication is not about *generating* new ideas, but about distributing information and meaning about a new solution that already exists (see Sect. 4.3).

The second understanding of communication as a process of reality construction does not focus on the *result,* but on the *process* of innovation and the creation of meaning

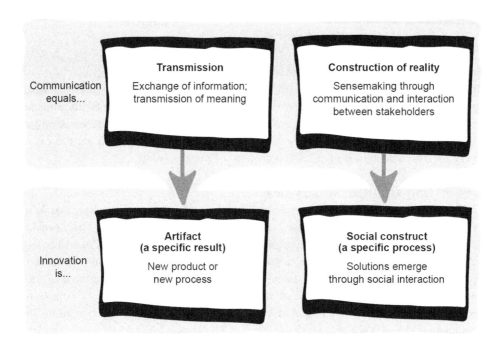

Fig. 2.6 Innovation: artifact or social process? (own illustration based on Angar Zerfass, 2009 [45])

through social interaction. In this view, new technologies or new products are the *result* of the "social construction of meaning and reality as well as an interest-driven action of the players" [45]. Innovation itself is a *social construct* created in by human interaction (see Chap. 3).

Ambidextrous Leadership Is Based on the Two Natures of Communication
For leadership in the innovation context, these two different dimensions are of crucial importance: If—as is often the case—only the dimension of information transfer is applied, it quickly becomes clear that this does not drive the emergence of new ideas. If the focus is on demand and control, the teams are not encouraged to find creative interdisciplinary solutions and to come up with their own ideas.

What leads to results in an efficiency-driven environment can have the opposite effect in the search for radically new solutions. It is therefore important to use *both* dimensions in one's own leadership style depending on the situation and context. How the respective communication styles differ is discussed in more detail in the following section. You will find concrete courses of action in Chaps. 3–5.

2.3.3 Ambidextrous Communication

2.3.3.1 Research Project in Industry 4.0

The principle of the two natures has now been introduced. But what exactly does that mean for communication in everyday life? And is this approach really suitable for the simultaneous pursuit of exploitation and exploration? To clarify this question, the research project "Ambidexterity, leadership and communication" [7] examined the innovation process of ambidextrous companies from a communication science perspective.

Ambidexterity Is a Dynamic Capability

The research project builds on the understanding of ambidexterity as a *dynamic capability* of companies to be able to exercise both exploration *and* exploitation. The *Dynamic Capabilities View* [46], a research approach coined by the renowned New Zealand economist David J. Teece, deals with an entrepreneurial environment of change and the question of how companies can best adapt to it. When markets change continuously and price competition intensifies, when proven products are disrupted by new technologies due to the digitalization, only those firms will survive that are able to adapt to ever new conditions and continuously change their resource base.

David Teece's research focuses primarily on the role of managers. The activities of top and senior managers at the micro level of organizations lead to a company's ability to master the leap into the future. Teece sees ambidexterity as a necessary dynamic capability that companies can create through the actions of their leaders.

He describes executives who find new strategic courses of action again and again, who at the same time drive the implementation of existing strategic goals and who simultaneously manage to configure and reconfigure the existing company set-up.

However, there is little knowledge about *how exactly* leaders can exercise these dynamic abilities on a daily basis. The research project "Communication, Leadership and Ambidexterity" by Julia Duwe [7] offers an interdisciplinary solution to that question.

Study "Communication, Leadership and Ambidexterity"

The case study-based research project in the German mechanical engineering industry focuses on product launches of large international companies. It asks what contribution managers can make in their daily work to ensure that companies remain competitive in the long term in a dynamic market and technology environment. As part of a qualitative research project, managers from German industrial companies in the environment of Industry 4.0 and digitalization were interviewed between 2013 and 2015. The results of the study are based on expert interviews with top and senior managers (board members, upper management levels) from German industrial companies in the high-technology sector. Only managers were selected for the interview, who were active either in the environment of exploitation or in the environment of exploration or in both worlds. The managers provided information about the leadership and communication patterns they used to achieve their innovation goals in everyday working life. The results made it clear that the communicative actions of the managers fundamentally differed depending on the strategic goal behind—exploration *or* exploitation.

The behavior of the managers either was focused on the exchange and distribution of strategic content. Or it reflected the social process of negotiating reality. It ranged from strictly hierarchically organized communication management to the loose orchestration of open networks. Communication patterns emerged that were used for implementing of defined strategic goals and others that were used for the creation of a "green field" and for entering new territory. At the same time, specific communication patterns emerged that supported both strategic approaches and that balanced exploration and exploitation activities of an organization. Thus, by their communicative behavior the managers where able to control whether they supported exploration *or* exploitation or whether they promoted the balancing act necessary for contextual ambidexterity of the organization through their different communication behaviors. Their behavior thus reflected the bimodal nature of communication.

Connecting the Worlds Through Communication

The results of the research study have been summarized in a communication-based model of ambidextrous leadership, which takes into account the demand for change and adaptability of organizations. The model reflects the twofold conceptualization of communication as both distribution/ transmission of knowledge *and* generation of knowledge. It describes how the different natures of communication support leaders to continuously adapt their own actions and thus bring about dynamic capabilities in companies.

The model provides answers to the question of *how exactly* managers can use existing strengths in an area of conflict between exploration and exploitation via communication, how they can identify new fields of action and, if necessary, change and reconfigure the existing resource base of a company. It shows how managers can influence radical and incremental innovation simultaneously through their daily communicative actions and how they can profitably combine both worlds (Fig. 2.7).

Building on the research findings, this book looks at the opportunities and chances of leadership in the environment of different innovation projects. Chapters 3–5 provide simple recommendations for leading in an increasingly complex, dynamic and ambivalent world. They offer courses of action to easily create an innovative internal environment through communicative action, and to successfully combine exploration and exploitation where necessary.

Communication Shapes Innovation Culture

While previous research on communication of managers has rarely focused on the design of innovation-specific actions, communication moves to the center of leadership in innovation contexts. Leadership communication shapes the culture of innovation and actually can initiate change in teams. The German Academy of Science and Engineering Acatech [47] predicts: "It is likely that work in Industry 4.0 will bring significantly

Ambidextrous leadership

Fig. 2.7 Ambidextrous leadership through communication

increased complexity, abstraction and problem-solving demands to the workplace." The successful integration of future technologies requires "to intelligently embed it in an innovative social organization".

The development of an innovative social organization called for here begins first and foremost with the people and the culture of a company. And managers have a decisive influence on the culture. Because it is precisely the design of communication between managers and employees or the facilitation of communication in teams that is important for motivation and mutual understanding. It is also a prerequisite for new ideas to emerge in the first place.

2.3.3.2 The Model of Ambidextrous Communication

"Innovation is networking, neural network, corporate culture" is how an expert from a German industrial company describes the importance of exchange and interaction in the company [7]. An open culture is seen as a prerequisite for innovation. Innovation can only be achieved through corporate culture. Innovation paves its way when it is possible (and desired!) to *discuss ideas* in the corridors and across departmental boundaries and hierarchical levels. An important lever for changing a culture lies in the communicative culture of a firm [37].

The communication model presented in this book shows that leaders have to act *differently* depending on the innovation context—exploitation, exploration or both. They can empower and institutionalize internal ecosystems and decentral communication networks for new business through different types of communicative action. This is even possible in the midst of a hierarchy-driven top-down culture of existing business fields.

Let us first look at the distinction between exploitation and exploration: Efficient management of the innovation process in the environment of incremental improvements and the optimization of the existing business requires clarity in the instructions for action (exploitation) on the one hand. On the other hand, this clarity is usually not available in the exploration environment and with regards to new technological solution spaces.

In everyday life, from a communication perspective, centralized communication processes meet numerous decentralized solution-finding steps based on exchange and interaction. Communication geared towards integration and homogeneity for strategy implementation meets the orchestration of heterogeneity and the variety of possible solutions. Narrow implementation scopes and process efficiency compete with solution spaces for radical innovation. We therefore base this book on the following principle:

▶ **1. Radical and incremental innovation requires different communicative actions from leaders.**

Table 2.3 provides initial indications of the different courses of communicative action by leaders in an ambidextrous organizational environment. Communication in the context of *radical innovation* (right column) appears as distributed, autonomous and bottom-up. In such an environment, it is mostly the vision that is communicated top down and controlled by management. Even more, the construction of new reality with regard to emerging solution spaces is at the center of attention. Communication structures are agile in nature. They emerge and evolve in the ongoing process. Leaders do not control but they promote decentralized, cross-departmental and cross-hierarchical communication activities of the teams (see Chap. 3).

Communication in the context of exploitation and *incremental innovation* (Table 2.3, left column) is rather centralized. The contents are derived from the corporate strategy. Information or instructions for action are sent top-down from above to the workforce. Clearly predefined structures, e.g. hierarchical levels, as well as the official means and channels of corporate communication can be used to distribute information. In the environment of exploitation and the improvement of existing products, processes or solutions, it is assumed that the necessary information and knowledge to act effectively is available and that efficiency is increased through the rapid distribution and execution of instructions for action (Chap. 4).

If managers work in an ambidextrous organization, they can use one *or* the other side of the communication toolbox, depending on the context. However, the model of

Table 2.3 Differences in communication for exploration and exploitation

	Exploitation	Exploration
Corporate strategy	Core business/ core component of corporate strategy, top-down initiative	Not (yet) part of corporate strategy, often a bottom-up initiative
Nature of communication	Communication is transmission; formalized, organized, centralized, official, hierarchy-centric	Emergence of new reality through interaction; informal, less tightly organized, decentralized, unofficial, cross-departmental and cross-hierarchical
How communication is organized	Clearly predefined communication structures: pyramid, communication cascades, centrally controlled top-down communication, classic instruments of internal corporate communication	Agile, adaptive, growing communication structures: ecosystem management bottom-up communication, horizontal and decentralized network communication, agile communication kit, design thinking
Target groups	Broad communication: e.g. all employees	Initially, communication with a defined group of people; depending on the maturity of the technology, the circle of addressees grows
Content	Corporate strategy, efficiency, costs, volume business, process innovation	Customer benefits, potentials technological innovation, business model innovation, new contents only emerges
Objective	Execution of the strategy, increasing efficiency, homogeneity, achieving a common denominator in the organization	Finding new solutions, creating customer value, out-of-the-box thinking, networked working, willingness to take risks, heterogeneity, promoting diversity and networking
Leadership culture	Omniscient manager, leadership by authority, hierarchy to improve efficiency	Promoter, orchestrator, networker, bridge builder, leading through communication and promoting communication

ambidextrous communication contains additional, *connecting* tools beyond the communication options for exploration *or* exploitation. This is the basis of the second principle of this book:

▶ **2. Ambidexterity is more than the ability to navigate either exploitation or exploration. In the ambidextrous organization, leaders use additional communication tools for balancing, orchestrating, and connecting *both* worlds** (Fig. 2.7).

Table 2.4 Communication to promote ambidexterity

	Ambidextrous organization
Corporate strategy	Communicate ambidextrous vision and strategic actions for *both* worlds; implement innovative bottom-up activities in your strategy communications
Nature of communication	Distribute information on vision and goals top-down *and* make connections between both worlds (reconfiguration)
How communication is organized	Use clearly predefined communication structures to communicate vision and strategy. Additionally, create new communication and network spaces for both worlds
Target group	Employees of *both* worlds
Content	Justify and explain why exploration is necessary even though today's business is successful; communicate ambidextrous vision and strategy (= both worlds as context for action); explain the goals of one world against the background of the other; show mutual benefit
Objective	Gain acceptance, understanding, commitment for both worlds and for necessary transformation; generate and institutionalize exchange between both worlds, create new links, prepare redistribution and recomposition of resources
Leadership culture	Ambidextrous and adaptive understanding of leadership (both worlds in focus), balancing and adapting according to the innovation context, top-down communication *and* reconfiguration of the organizational setting

When leaders are ambidextrous, they manage to make the *connection* between activities for the present and for the future. Because when 70, 80, 90% of sales are generated by a company's well-known, successful core business (exploitation), if companies report successful annual financial statements, why should people in organizations accept change?

Ambidextrous leaders have an answer to this question. They justify why changes are urgently needed for the future, even though a company is extremely successful today. They sit in the middle of the worlds shown in Fig. 2.7 and they connect the left and right sides of the organization. Through their communicative actions, they shape the corporate culture and the mindset of the ambidextrous organization and, in their daily interaction with the people of a company, they create the appropriate context of meaning for the two worlds to coexist and cooperate. And finally, they know how the boundaries between exploitation and exploration can finally become blurred (Table 2.4).

The first promising step in ambidextrous leadership is to question one's own patterns of thought and action: Even before expectations are placed on the teams, you communicate the ideas, goals and intentions of a "two-world space" (Chap. 5) in a truly credible and comprehensible way. This includes the presentation of a clear vision of the future. The vision spans a space in which the *interconnectedness* of the two worlds becomes clear. You explain and clearly communicate *why* the company needs opposing goals, what strategic measures need to be implemented to achieve them, and how both worlds benefit from each other. For the latter, simply sending out messages is no longer enough. Managers must build connections, i.e. opportunities for communication and exchange. By actively connecting people from different innovation contexts, they can prepare a reconfiguration and redistribution of resources—and of mindsets.

Reconfiguration: Connecting People in the Network

The abstract understanding of leadership as 'reconfiguration' and as 'the connecting of worlds' can be accomplished through very simple measures. They establish exchange between groups of people who were previously not in touch: From the cross-disciplinary use of company spaces, to the introduction of a business partner model, or the creation of a common resource base for both worlds, different approaches will work. The task of leaders in this context is to connect people in a network. Networking and interaction require that you plan and prepare (institutionalize) communication between groups of people.

The goal is that the employees from both worlds *accept* each other and that they understand their own role in the overall system. In addition, against the backdrop of future business opportunities, new core competencies must be developed and existing competencies will have to be reconfigured. It is exactly this redistribution, reconfiguration, reallocation of resources that leaders must prepare systematically. It is not enough to offer coffee spaces and meeting points for "casual" exchange in the company. The exchange between technology and competence teams must be consciously prepared and planned against the background of a new business or business model, as the following examples of reconfiguring measures show.

Example

Example 1: Cross-Divisional Interdisciplinary Project Organization

A supplier of components for machinery and equipment has established a project-based organization within the existing structures of the company to digitize one of its core technologies. Steered and led by a central project management team, company-wide sub teams are being set up to drive the technological change, the potential change in the business model, and the necessary cultural change.

The project goal is to establish a cross-divisional and cross-national ecosystem for the market launch of a new technology. To this end, the company's existing core processes are being used where possible, such as in hardware development, production or marketing. In addition, new processes and interdisciplinary teams will be set up by the project team, which will take over partial tasks of the new digital business. The guiding principle here is the use of the best processes from the existing world and the introduction of new processes and methods where the existing ways do not work. Reconfiguration arises here through the cross-departmental development of new structures and the connecting of interdisciplinary teams in the midst of the existing organization. By networking units that have not worked together directly up to now and by reconnecting the company's existing know-how, solutions are created that pave the way for the new business.

Example 2: Connecting Technologies Through an Ideal Use of Space

A manufacturer of machines for industrial manufacturing changes its use of corporate spaces in order to support the shift towards a new business model. The company plans to connect employees from different areas. The firm, which on the one hand is successful with the sale of single machines (product-centric approach), is also implementing a platform-based business model that supports the entire production process of its customers (solutions-centric view). In addition to the optimization and incremental further development of existing hardware products, a new range of networked Industry 4.0 solutions is to be created. Connecting the individual machines in the production process will increase the customer value many times over.

However, the teams, which were previously divided according to single machine technologies (= silos), must work together in a completely different way for this purpose. But this was made difficult by the existing R+D infrastructure which was organized according to technologies. The desired software-based horizontal networking of the machines and technologies was initiated in the test area of the research and development division by bringing together the people working on the individual technologies in a new location. Against this background, the test facilities were redistributed and relocated and with regards to the new business field, teams were reassembled by relocating the workplace of the individual employees.

Additional breakfast rooms led to the exchange of people who previously did not get in touch with each other simply because of the spatial separation. This spatial reconfiguration brought about completely new connections between the teams that were profitable for the company's future business.

Example 3: Building a Common Competence and Resource Base

An automotive supplier describes how the R+D resource base, which has been firmly anchored in a business unit for decades, is being removed from the original structures and transferred to a central unit outside the traditional business units in the course of establishing a new future business. The new central unit itself will be transformed in such a way that it will offer development and qualification services for existing as well as new business units after the separation. In the newly created competence and resource pool, existing competencies will be further developed and new IoT and digitalization competencies will be built up. This approach is based on the assumption that the company's existing valuable know-how can also bring profit in completely new markets. At the same time, the new IT and digitalization know-how can also be implemented into the existing business in existing markets.

This approach shows the *structural* separation of business areas, which however access a common research, development and qualification infrastructure. By 'merging' the R+D resource base, new linkages will emerge that provide added value for all business areas. ◄

All of the approaches and measures just described serve the same purpose of expanding the daily context of meaning for employees in organizations with regard to new business areas and to initiate the transformation. All three examples require intensive support from leaders at all levels.

Because such simple interventions (project organization, new use of space) up to serious ones as in Example 3 (complete reorganization) will only be successful if the leadership culture, the understanding of leadership, the understanding of roles at all levels also change. The importance of a cultural change cannot be emphasized enough. Because the culture is shaped by leaders and organizational change is either massively blocked or enabled by their actions.

For the time in the transition mode, when the two worlds have to be connected in a profitable way, this book presents concrete communication-based leadership tools that help to shape a new culture (Chap. 5). These core elements, based on communicative action, make it easier to actually implement an ambidextrous leadership style in a hybrid world.

Summary: Communication Promotes Ambidexterity

Corporate communication can be described on the basis of three different fields of action: Market communication and public relations aim at a homogeneous external image of an organization. Internal communication deals with internal information flows and communication events within a company. It channels the diversity and heterogeneity of voices and opinions for the joint provision of services based on the division of labor. In this book, we delve into the internal communication of leaders.

In principle, two types of communication can be assumed in the communicative actions of leaders: On the one hand, communication serves to *transmit information* and, on the other, to *construct reality*. Especially in the environment of innovation, both natures must be actively used, since communication has this 'innovation-creating' character beyond the mere transmission of content: Through communicative interaction, people from the most diverse disciplines can negotiate common perspectives and thus bring an innovation, an object, a business model to life.

We can use the knowledge of the two natures of communication in a targeted manner in the environment of existing and new business. This is the essence of the German research project from 2015 "Ambidexterity, Leadership and Communication" presented here. Depending on the innovation context—exploitation or exploration—leaders need to act differently. Even in the midst of a hierarchical top-down culture of existing business fields, they can establish and institutionalize internal ecosystems and network communication for new business fields.

Ambidextrous leadership, however, goes beyond the combination of action patterns for exploration or exploitation. It additionally requires specific *balancing* and reconfiguring patterns that expand the comprehensive context of meaning for employees in organizations with regard to existing and new business areas and thus trigger the transformation process. ◄

2.4   Conclusion: The Gift for Something Completely New

Let us go back to the questions posed at the beginning: What is ambidexterity? Why do we need it in companies? How does the concept change today's understanding of leadership? And how can I as a manager implement an ambidextrous leadership style?

To clarify these questions at the very beginning of the book, this chapter has introduced the concept of organizational ambidexterity. Ambidexterity provides answers to a phenomenon that can be observed in many places and with which numerous companies are confronted in the environment of digital transformation. They rely on existing technologies in their "cash cow business", while in the background, these technologies are to expire sooner or later. Yet all resources are tied up in today, even though we know that the future is not waiting for us.

This area of tension is of the utmost importance for the upper management of companies. Because they are confronted with both challenges on a daily basis. They have to make decisions about the future of the company. If they focus too much on new solution worlds, in extreme cases the solid basis of the workforce will be alienated. If the focus is too strongly on today's business, it is only a matter of time before a company loses its connection to the future. The concept of organizational ambidexterity provides a scientific explanation and a viable model for strategizing and navigating in this situation. It describes companies that manage to balance both worlds: They drive the evolution in order to finance the revolution. At the core of the concept is the parallel orchestration and balancing of *exploration*, which is entering new technological territory, new business models and new markets, and *exploitation*, the expansion and evolutionary development of the existing business. The goal is to find a way to transform the difficult "exploration / exploitation trade-off" into a synergetic co-existence.

Patterns of Action for Orchestrating the Worlds
Companies have developed very different patterns of action for this purpose. The more advanced they become, the more they require ambidextrous leadership from their managers—right through to all the players in an organization. Whereas initially a temporal, sequential separation of exploration and exploitation was favored—we do one first, followed by activities for the other—the intensified pressure of a highly dynamic market and technology environment no longer leaves time for such an approach. Today, both worlds—core business and future business—have to happen simultaneously. This is why in many places a structural separation of existing and new business areas can be observed. Dual structures are then created so that the two opposing worlds do not hinder each other and allow a clear assignment of people. Only a few people at the top then have to balance both worlds.

But here, too, reality shows that a strict separation usually does not lead to a company's success in the long term. At the latest when the same resources and competencies are needed in both worlds, the boundaries become blurred and the acid test conquers everyday management at all levels of an organization. This state is described in the concept of *contextual* ambidexterity. It makes a permanent balance and orchestration of both innovation contexts necessary. Managers have to deal with conflicting demands every day. They have to balance the tensions and achieve an equilibrium. Ambidexterity is thus no longer just an organizational capability but a competence that every individual must have in everyday leadership. But how?

Change in the Understanding of Leadership

To approach this question, this chapter has taken a deeper look at leadership theories. If ambidexterity is an elementary leadership task, what principles underlie leadership? The core ideas of ambidexterity research first enabled us to get started. It explained that ambidexterity presupposes a corporate identity in which contradictory fields of action are mapped. It requires different criteria and performance indicators for exploration and exploitation and the willingness of management levels to engage in both worlds and to give up feudal approaches. The change in the understanding of leadership goes so far that leaders not only find themselves caught between existing and future business. Moreover, they must be prepared—at least in part—to break away from a pre-defined position of managerial authority—a fundamental rethinking process. Because a rigid understanding of leadership no longer does justice to the situation of companies in the digital transformation. Instead, managers must continually adapt their behavior in an innovation-driven environment depending on the innovation context and, first and foremost, give up their personal, emotional attachment to a formal function.

The 'second hand' of leadership is needed at this point. It is based on an understanding of leadership as *detached* from an assigned authority and rather as the result of a complex process of social interaction. When the interaction between people in the company moves at the center of attention of leaders, communication and exchange between individuals also take on a whole new significance. Communication becomes a powerful element of leadership work.

The Solution: Communication

The central approach of this book takes this shift in meaning into account. It places leadership communication at the center of the consideration. Accordingly, the fields of action of communication in the company were first shown and the essence of internal communication in the company was presented in detail. In alignment with its two fundamental natures, communication does not only serve the mere one-way transmission of existing information. Rather, it has the potential to create new reality. Both facets must be institutionalized in ambidextrous leadership work.

The model of ambidextrous leadership communication explains how leaders can bring ambidexterity into the organization through their daily communication. It aims to make the two natures of communication visible and to institutionalize them in everyday corporate life. The model shows offers different courses of action that are available depending on the innovation context. The instruments are described in detail in the practical part of this book, in the following Chaps. 3, 4 and 5.

The Gift for Crossing Disciplines

Let us jump back to brain researcher Nancy Andreasen's thoughts to close this chapter. Because what she shares is more than encouraging to take the step into ambidexterity. Andreasen describes people who, in addition to their known talents, successfully delve into completely unrelated fields. They then produce cross-disciplinary skills and make exceedingly profitable new connections between areas [20]. "So I made the transition," the scientist explains. "And what I discovered was a tremendous gift for science that I would never have known about if I had not made that change" [21].

So if we dare to step into the unknown, if companies decide to make the change despite all the difficulties to be expected, if new territory is opened up from the strength of a firm's existing capabilities, then a fascinating new world will emerge. And who would not like to know what awaits us there? So let us move on to Chap. 3.

References

1. Osterwalder, Alexander; Pigneur, Yves (2011): Business Model Generation: Ein Handbuch für Visionäre, Spielveränderer und Herausforderer. Frankfurt/Main: Campus.
2. S-Kurven-Konzept. In: Gabler Wirtschaftslexikon. Online: https://wirtschaftslexikon.gabler.de/definition/s-kurven-konzept-43411/version-172224 [Accessed: 23.05.2020].
3. Amberg, Michael; Bodendorf, Freimut; Möslein, Kathrin M. (2011): Wertschöpfungsorientierte Wirtschaftsinformatik. Heidelberg: Springer.
4. Schilling, Melissa A. (2013): Strategic Management of Technological Innovation. 4th edition. New York, NY: McGraw-Hill.
5. Zetsche: Elektroautos erst 2025 wettbewerbsfähig. Interview mit Daimler-Chef Dieter Zetsche. In: Deutschlandfunk, June 25, 2017. Online: https://www.deutschlandfunk.de/elektromobilitaet-zetsche-elektroautos-erst-2025.868.de.html?dram:article_id=389524 [Accessed: 23.05.2020].
6. Angriff auf Tesla und Google: Daimler, VW und BMW entwickeln eigene Betriebssysteme. Handelsblatt, May 25, 2020. Online: https://www.handelsblatt.com/unternehmen/industrie/softwareplattformen-angriff-auf-tesla-und-google-daimler-vw-und-bmw-entwickeln-eigene-betriebssysteme/25847494.html [Accessed: 29.05.2020]
7. Duwe, Julia (2016): Ambidextrie, Führung und Kommunikation. Wiesbaden, Springer Gabler.
8. Birkinshaw, J.; Gupta, Kamini (2013): Clarifying the Distinctive Contribution of Ambidexterity to the Field of Organization Studies. In: Academy of Management Perspectives 27 (4), p. 287–298.
9. Tushman, Michael L.; O'Reilly, Charles A. (1996): Ambidextrous Organizations: Managing Evolutionary and Revolutionary Change. In: California Management Review 38 (4), p. 8–30.
10. Wissenstransfer in der Industrie muss keine Einbahnstraße sein. Interview mit Dr. Heinz-Jürgen Prokop, Vorsitzender des VDW. In: Maschinenmarkt, July 18, 2017. Online: http://www.maschinenmarkt.vogel.de/wissenstransfer-in-der-industrie-muss-keine-einbahnstrasse-sein-a-625782/ [Accessed: 23.05.2020].

11. Henderson, Rebecca M.; Clark, Kim B. (1990): Architectural Innovation: The Reconfiguration of Existing Product Technologies and the Failure of Established Firms. In: Administrative Science Quarterly 35 (1), p. 9–30.

12. Tushman, Michael L. & Anderson, P. (1986): Technological Discontinuities and Organizational Environments. Administrative Science Quarterly (31), p. 439–465.

13. Raisch, S.; Birkinshaw, J. (2008): Organizational Ambidexterity: Antecedents, Outcomes, and Moderators. In: Journal of Management 34 (3), p. 375–409.

14. Duncan, Robert B. (1976): The Ambidextrous Organization: Designing Dual Structures for Innovation. In: Ralph H. Kilmann, Louis R. Pondy und Dennis P. Slevin (ed.): The Management of Organization Design. New York [u.a.]: North-Holland, p. 167–188.

15. March, James G. (1991): Exploration and Exploitation in Organizational Learning. Organization Science, 2 (1), p. 71–87.

16. O'Reilly, Charles A.; Tushman, Michael L. (2004): The Ambidextrous Organization. In: Harvard Business Review 82 (4), p. 74–81.

17. O'Reilly, Charles A.; Tushman, Michael (2013): Organizational Ambidexterity: Past, Present, and Future. In: Academy of Management Perspectives 27 (4), p. 324–338.

18. Gibson, C. B.; Birkinshaw, J. (2004): The Antecedents, Consequences, and Mediating Role of Organizational Ambidexterity. In: Academy of Management Journal 47 (2), p. 209–226.

19. Birkinshaw, J.; Gibson, C. B. (2004): Building Ambidexterity Into an Organization. In: MIT Sloan Management Review 45 (4), p. 47–55.

20. Andreasen, Nancy C. (2005): The Creating Brain: The Neuroscience of Genius. New York: Dana Press.

21. Creativity, Learned or Innate? Interview with Dr. Nancy Andreasen. In: NPR.org vom 15.12.2006. Online: http://www.npr.org/templates/transcript/transcript.php?storyId=6631146 [Accessed 23.05.2020]

22. Andreasen, Nancy C. (2017): "Super Leute" – Interview. In: brand eins, Thema Innovation 4 (7), p. 66–71.

23. O'Reilly, C. A. & Tushman, M. L. (2008): Ambidexterity as a Dynamic Capability: Resolving the Innovator's Dilemma. Research in Organizational Behavior, 28, p. 185–206.

24. Top 50 Crossovers of NBA 2016-17 Season. In: World of Basketball 2, Youtube Kanal. Online: https://www.youtube.com/watch?v=LnyZBATX-wM [Accessed: 23.05.2020].

25. Tushman, Michael L; Smith, Wendy K..; Binns, Andy (2011): The Ambidextrous CEO. In: Harvard Business Manager. June 2011. p. 74–80.

26. Gassmann, Oliver; Sutter, Philipp (2016): Digitale Transformation im Unternehmen gestalten. Geschäftsmodelle, Erfolgsfaktoren, Handlungsanweisungen, Fallstudien. München: Hanser.

27. Lang, Rainhart; Rybnikova, Irma (2014): Aktuelle Führungstheorien und -konzepte. Wiesbaden: Springer Fachmedien.

28. Winkler, Ingo (2010): Contemporary Leadership Theories. Enhancing the Understanding of the Complexity, Subjectivity and Dynamic of Leadership. Heidelberg: Physica-Verlag HD.

29. Avolio, Bruce J.; Bass, Bernard M. (2015): Developing Potential Across a Full Range of Leadership TM: Cases on Transactional and Transformational Leadership. Mahwah, New Jersey: Lawrence Erlbaum Associates.

30. Fraunhofer Gesellschaft (2014): Führung bei Fraunhofer. München: Fraunhofer Gesellschaft.

31. Rosing, Kathrin; Frese, Michael; Bausch, Andreas (2011): Explaining the Heterogeneity of the Leadership-Innovation Relationship: Ambidextrous Leadership. In: The Leadership Quarterly 22 (5), p. 956–974.

32. Fairhurst, Gail T.; Connaughton, Stacey L. (2014): Leadership: A Communicative Perspective. In: Leadership 10 (1), p. 7–35.

33. Giddens, Anthony (1984): The Constitution of Society. Outline of the Theory of Structuration. Berkeley: University of California Press.
34. Likert, Rensis (1961): New Patterns of Management. New York: McGraw-Hill.
35. Zerfass, Ansgar (2014): Unternehmenskommunikation und Kommunikationsmanagement: Strategie, Management und Controlling. In: Ansgar Zerfass und Manfred Piwinger (ed.): Handbuch Unternehmenskommunikation. Wiesbaden: Springer Fachmedien Wiesbaden, p. 21–79.
36. Mattmüller, R. (2012): Integrativ-Prozessuales Marketing: Eine Einführung Mit durchgehender Schwarzkopf&Henkel-Fallstudie (4th edition). Wiesbaden: Springer Gabler.
37. Mast, Claudia (2013): Unternehmenskommunikation (5th edition, Bd. 2308). Konstanz: UTB.
38. Mast, Claudia (2014): Interne Unternehmenskommunikation: Mitarbeiter führen und motivieren. In A. Zerfass & M. Piwinger (ed.), Handbuch Unternehmenskommunikation (p. 1121–1140). Wiesbaden: Springer Fachmedien.
39. Taylor, James R.; van Every, Elizabeth J. (2000): The Emergent Organization. Communication as Its Site and Surface. Mahwah, New Jersey: Lawrence Erlbaum Associates.
40. Shannon, Claude E. (1948): A Mathematical Theory of Communication. Bell System Technical Journal, 27 (3), p. 379–423.
41. Cornelissen, J. P.; Durand, R.; Fiss, P. C.; Lammers, J. C.; Vaara, E. (2015): Putting Communication Front and Center in Institutional Theory and Analysis. In: Academy of Management Review 40 (1), p. 10–27.
42. Weick, Karl E. (1985): Der Prozess des Organisierens. Frankfurt am Main: Suhrkamp.
43. Daft, R. L.; Weick, K. E. (1984): Toward a Model of Organizations as Interpretation Systems. In: Academy of Management Review 9 (2), p. 284–295.
44. Weick, Karl E.; Sutcliffe, Kathleen M.; Obstfeld, David (2005): Organizing and the Process of Sensemaking. In: Organization Science 16 (4), p. 409–421.
45. Zerfass, Ansgar (2009): Kommunikation als konstitutives Element im Innovationsmanagement. Soziologische und kommunikationswissenschaftliche Grundlagen der Open Innovation. In: Ansgar Zerfass und Kathrin M. Moeslein (ed.): Kommunikation als Erfolgsfaktor im Innovationsmanagement. Strategien im Zeitalter der Open Innovation. 1st edition. Wiesbaden: Gabler, p. 23–55.
46. Teece, D. J. (2009): Dynamic Capabilities and Strategic Management. Oxford: Oxford University Press.
47. Acatech. (2013): Umsetzungsempfehlungen für das Zukunftsprojekt Industrie 4.0: Abschlussbericht des Arbeitskreises Industrie 4.0. Frankfurt am Main. Online: https://www.bmbf.de/bmbf/shareddocs/downloads/files/umsetzungsempfehlungen_industrie4_0.pdf [Accessed: 23.05.2020].

Breaking New Ground

3

Abstract

In the past, when we spoke about *innovation*, we meant the creation of new products and solutions for a specific market. Today and in the future, innovation will be about designing global *digital ecosystems around a specific customer value*. Ecosystems consistently place the user at the center of value creation. They offer the chance to leave the 'red ocean' of price competition and commoditized products. Instead, they open up a 'blue ocean' with new digital solutions and new rules of the game in global markets.

This chapter introduces you to an ecosystem-based leadership approach that is tailor-made for the world of digital platforms and ecosystems. You will learn how leaders can build ecosystems for innovation inside an organization and thus break new ground towards the unknown. The more a solution, e.g. in the Industry 4.0 context, is itself determined by autonomous, networking units, the more precisely these abilities must be activated in the innovation teams. It is essential to bring about diverse individual interactions, offer open working spaces, and use the output of the emerging interactions to gain competitive advantages. In this world, communication will be at the very heart of your workplace.

You will now quit the organizational *pyramid* with one person in charge at the top and you will enter the world of adaptive dynamic ecosystems instead. Against this backdrop of a new organizational paradigm, the chapter will examine how leaders will have to adapt their role in the environment of new working methods and philosophies. For this purpose, three communication-based courses of action will be presented. First, the systems-oriented approach of *ecosystem management* is introduced. Second, an excursus into agile working methods discusses the role of communication in agile, autonomous, self-organized teams. Third, the section on design thinking dives into a

© Springer-Verlag GmbH Germany, part of Springer Nature 2022

J. Duwe, *Ambidextrous Leadership*,

https://doi.org/10.1007/978-3-662-64032-6_3

practical approach to enhance creativity through interdisciplinary collaboration and describes how leaders can shape a new mindset in organizations.

3.1   In the Blue Ocean

3.1.1   New Processes for the Digital Transformation

Many industrial companies have built innovation and technology leadership into their DNA. They have once started with new ideas and have grown successfully over decades. However, when the enterprise has reached a certain size, maturity of products and has met increasing competition, the vision of shaping the future is neglected. Instead, we focus on *running* the present business. Aggressive price wars in global markets and products threatened by commoditization require a great deal of our attention. Manufacturing costs must be reduced, processes optimized, and economies of scale achieved while you continuously invest in improving of the existing business. The goal is to increase your company's contribution margins. Welcome to the *red ocean*.

In their book "Blue Ocean Strategy" [1], INSEAD Business School professors W. Chan Kim and Renée Mauborgne divide global markets into 'blue and red oceans'. The term *red ocean* describes well-known markets in all industries. Red oceans are characterized by saturated markets with clearly described rules and boundaries. At a certain point of time in their lifecycle, high-end products develop into mass-produced goods in red oceans. Commoditization and price wars among market participants are a daily occurrence here. The objective or rather the only chance of survival is to beat each other and divide up the market in your own favor. This battle consumes enormous amounts of your corporate energy. The task here is to manage the present. In the red ocean, there is hardly any time or resources left to think about the future.

In the Blue Ocean There Is No Competition
But unforeseen possibilities abound. To generate true innovative power and competitive advantage, Kim and Mauborgne push organizations *not* to swim in the red ocean, but to seek entirely new markets and open up new territory. They call this new territory the *Blue Ocean*.

A blue ocean company is not focused on attacking the competition. It leaves the competition far behind. In a blue ocean, the focus is *not* on existing markets and existing business areas. The attention is on opening up new territory: "It is about creating new land, not dividing existing land" [2]. In a blue ocean, there is no competition.

Companies in the blue ocean do not put the competitor, but the USER at the center of their attention. In contrast to the conventional idea of a trade-off between the lowest possible costs for the company and the greatest possible benefit for the customer, companies tap into the blue ocean when they *both* improve their cost structure *and* achieve added value for the customer. They thus create a 'value innovation' as opposed to a purely technological innovation.

Digitization Comes Just in Time

For the blue ocean, digitization comes at the right time. It offers companies the chance to combine both approaches, i.e. to optimize the cost structure *and* customer value. It provides approaches for radical cost reduction, e.g. through the digitization of services or hardware functions and at the same time helps to generate customer value.

In this way, machine builders and plant operators in the Industry 4.0 environment achieve their productivity goals significantly faster thanks to end-to-end digital solution offerings. From optimized machine designs thanks to a digital twin of a real plant, the simple commissioning and configuration of app-controlled components and cloud-connected machines, to the overall process and data management of plants that provide status information in real time, that are maintained online without downtime and that can be reconfigured or expanded at the touch of a button: Features or services that were expensive to implement via different hardware products or the use of human labor can now be provided digitally and in real time. For companies, digital technologies and business models can significantly improve the cost structure *and* customer value—a *paradise* for those seeking the blue ocean.

Blue Ocean Requires a New Mindset

However, according to experts Kim and Mauborgne, if you decide in favor of a blue ocean strategy you will meet *massive* changes within your organization and its processes [1]. The implementation of a blue ocean strategy is both a difficult experience and a fundamental transformation for companies. However, Harvard Business School professor Gary P. Pisano [3] confirms that a change in internal processes is extremely important in order to generate real innovations: "Your process shapes the product". The *same* process will always produce the *same* products—a core principle that the professor memorably illustrated in a conference lecture in 2015 using a photograph of a spaghetti machine (see Fig. 3.1).

A process must match with the result that is to be produced by it. If a process is designed to develop single machine components that are sold in simple one-time transactions, it will probably not produce a whole system of the same quality that accompanies the customer's entire production process end-to-end and is based on hardware, software and service components. In the same way, a process for the development of combustion engines will not satisfy the altered mobility needs of today's users. Everyday experience shows that only a paradigm shift opens up the opportunity for companies to create radically new solutions that lead to a 'blue ocean'. In an interview, Porsche CEO Oliver Blume points out the profound impact of digitalization on products and processes: "In the automotive industry, digitalization is causing an epochal change. Our products, production, processes—everything is being questioned" [4].

Fig. 3.1 The process shapes the product (own illustration based on Gary P. Pisano [3])

The competencies of individual business units are no longer sufficient to produce new e-mobility solutions. Instead, the merging of hardware, software and services and the emergence of business ecosystems on global markets lead to a multitude of disciplines and faculties involved in the innovation process. They can no longer be mapped in individual departments and divisions. And they additionally require intensive cooperation with partners outside of companies.

Digital Transformation: Investing in Ecosystems
In order to be fast on the market and to withstand competitive pressure, it is almost impossible to build up the necessary new know-how within one's own organization in the shortest possible time. Companies must ensure that they integrate knowledge: across units, e.g. from other internal divisions up to external partners and customers far beyond the boundaries of the company. The sports car manufacturer is also investing in the development of digital ecosystems: "In order to hold its own against traditional and new competitors, Porsche is opening up and working on building an ecosystem with suitable partners" [5].

To gain access to diverse digital resources and competencies, organizations are well advised to open internal boundaries and silos and to shape open structures that are project-based and network-like instead. In addition, corporate boundaries will also open up. Collaboration with external partners, with customers and suppliers, with start-ups, research institutes or universities will become increasingly important for remaining competitive in the long term. If the rules of the game in global markets are changing so dramatically, what changes are inevitably coming to leaders in this environment?

3.1.2   Demand for New Leadership Skills

When we talk about *product* innovations today, tomorrow companies will have to deal with innovation ecosystems and combinations of solutions from different partners. Instead of single products, a whole space of solutions consisting of hardware, software, and numerous services will be offered.

Whether Apple with iTunes, IBM with the supercomputer Watson, Vorwerk with the kitchen wonder Thermomix or the American online magazine Huffington Post—numerous companies are setting an example. They manage to build an entire universe, a *business ecosystem*, around a technological hardware or software platform. At the same time, they are reinventing their business models. Instead of relying exclusively on one-off hardware / software sales, they provide their community with free and paid '*vehicles*' to move around in this cosmos and continuously generate value.

▶   **How can companies profit from dynamic, networked, self-organized business ecosystems when they themselves do not think and act in terms of adaptive structures?**

If you want to be the keystone of a business ecosystem in the market, you must also introduce this paradigm to your organization. According to the statement of researcher Gary Pisano (Fig. 3.1), the design of the innovation process will directly impact the outcome. The process shapes the innovation. Intelligent adaptive platform innovations will only emerge in teams that possess these characteristics and work highly networked themselves. Business ecosystems will only emerge in organizations that have understood the mechanisms of such systems and implemented them in their own processes. But such structures and processes do not emerge on their own. For them to develop and grow at all, someone has to sow the seeds. Who can do this if not the leaders of an organization? Who, if not you?

▶ **Business Ecosystem**   In their Harvard Business Review article "Strategy as Ecology" [6], Marco Iansiti and Roy Levien characterize business ecosystems as "a large number of loosely interconnected participants who depend on each other for their mutual effectiveness and survival." They cultivate symbiotic, complementary relationships. The boundaries of these alliances are fluid.

Similar to biological systems, the experts speak of the "keystone players" of an ecosystem: "Keystones exercise a systemwide role despite being only a small part of their ecosystems' mass." [6] With their platform, they provide the linchpin in the ecosystem and can shape the rules of the entire system. They increase the productivity of a system by using the platform to connect members. They strengthen the ecosystem by creating and sharing value with it. By optimizing the overall system far beyond the own direct operating range and by involving the players in the ecosystem in the process of collaborative value creation, the keystones also create the greatest possible value for themselves in the long term [6].

Although business ecosystems increasingly determine global markets, Iansiti and Levien note that the mechanisms behind them are still far too little understood and managed [6]. But if global markets are increasingly characterized by dynamic, loose networks, companies urgently need to prepare themselves for this.

They also must face another reality: In the ecosystem environment, the all-knowing boss is threatened with extinction. The manager who has all answers to a technical problem or a design of a process, who issues clear instructions to the teams for implementation, will hardly survive in the world of complex ecosystems. The knowledge of one single person will hardly be sufficient to develop and operate a platform-based product-service-system. The complexity of tomorrow's customer-centric solutions has become far too high.

Instead, leaders are asked to admit that they don't have all the answers anymore. And that is the first step. The digital transformation is a unique occasion to rethink and redesign one's own leadership role (Fig. 3.2).

More than they ever notice, leaders shape the processes, structures and the culture of their organization. It would therefore be a wasted opportunity to just passively chase digital change and join the networks and rules of the game from other players in the market. Instead, actively shaping change and being a keystone player means that executives in organizations take responsibility for the future. They have to think far beyond their own product and take services, business models and processes into account. They create the appropriate structures for tomorrows business. At an early stage, they start to get their organization prepared for the revolutionary developments that take place *outside*.

Fear of Flat Hierarchy Unfounded
The fear of flat hierarchical structures is completely unfounded. The fear of losing control in times of autonomous self-organized teams is groundless. After all, in the digital transformation, leaders have a new, pioneering role to play: *They* are the ones to transform the corporate culture, redesign processes and create structures for breaking new ground. *They* are the ones who decide whether a company will become a keystone or a niche player in the digital ecosystem.

For leaders the innovation process, a new, system-oriented management style is recommended. It directs the spotlight beyond the boundaries of one's own area of responsibility: You are a little less of a specialist with a detailed view and a little more of an architect with a system view. Instead of focusing on one's own area or department as a line manager, leaders in the digital transformation must keep an eye on the overall systems (organization and market) and the entire innovation process that extends beyond the boundaries of the firm.

Summary: Keystone Leadership
Strategy experts Kim and Mauborgne divide the global markets into "blue and red oceans". Red oceans are characterized by saturated markets, commoditization, and price

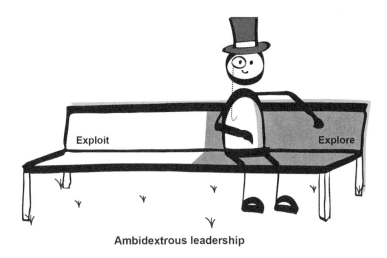

Fig. 3.2 Leading exploration

wars among market participants. In the blue ocean, on the other hand, companies leave the competition behind. This is where digitalization comes into play: In many places, digital technologies can significantly improve cost structures *and* increase customer value—a paradise for those seeking the blue ocean. But companies still underestimate the mechanisms and rules of the new digital ecosystems. Processes are still geared to today's world. But how can an organization profit from dynamic business ecosystems if it does not think and act in an ecosystem-friendly way? If you want to be the keystone in the market, you have to start inside of your company. And this is where the leadership task begins.

To tap into a blue ocean of new opportunities, companies must change their processes and their leadership culture first. Because radical digital innovations require collaboration of various disciplines and stakeholders. They need an open corporate culture that stretches far beyond organizational boundaries. Orchestrating communication and interactions in networks and ecosystems are becoming the new leadership tasks. Leadership that wants to *transform digitally*, whether in research, development, sales, purchasing, production or logistics, requires an ecosystem-based approach. The actions of a leader have to facilitate and enable collaboration across disciplines. Through their thinking and actions, leaders will determine whether a company will chase the digital transformation as a niche player or rise to become a keystone player. ◀

3.2   Leaving the Organizational Pyramid

3.2.1   Pyramid, Network, Ecosystem

Digitization not only revolutionizes the technological world. Due to its interdisciplinary nature, it massively shakes up existing processes and cultures of companies. Instead of sticking to the well-known closed value chains, in the future you'll have to manage open, self-organized innovation ecosystems. To meet the desired customer value, complex product-service-systems will emerge through collaboration across the company and beyond its boundaries. A paradigm shift.

Instead of managing departments or divisions in the classic organizational hierarchy, you as a leader will be challenged to manage value creation networks across divisions and disciplines or even to orchestrate entire ecosystems. These are systems that are geared towards customer value, that adapt continuously and dynamically. They sometimes even evolve unexpectedly and grow far beyond the boundaries of the company. But how exactly is this supposed to work? And what leadership skills are required for it?

Figures 3.3 shows a hierarchical organization compared to a network structure and an ecosystem approach (Sect. 3.3). While decisions in a pyramid organization are made at the hierarchical levels and communicated "downwards", decision-making processes in the network structure shift from upper management levels and supervisory authorities to the level of the employees and teams.

Comparable Change in the World of Manufacturing
A comparison with the world of manufacturing serves as an illustration: "The classic automation pyramid with its hierarchy levels will no longer be up to date," is how the industry magazine IEE explains the change in Industry 4.0 on the occasion of the Hannover Messe 2016 [7]. Instead, decision-making processes in factory control are increasingly

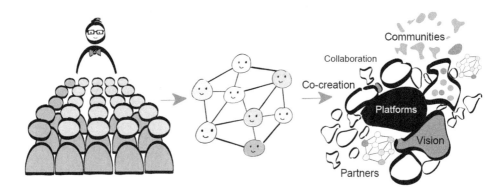

Fig. 3.3 Paradigm shift: organizational pyramid, network and ecosystem

being shifted from the upper levels of the automation pyramid to the lower levels. Festo, a manufacturer of components for industrial automation, describes this process: "Production systems will in future be based on autonomously functioning mechatronic assemblies. These are also called intelligent components. Data processing is increasingly taking place at local levels, and an increasing number of functions are directly integrated on the modules. They network, organize and configure themselves in order to take on orders from the superordinate control level" [8].

Due to the increasing networking of all entities involved in value creation, communication in the network is becoming the focus of Industry 4.0: "Network communication is an important element in the change of the classic industrial manufacturing pyramid to a continuous network of distributed systems", is how the German initiative *Plattform Industrie 4.0* explains the need to promote communication between Industry 4.0 components via technologies, networks and protocols [9].

Danger: Internal Communications Is Underestimated

However, while communication infrastructures of industrial production have become a core component of the reference architecture model for Industry 4.0 (RAMI 4.0) [9], the same efforts are not being made to change internal organizational control and communication processes. In fact, it must be assumed that highly networked digital solutions for the internet of things can only emerge in organizations that think and work in networks of distributed systems.

If leaders want to establish networks within existing organizations they will have to break silos and open intraorganizational boundaries (horizontally). Additionally, they must break down the boundaries between hierarchical levels (vertically) within the line organization.

Only by opening up vertically as well as horizontally can you ensure that innovation networks form and that the right disciplines connect. If companies want to master the increasing complexity at all, 'network communication' must become a core element in their transformation. Just as in the transformation of the automation world described above. Communication in the network, one of the core ideas of this book, will become the linchpin of leadership in Industry 4.0 and other digital businesses.

3.2.2 Network Communication for the Organization 4.0

Let's call it a new *leadership paradigm* where communication is the core competence for action. This type of communication is characterized in its basic nature by the network. Through network communication, self-organized teams and communities can be connected in a loose structure. Through network communication, the internal precursors of business ecosystems can emerge in an organization.

The architects of such internal ecosystems have the role of connecting the stakeholders through a common vision and a common culture. The first step toward an open culture of innovation and toward working in dynamic intraorganizational and interorganizational networks lies in a shared understanding of communication among all stakeholders. It also is based on the organized exchange between the members across departmental and company boundaries (see Sect. 3.3).

Network communication fosters openness. It takes place in real and virtual networks. Personal communication between people is the most sustainable but not the only way to create connections. Leaders, and especially upper-level leaders, have the opportunities to shape this open culture in a company. They can create and grow a culture of open doors, collaboration and cross-functional interdisciplinary exchange by starting it themselves.

Digital Transformation Needs Leadership

As a leader in a company with a long and successful tradition, truly committing to the digital transformation means breaking new ground *despite* the previous success. The step to build new structures means entering uncertainty and contrary winds. Committing to digital transformation does not mean having the right answer every day. Rather, it means harnessing the potential of the (still) unknown and creating completely new connections for it.

The step out of the present and into the digital future requires courage from you as a leader. Because in the present you are safe. You know your environment, your tasks, your goals. But what do these look like when it comes to breaking with precedent? When real leaps in development are to happen? How does your role change when you are no longer 100% familiar with a technical solution and when you need partners for the realization of a vision? When you leave the old behind without being able to define the new exactly?

To lead in uncertainty, you need a strong vision. You'll need a willingness to take risks, and the confidence in the abilities of the people working together to achieve the vision. Leadership in such an environment means creating the conditions for the unexpected. It is about providing the conditions in which the *exception to the rule* can happen *with certainty*. These conditions resemble a reference architecture for the Organization 4.0. This organization has communication and interaction at its core. And the well-defined use of communication in turn provides you as a leader with a stable plan in a volatile environment.

The Curators of the Blue Ocean

There is *no doubt* that the heterogeneity in the teams, if brought together properly, leads to innovative new solutions. There is no doubt that each team member will add unique skills. And there is no doubt that there are methods and leadership tools to profitably harness these unique skills for an organization. Like curators in an art exhibition, leaders in the digital transformation are the ones who create the space and context for multiple interactions and communications, thus multiplying the likelihood that a blue ocean will emerge.

Summary: A New Leadership Paradigm

Digitization not only revolutionizes the technological world. It massively shakes up existing processes and cultures of companies. Instead of managing departments or divisions in the classic organizational pyramid, leaders in the digital world are increasingly called upon to manage value creation networks across divisions and disciplines or even to build and orchestrate entire ecosystems.

But while the infrastructures for communication and networks have become a core component of reference architectures in the Industry 4.0, the same efforts are not being made to change internal management and communication processes of organizations. However, we urgently need a new leadership paradigm in which communication becomes a central ingredient. Because through targeted internal communication in the network, organizations can develop the precursors of business ecosystems. Leaders can take on the role of shapers or key players of internal ecosystems. By creating the conditions for the networking of disciplines and by offering platforms and spaces for exchange, leaders enable digital solutions to emerge around a customer value and to continuously grow. ◀

3.3 Courses of Action

3.3.1 Ecosystem Thinking

What follows is a practical guide to building and maintaining internal ecosystems. We do *not* venture into the scientific depths of systems theory. Nor do we attempt to comprehend cybernetics, the scientific study of the control and communication of complex dynamic systems. However, to better understand ecosystem-based leadership, the basic assumption of the originator of cybernetics, Norbert Wiener, is used at this point: a system becomes controllable when all parameters of the system and their relationships to each other, referred to by Wiener as "communication", are known [10].

Everyday leadership shows: ecosystem management is communication management. It is based on the basic philosophy of thinking and acting in communication and network structures [11]. This ecosystem-based approach to leadership is referred to below as *ecosystem thinking*. *Ecosystem thinking* is based on an understanding of leadership that takes into account the new rules of highly networked global markets and digital data- and service-oriented business models. Although the world outside in the market is increasingly organized in business ecosystems, and even though the economic success of this development can hardly be overlooked, ecosystems still hardly play a role in the management of companies. Far too little attention is given to the mechanisms of loose interconnected networks. Far too seldom is it asked how leadership must change so that business ecosystems do not emerge everywhere else in the world, but in the midst of one's own company.

3.3.1.1 Innovation Ecosystems for the Commercialization of Disruptive Technologies

To help a business ecosystem grow in the market, it is advisable to have a 'test-run' within your own organization. With an internal innovation ecosystem, you can pursue the goal of commercializing disruptive technologies or business models. In practice, building and "running" an internal ecosystem turns out to be a promising way to bring new digital solutions to market. It becomes the *only viable* path when it comes to tapping into a blue ocean. When you want to implement a radically new business model and position yourself as an innovation leader or keystone player in the digital world. At this point, we briefly repeat the definition and concept of business models from Sect. 2.1, as the term will be used more often:

▶ **Business Models** Alexander Osterwalder and Yves Pigneur define a business model in their book "Business Model Generation" as the basic principle "of how an organization creates, delivers, and captures value" [12]. The *Business Model Canvas* designed by the authors describes an organization's key resources and activities, partners, cost structure, value propositions, customer relationships, customer segments, distribution channels, and revenue streams. The canvas serves as a basis hands-on tool to question, revise or redevelop a business model "from the perspective of value creation, customers and cost structure" [12].

In order to bring forth new digital business models and software- and data-driven solutions, the ability of leadership teams to orchestrate ecosystems is increasingly required. They must be able to recognize the potential for value creation in ecosystems, build ecosystems, boost their growth, and keep the systems running towards a shared vision.

In a complex, network-based environment, leadership no longer works in a hierarchical way. Instead, it requires new competencies for managing dynamic intra- and interorganizational networks [13]. In doing so your ecosystems for innovation will grow far beyond the organizational boundaries and establish themselves there as business ecosystems. And this is precisely where you will find added value, when you want to commercialize new solutions. Leadership means supporting these collaborative systems so that they can eventually organize and regulate themselves in a way that is profitable for your organization.

▶ **Ecosystems for Innovation** The word ecosystem goes back to the ancient Greek term oikos and means 'house'. It describes a habitat and the living beings that inhabit it [14]. Ecosystems for innovation are defined in this book as dynamic social organisms that serve the successful introduction of new technologies and their commercialization via a sustainable business model. Innovation ecosystems become meaningful due to the fact that innovations today are no longer generated in a technology-centric manner by individuals or groups of individuals within an organization. Rather, innovations emerge in a highly user-centric context. They emerge from complex interactions between individuals and disciplines inside and outside the organization.

If managers want to build such a loosely connected system, e.g. around technological platform, the motivation and objective should be to bring together participants inside and outside the enterprise in a collaborative value creation process. You enable interaction and collaboration between stakeholders that are relevant to the commercialization of your platform [6]. Innovation ecosystems accordingly appear as value creation networks of loosely connected participants.

The participants (e.g. employees, sales companies, customers, suppliers, development partners) join when they consider the networking to be helpful for achieving their own goals. In contrast to conventional rigid organizational or project structures, the boundaries of such networks are fluid. They adapt independently to the respective tasks and customer benefits and grow by providing added value for the participants, e.g. information, services or connections. A central player, similar to the keystone player in the business ecosystem [6], must be concerned about the state of the overall system—an ideal role for executives in the digitalization environment.

3.3.1.2 Managing Adaptive Structures

Central to ecosystem management is identifying the opportuneness for such a system, establishing it and nurturing it by generating added value for the system's participants [15]. Comparable to biological systems, in which cooperation is beneficial for the living beings involved, an incentive system must also be developed in innovation ecosystems. It offers the connection of members and leads to a growing number of participants who, by being organized in a network, generate higher customer value than is possible for them alone [16].

Compared to the management and control of project organizations in companies, ecosystem management is a highly dynamic process that focuses on customer and partici- pant benefits. Although most companies today work in a network- and project-based manner and divisional boundaries are increasingly opening up, management methods are still conventional in nature. If you, as the project leader, have budgetary sovereignty and an official mandate from senior management, including decision-making authority, then the teams will follow you. In ecosystems in which participating units can also be located outside the company boundaries (or out of scope when an internal initiative must first be brought to the attention of management from the bottom up), budgets and decision-making processes are highly decentralized.

Difference to Traditional Project Management

The only tool you can rely on as a leader in an ecosystem context is your ability to use communication purposefully and to orchestrate it between participants. Because applying pressure will not work in ecosystems. The participants decide voluntarily whether they want to take part. And they'll do as long as they see a personal benefit. Managing an ecosystem means facilitating highly dynamic interactions between participants. It is about enabling people to interact via interfaces and platforms, and constantly gaining new participants who serve the health of the overall system.

In contrast to a conventional project, e.g. a development project with a linear stage-gate process, an ecosystem works according to other rationale. It breathes, moves and changes continuously. It lives. The participants come and go, depending on the benefits that the ecosystem—the living space—provides for them. The objective is to engage all participants and their collective entrepreneurial actions in an overarching vision of an enterprise. This goes beyond pure networking activities. It requires leaders as keystone players ("keystone leadership") to act consciously and at the same time intuitively in an environment of dynamics, uncertainty and unpredictability.

Resilience Through Communication
However, building innovation ecosystems becomes an extremely powerful leadership tool when self-organizing subsystems emerge that are connected and governed solely by a shared raison d'être and vision. A resilient association of participants emerges with the common goal of commercializing an innovative solution. And the likelihood of success of the potential innovation increases as the technology evolves and is optimized, as it does with each additional participant, their relationships, and their contribution to the strategic objective. Just as in nature a growing ecosystem becomes more and more resilient as the chances of survival of its creatures increase.

Create Access to Other Areas and Companies
The larger a company is and the more areas you touch with your topic, the more difficult the task of orchestrating an ecosystem becomes. Against this backdrop, what contribution can you make as a leader? To create a radically new product or a pioneering new solution for customers, you need to gain access to a wide variety of areas, right through to external partners and customers. Because the different disciplines you need will no longer be able to be mapped in your department or a single division due to the increasingly complex requirements (see Fig. 3.4).

Rather, the process of finding a solution will be successful when participants from other areas, external partners such as universities, suppliers and customers can enter your ecosystem for a period of time X and leave again when their purpose is fulfilled or they no longer see any benefit in it.

Leadership that follows the basic idea of ecosystem thinking adds another element to the approach of "network thinking" [17] coined by Ulrich Weinberg, head of the HPI School of Design Thinking. *Ecosystem thinking* is based on the same assumption that knowledge is a decentralized resource distributed in "wide-spread networks" [17] that needs to be harnessed. In doing so, Weinberg emphasizes the urgent need for a transition from "*Brockhaus* thinking that we've known for decades to a networked culture in the twenty-first century world" [18]. He describes three core elements of network thinking that need to be permanently worked on: (1) focusing on the team and on diversity instead of the

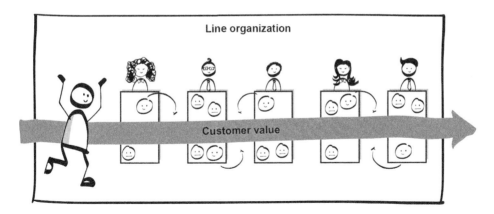

Fig. 3.4 Across the organization: creating access to other resources

individual, (2) breaking out of mere linear thinking and (3) enabling collaboration between people [18]. Leadership based on these three pillars requires that leaders have an understanding of the overall system and know how to link the right disciplines at the right time.

Ecosystem thinking further means 'feeding' such interconnected systems and continuously ensuring the health and balance in the system [16]. It means constantly reassessing and ensuring that all participants find their personal added value and benefit and therefore "voluntarily" join a system. Beyond the networking task, ecosystem leadership requires people who see their overall duty as a supportive, nurturing, connecting activity. *Ecosystem leaders* continuously create added value for the system's stakeholders. They communicate an open and user-centric vision of the future. They actively manage relationships and communication. And they promote a global exchange of experiences by providing knowledge, interfaces and information.

▶   **Book Recommendation: Your Strategy Needs a Strategy: How to Choose and Execute the Right Approach**
      The authors from Boston Consulting Group, Martin Reeves, Knut Haanaes and Janmejaya Sinha, add a new approach to their strategy palette that creates the conditions for building ecosystems [19]: They use the term "shaping" to describe the strategy approach that seeks to open up new markets and set the rules that do not yet exist. In a constantly changing organizational environment, strategic planning cycles must be shortened or transformed into an iterative process. Target positions need to be adjusted or redefined, tactics to be changed, and resources to be reconfigured continuously. In contrast to efficiency-driven strategy, the *shaping approach* pursues the goal of gaining flexibility, adaptability and innovative strength. "Shaping firms mold or reshape an industry by influencing the development of a market in its favor through the coordination with other players" [19].

3.3.1.3 The Seven Steps of Ecosystem Management

Back to the initial statement: ecosystem management is communication management. In order for ecosystems to create a new culture of innovation in the company that enables the collaborative commercialization and marketing of digital innovations, it is the basis of leadership to ensure *nurturing connections*. This is possible with the help of well-planned communication and the initiation of communicative interaction between the ecosystem players.

In practice, recurring patterns of action have emerged that are based on the two natures of communication, (a) the distribution of information and (b) the generation of knowledge through social interaction (see Chap. 2). Based on these tried and tested patterns, a guideline has been developed. It provides you, as a keystone player, with orientation and concrete courses of action when setting up and shaping an internal ecosystem. Ecosystem management is based on seven main steps:

1. Provide a compelling vision based on your future business model
2. Identify and communicate main fields of action for the ecosystem
3. Build an open network
4. Enable and encourage self-organization in teams
5. Create and offer platforms for communication and collaboration
6. Change the operating system. Implement an agile operating system
7. Attract supporters, sponsors and mentors

The steps shown in Fig. 3.5 are not implemented once, but can be run through continuously and used multiple times as needed. The seven steps of ecosystem management describe an iterative, adaptive process. It enables leaders to act as keystone players and to shape and design the ecosystem, while at the same time constantly adapting and responding to new requirements from the system.

This is because new requirements arise continuously in the ecosystem and require the strategy to be reviewed in an iterative process. If, e.g., a development team understands during a meeting with a customer that a different licensing approach would be beneficial for the product, or that previously neglected features are of utmost importance to the customer, the strategic plan should be adapted accordingly and again distributed to the teams. Perhaps new access points to the ecosystem need to be created for new groups of people, or new sponsors and mentors need to be recruited. Ecosystem management (Fig. 3.5) keeps an iterative planning and control process going. This makes it possible to react quickly to customer wishes and reconfigure teams accordingly by continuously reviewing and adjusting your strategic goals.

Step 1: Provide an Integrated Vision Based on Your Future Business Model

The process of establishing an internal ecosystem around a potential innovation begins with the communication of a comprehensive and integrated vision that is linked to the

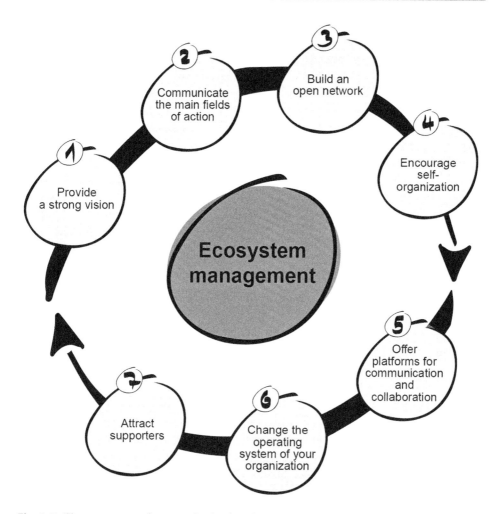

Fig. 3.5 The seven steps of communication-based ecosystem management

overall system of the ambidextrous organization. It contains the starting points for the future business model and shows which opportunities and risks will arise in the future. The vision of a hardware manufacturer, e.g., can depict how its current core business will only contribute *a* share to total sales in the future and that new platform and service-based revenue sources will be added.

The vision of your future business and value generation for your customers is at the center of the overall architecture of your ecosystem. This vision differs significantly from a vision that relates to a single product of a company, e.g. market leadership for a product range. Instead, it describes a complex ecosystem of products and services and provides space for the network described to develop dynamically in the innovation process.

Redefine and Communicate the Frame of Reference

The vision is the essential starting point of the ecosystem. At this point, the strongly pronounced internal view and the thinking in separate individual departments, in separate individual technologies, in separate individual companies must no longer prevail. Rather, a vision for an ecosystem is based on a larger, overall architecture across companies that draws connections across corporate boundaries. This means that components of the overall vision can lie outside of the company's own boundaries, that some of the business can be done outside, for example, with partners. To illustrate this approach, Fig. 3.6 uses the well-known "nine-dot problem" first published by the Gestalt psychologist Martin Scheerer [20] in 1963.

Scheerer demonstrates with a simple test that solutions often lie outside our known frame of reference. The task of connecting all the dots drawn on the left-hand side of Fig. 3.6 with four straight lines without interruption cannot be solved if we remain within the boundaries that are spontaneously visible to us and defined by the four corners. We are so focused on the square that we do not consider looking for a solution outside it. If we consider the space outside the dots, the solution is suddenly easy.

In order for us to be able to build an ecosystem at all, a vision is needed that goes beyond the frame of reference we are familiar with. The vision leaves evolutionary thinking behind and shows a scope of action that goes beyond the boundaries of the company.

Building an ecosystem requires that such a big-picture vision exists and can be communicated to the company's stakeholders. "You need the big picture, otherwise people won't go for it," is how the CEO of mechanical engineering company Bosch Rexroth described the need for a vision in an interview in order to innovate in an environment of epochal change [21]. As in the construction of houses and large buildings, this requires the role of an *architect* who acts and communicates in the context of the overall system.

At the same time, this initial setting of a framework by the senior management is of the utmost importance in another respect: For the teams within the organization, it helps to rate the risk of a radical project as low as possible. It also supports you to get all participants involved in the overall objective. A vision does not have to provide clarity for the concrete implementation of a task, because the detailed design of technology and solution space is decided in the community. Instead, the vision must clearly convey the central customer value. It must be continuously developed in exchange with all players of the ecosystem so that the participants understand and can actively shape their raison d'être at all times.

In the context of ecosystem management, communicating the vision is therefore not a one-off communicative action. It is an iterative process. The initial communication of the envisioned future is followed by a continuous process of sensemaking and providing orientation. Because every change brings uncertainty with it and automatically requires a higher level of communication. The increased use of communication is *even necessary for the survival* of organizations against the backdrop of the massive changes of the digital transformation. It is essential to create trust through a clear vision of the company, to achieve understanding among all those involved and to actively integrate them into the shaping of the vision in an iterative process.

Fig. 3.6 The nine-dot problem. The solution is outside our frame of reference (own illustration inspired by Martin Scheerer [20])

Communication task for leaders:

- Communicate vision to internal stakeholders; thereby broadening the organization's frame of reference and opening up the space for a cross-organizational ecosystem.
- Continuously communicate the vision via different channels (not a one-time action)
- *Sustaining* stakeholder buy-in and involvement, listening to and testing their ideas, and expanding and re-communicating the picture of the future.

Step 2: Identify and Communicate Main Fields of Action for the Ecosystem
When building an ecosystem for innovation, it is important to think not only in terms of individual products or individual technologies, but also in terms of technological solution spaces. The keystone player in an ecosystem often provides a technology platform for this purpose. The participants in the system generate added value for themselves by operating on this hardware or software platform. In return, the keystone provides a certain openness of the platform that leaves room for further development of the technology. The actual

added value generated by the ecosystem is not the platform itself, but the growing knowledge and the ever new strategic fields of action that arise around the platform [22].

In this second step, the strategic fields of action that serve the commercialization of the new technology must be continuously identified and specifically launched in the organization. A system-oriented vision that describes entire *worlds* instead of individual products (see step 1) is a helpful starting point for strategic fields of action. If, e.g., an intelligent hardware platform is developed in your company, e.g. an electric vehicle, a programmable kitchen aid or a transformable automation platform, numerous other objects and complex networks of relationships can gather around these technology platforms, e.g. the future users or app developers, but also customer interfaces, programming interfaces, online shops, hardware accessories, software accessories, etc. Derived from the business model by asking the simple question "How can we earn money with this?", ecosystem managers continuously identify the next fields of action from the overall system and communicate them to the ecosystem players.

If we compare this with the conventional way of developing strategies and associated programs once and then rolling them out over a period of several years, it becomes clear how much ecosystem management requires a different type of iterative strategy making. An agile, adaptive strategy process [19] runs continuously, in iterative steps, in parallel with the development of the ecosystem. It takes into account new, emerging fields of action along the way (including their monetization approaches) as well as new participants to be integrated. Strategy changes or adjustments must be continuously accompanied by communication and distributed among the relevant stakeholders. The strategy process is more like the continuous release management of the software world than the one-time introduction of a traditional hardware product.

Communication task for leaders:

- Derive profitable fields of action from the vision and communicate them
- *Release management*: picking up, developing and launching changes, new fields of action or changes in strategy

Step 3: Build an Open Network

1. Approach: In the third step of ecosystem management, you are in search of new participants for the ecosystem. For the implementation of your strategy, you need people who participate, whether in the process of value creation itself or in the financing of the innovation project. In order to enable an ecosystem to grow and flourish, the continuous search for helpful participants, i.e. users, developers, sellers, buyers, mentors, supporters and financiers, must be the focus of your daily activities.

   This includes reaching out to potential stakeholders in the system who are enthusiastic about an innovation or can contribute skills that are necessary and useful for the introduction of an innovation—from internal research and development to external customers and partners. These connections build on a win-win situation for all parties involved, because knowledge is shared in the ecosystem. This requires a certain openness of the system [22], which you as ecosystem manager ensure.

2. Access: The still widespread desire to be the inventor of an innovation and the rejection of others' ideas, also known as the "not-invented-here" syndrome, seem downright old-fashioned in this environment. Ideas, knowledge and information are shared in order to make progress as quickly as possible by combining different approaches. It is all about using and reusing information. The key resource in ecosystem management is *knowledge*.

   Against this backdrop, ecosystem management means that you provide the constantly new players with *access to* the system with its technology, information and exchange platforms. In order to develop ecosystems, you need transparent and open communication that ensures the distributed exchange of knowledge and information. Provide start-up assistance in the use of communication platforms, moderate communication and make it as easy as possible for the players to contact each other.

3. Networking: For this purpose, it is important that all communication participants know about each other, are given the opportunity to exchange information with each other at any time and have access to necessary information. As the designer of the ecosystem, your role is to enable communication between the participants.

   Within the organization, hierarchical levels take a back seat in ecosystems and knowledge and disciplines come to the fore. Cross-functional and cross-company networking, actively breaking down structures through communication, promoting cooperation and breaking down barriers is another main task of leadership in ecosystems.

4. Configuration: The more complex a project, the more important it becomes to bring together the right disciplines, business units and partners. This involves the constant reconfiguration of resources in the innovation process. As a *keystone player* in the innovation process, your task is to track down and network the right players across the organization and beyond its boundaries. Rigid processes and structures cannot be used here, because depending on the problem, you always need to get new faculties involved. Those responsible for ecosystems continuously ensure that many different disciplines come together and form knowledge networks, and that the space of possibilities of a solution constantly grows due to a growing diversity of involved disciplines and players.

Communication task for leaders:

- Continuously contact helpful participants (approaching the stakeholders)
- Establish communication platforms and connect participants to it (give access)
- Establish and enable connections between participants (networking)
- Make distributed knowledge usable, break down silos, create ever new connections through open communication between areas and hierarchical levels (configuration).

Step 4: Encourage Self-Organization in Teams

The more complex the relationship networks of your ecosystem become over time, the more distributed the teams, decision-making processes, and budgets, the more difficult it will be for you to lead and control an innovation project in the conventional sense. Now, if you stick with the old governance model and claim full control of the overall system, the growth of the system ends at that point. You become the administrator.

In this fourth step, the difference to conventional project management becomes very clear. In the ecosystem, leadership means placing trust in the teams and letting go. Incidentally, the business magazine *brand eins* dedicates an entire issue to the various forms of *letting go* in everyday working life [23]. *Letting go* in ecosystem management means that the self-organization of the participating teams is not only accepted but enabled and decision-making processes are actively decentralized.

For the initiator of an ecosystem, it means getting out of the decision-making role and into the role of the mentor and coordinator. For managers who have "handed over" their employees to an externally initiated ecosystem, it means the same thing. Leadership does not become less important; it just takes on a different focus and it is based on trust. Because this is increasingly important if you want to manage a complex internal network of relationships.

It is almost impossible to consistently make the decisions yourself in a complex system, to make the announcements or have the final say. That is why leaders have to consciously put their teams in the *driver's seat* right from the start and decide to actively decentralize the decision-making processes. All participants maintain an overview through active connection to communication platforms.

Communication task for leaders

- Create transparency, make visible why, which decisions are made and who decides
- Have confidence in the teams and actively communicate and interact
- Allow self-organization and make the progress of all fields of action visible by offering communication platforms
- Allow and enable decentralized decisions, do not always make the announcements yourself

Step 5: Offer Platforms for Communication and Collaboration

If you want your organizational members to organize themselves along the innovation process (step 4), you as an ecosystem manager must create structures that enable rapid communication between the participants, at the same time create transparency about the many different individual activities, and fuel the work on an innovation project. If people like to visit certain 'spaces' and go there again and again, this is a good prerequisite for the progress and growth of an idea.

As an ecosystem manager, you must therefore ensure that attractive exchange platforms (physical as well as virtual) such as co-creation spaces or innovation labs are available. You will ensure that there are spaces where information can be exchanged, progress can be reported, contacts can be made and joint work can be carried out. You can make it your very own business to enable interaction, collaboration and co-creation between teams and customers. Because that is exactly why teams need a place to meet and share. They need a marketplace or space of possibilities where the solution to a customer problem can grow and evolve. This can be real or virtual spaces.

A shared space evolves when all users have the same understanding of the meaning and purpose of the infrastructure offered. If platforms are made available, the central task is to ensure dynamics and to fuel and moderate the exchange.

Communication task for leaders:

- Create spaces, laboratories, temporary meeting places to enable communication and collaboration
- Actively offer rooms for use and communicate rules for use
- Ensure dynamics and exchange in the offered spaces through moderation and regular events

Step 6: Change the Operating System
While existing product portfolios have grown over years in existing stable structures and processes, new digital solutions often require a different mindset. This is where the concept of agile working comes into play. Agile comes from the Latin term "agilis". *Agile* usually refers to a flexible and adaptive behavior. In companies, agile stands for personal responsibility and for increased transparency in the team. It restructures the daily work routine. A new form of communication, which no longer takes place from the top down, but appears networked in the self-organized team, enables teams to reach their goals faster and more creatively and also to complete difficult tasks or a barely feasible workload at high speed.

Whereas in the organizational context of implementing agile approaches, terms such as method, instrument or process fall short of describing the extent of the change, John P. Kotter proposes a more suitable term: He calls agility an *operating system* for organizations, in contrast to today's widespread operating system of the "management-driven hierarchy" [24, 25] (see also Sect. 5.1). In the agile operating system, the manager abandons the role of the all-knowing expert who makes top-down announcements and knows everything. Instead, they become coaches and mentors and create the framework for the right people to come together.

Agile working is, in its basic nature, communication-based working. What originally started in software development [26] is now applied in many areas of companies and in different manifestations. So as an ecosystem manager can implement it directly in your teams and culture. We will delve into this topic in the following sections.

Communication task for leaders:

- Introduce agile operating system, increase transparency through daily exchange and increased communication

Fig. 3.7 Bottom-up initiatives need a tail wind

- Use design thinking for interdisciplinary collaboration and for the iterative processing of development tasks

Step 7: Attract Supporters

Once an idea has grown to a corresponding size, it is time to bring prominent supporters and mentors on board. These can be board members or senior managers. Important customers are also helpful. You need clear backing from the top (and probably funding) so that an initial bottom-up initiative gets tail wind from a strategic top-down decision. Without this tail wind, the climb (Fig. 3.7) can become arduous....

At the same time, you need mentors from different areas and from the company management who accompany and support the teams not only selectively but continuously on the new path in everyday life. To do this, you need to involve managers from all areas of the company, inform them regularly and place them visibly as supporters in the ecosystem.

Communication task for leaders:

- Contact prominent supporters and visibly integrate them into the system
- Connect supporters with ecosystem participants
- Keep supporters informed about the status and progress of a project

Example

Example 1: Ecosystem Management for the Market Launch of an Industry 4.0 Platform

For the global market launch of an intelligent automation platform for Industry 4.0 [27], Festo AG & Co. KG is relying on a network-based organizational structure. With the fundamental change in organizational understanding away from the pyramid and a rigid process world towards a dynamic, user-centric innovation approach, a company-wide, continuously growing team is being set up. It is coordinated by a project management from R+D, which is to drive the market launch of the new digital solution world in a decentralized manner. In addition to the development team, sales companies and, through them, customers can join the global network and participate in the further development of the new technology platform.

Active community and communication management, the provision of knowledge and information on the new digital technology, and the facilitation of a global exchange of experience create added value for the interconnected players. They decide independently to use and expand the existing network structures, which are profitable for the individual and help the company as a whole to commercialize the new technology. Different agile working approaches, such as design thinking and elements from the agile method toolbox, support the teams in the various fields of action. Real laboratory spaces, in which cross-departmental and cross-company communication and collaboration between R&D, sales and customers can take place, are offered, as are internal online platforms that enable dialogue between the participants throughout the company.

Example 2: IBM Launches Global Ecosystem for Innovation

With the Watson Ecosystem, IBM (see also Sect. 6.7) is orchestrating an ecosystem for innovation around its artificial intelligence-based supercomputer, in which customers, partners, startups, universities and research institutes have access to the Watson intelligent platform [28]. Through the ecosystem approach, IBM is pursuing the goal of commercializing Watson. Building the Watson ecosystem first began with the deployment of the Watson Developer Cloud, a platform where developers worldwide can pilot and test business ideas while developing new programs for Watson. In February 2017, IBM opened real spaces for cross-company collaboration in Munich alongside the virtual space, opening a new chapter in collaborative technology development together with clients and partners. An entire world is being created around Watson; via co-allocation, customers and partners are now located in the Watson IoT Center in real terms.

Excerpt from the IBM press release of February 16, 2017: "With the global Watson IoT headquarters in Munich, IBM is breaking new ground in collaboration: In so-called collaboratories—a combination of the words "collaboration" and "laboratories"—IBM experts will work together with clients, partners and research institutions on new cognitive technologies and solutions. This open, cross-company and cross-border collaboration will at the same time become the nucleus of a new ecosystem for innovation," IBM explains [28]. ◄

If the seven steps of ecosystem management described above are followed in an iterative process, a resilient ecosystem can emerge. The stronger the connections between the participants in the ecosystem become, the more resilient the entire system becomes.

Connecting lines become more stable the more often the participants interact with each other—whether in personal contact or on virtual platforms. In order for the ecosystem to gain robustness [6], companies need ecosystem shapers who strengthen existing relationships by initiating and facilitating regular exchanges and continuously ensure the emergence of new relationship.

Focus on Business Model and Monetization Approaches

At the same time, the key players must also ensure that there is a healthy balance between the benefits for the participants and their own benefits as a platform provider. An initially critical development can be found in the following example of a well-known business ecosystem: In July 2012, the Sueddeutsche Zeitung wrote about the short-messaging service Twitter and the risk of open platforms [29]: "Today, an impressively large ecosystem exists that brings considerable additional benefits for many users, but no advertising revenue for Twitter." Twitter's mission is "to make it possible for anyone to create and share ideas and information instantly and without barriers." Up from 328 million *monthly* active users in 2017 [30], the platform can already boast 166 million *daily* active users in 2020, with annual growth of 24 percent [31]. It is thus a key player in a robust ecosystem. And while the company, whose open platform is funded by ad revenue, struggled with a decline in revenue in 2017 [30], Twitter cracks the billion-dollar mark for the first time in 2020 thanks to increased ad revenue [32]. In order for the establishment and maintenance of ecosystems to serve the commercialization of new technologies, it is crucial to consistently keep an eye on one's own business model and the approaches to monetizing services. After all, ecosystems are not an end in themselves, but a targeted strategic approach to radically reshape markets to one's own advantage in the long term (see Shaping strategy [19]). Transferred to the management of innovation ecosystems, it is therefore important to pay consistent attention to the potential monetization opportunities, despite all the benefits for the participants.

Summary: Resilience Through Ecosystem Management

Ecosystem management is communication management. In order for ecosystems to create a new culture of innovation that enables the collaborative commercialization and marketing of digital innovations, the foundation of leadership is to provide *nurturing connections*. This is made possible with the help of organized, well-planned communication and initiation of communication between ecosystem members.

Once the decision has been made to build an ecosystem, this has far-reaching consequences for the previous leadership approach of companies. This is because, like the vision, leadership must be rethought in a much larger frame of reference and beyond departmental, divisional and organizational boundaries. To this end, this section has presented the seven steps of ecosystem management with their respective courses of action for ecosystem leadership and design. From the overarching vision, to the strategic action items and their progress, ecosystem managers must continuously provide all relevant information in the open network. They must allow and encourage self-organization in teams, create communication platforms and implement an agile operating system with new working methods. Finally, it is important to permanently have the important supporters and mentors from all areas on board so that an ecosystem-based project also receives the necessary legitimacy and tail wind. If the steps are taken continuously, this will initially lead to a resilient internal ecosystem. It can become the ideal basis and preparation for a convincing introduction of a new technology to the market. ◀

3.3.2   Excursus: Agile, Communication-Based Operating System

Much has already been written about agile methods and suitable structures in companies. The sole aim of this short excursus is to highlight the connection between agile working and communication. Because agile working is essentially communication-based working. It *automatically* improves communication.

Pulsing

Agile working structures your everyday work. It provides new approaches to the design of projects. The idea is based on implementing shorter coordination cycles, i.e. a new temporal design of coordination processes, a rhythm. Simply by structuring the time of regular coordination between the participants it increases transparency in the team.

Packages

In agile working, goals to be achieved are broken down into manageable tasks and cut into the smallest workable units for everyday use (product backlog). The "tasks" to be completed directly are planned by the teams over a defined recurring period of a few weeks (sprint planning). In daily stand-ups, the team members inform each other about the progress of the work and the next steps. The degree of implementation of the tasks is reviewed at defined intervals, e.g. 2 weeks. The completed tasks are "delivered" in the review. In subsequent retrospectives (retro), the team members look back and evaluate what went well in the current sprint and what needs to be improved.

Customer Benefit

With agile working, the decision-making authority lies with the team. By regularly presenting intermediate statuses, the work is consistently oriented towards the requirements of the customer. This simple user-centric mechanism can be used in any work environment. It leads to processes becoming transparent, teams taking responsibility, picking up speed and working in a more motivated manner. The following excursion into journalism shows that the approach known as 'Scrum' in the software environment not only works in the engineering world [33], but also outside of everyday development work.

Agile Working in Journalism: A Comparison

If you follow the principles of the *Agile Manifesto*, journalism is an excellent example of agile working. Here, people have *always* worked in an "agile" way. Because journalists *always* have their ear to the ground. They are in *constant dialogue* with their audience. In online or newspaper editorial offices, people meet *daily,* often standing up directly at the editorial board (task board) for the first meeting and discuss the day (daily stand-up). Deliveries are made to clients at regular intervals and the feedback discussion (retro) looks at what has been published. Editorial conferences take place *regularly* (sprint planning). Here the next issues are being planned. Topics and articles are included and prioritized in editorial plans (product backlog) and it is defined which contributions are to be worked on for the upcoming publication period (sprint backlog).

While in agile software development the developers are asked to deliver functioning software features regularly within a few weeks [26], the journalist's product is the readable article that has to be delivered. As a rule, publication dates cannot be postponed any more than a presentation date at the customer.

Against this backdrop, it is all the more surprising that large publishing houses and media companies have recently been communicating that they are now "also" implementing agile working methods. Agility is in the nature of journalistic teams: working in sprints is part of the business simply because of the regular publication deadlines from weekly to daily to hourly to minutely.... Whether it is a letter to the editor or an opinion piece in real time—the consistent orientation towards the user determines journalistic action, because the user (the reader) is relentless.

In this environment, the head of an editorial team is ill-advised to make all the decisions himself in every journalistic contribution. In order to counter the flood of information and the exponentially increasing dialogue with the user, he *shifts* decision-making processes to the editorial teams all the way to the readership. Editorial teams are increasingly organizing themselves in a decentralized manner, all the way to authoring models in which the users themselves become producers.

An example of the latter is the American online newspaper *Huffington Post, which was* launched in 2005 *and has gradually transformed itself from an information platform to an interactive collaboration platform.* The editorial team provides the infrastructure and maintains the dynamics in the ecosystem of readers and authors by moderating the network: The terms of use state: "HuffPost provides a forum with a large, diverse audience for you to share your views and express your unique opinions and ideas." The portal delegates responsibility for content to their "independent users" [34]. Industrial companies can find good examples in the strictly time-boxed, highly decentralized work of the now numerous media platforms and be inspired by the culture of fast-moving and permanent change. For here there is an icy battle for attention. Those who do not differentiate themselves will perish. ◄

Agile working is, in its basic nature, communication-based working. The example from the media world shows that you do not have to develop products or services to introduce agile methods in your field. What originally started in software development and found expression in 2001 in the "Manifesto for Agile Software Development" has now spread across all areas of companies.

In this context, the "Agile Manifesto for Software Development" focuses on individuals, interactions and communication in the development process, collaboration with the customer, and a high level of responsiveness to change: "The most efficient and effective way to communicate information to and within a development team is through face-to-face conversation" [26].

Agile Working Is Communication-Based Working

Agile working is simple and can be implemented immediately, regardless of existing processes and routines. A suitable location for the daily meetings, which should last a maximum of 15 min, is ideally close to the teams' workplaces and enables personal exchange between people who are working on a common project. Team members present in turn what they have achieved since yesterday, what they are working on today and whether there are any problems—nothing more.

Agile understood as an operating system defines the working mode of an organizational unit and determines its performance. An agile operating framework provides certain courses of action for communication and collaboration that lead to more transparency, flexibility and efficiency. Agile working is communication-based working [35]. It turns out that increased transparency alone can also increase a team's efficiency and, at the same time, its ability to solve problems. Duplicated work is eliminated, frustration due to lack of information ("I have not been informed") decreases, successes—even the small ones— become visible and are rewarded by the team. The performance in the team, which is only possible through cooperation, becomes transparent and the team grows closer together through regular exchange.

Communication is of central importance in the environment of agile working methods [35]. A new form of communication, which no longer takes place from the top down, but is networked in the team working independently, enables teams to reach their goals faster and more creatively. Suddenly, they are completing tasks that are hardly solvable and a workload that is actually unfeasible at high speed. To work in an agile way, you do not need a system executed dogmatically according to the rules. Just the willingness to use a single element from an agile method toolbox, e.g. managers meeting every morning for the daily, improves the communication and the mindset of a team.

Agile stands for personal responsibility and increased transparency in the team. The manager himself leaves the role of the expert who makes top-down announcements and knows everything. Instead, she becomes more of a coach and mentor. She creates the framework for the right people to come together and for a stronger exchange between the disciplines to take place. The teams are then in permanent communication. The chance to talk to each other on a daily basis and at eye level not only leads to better results, but also to people suddenly "blossoming". Appeals and announcements cannot make this possible. Here, a natural drive from within and fun in simply trying things out arises. New ideas come "automatically".

This agile mindset is also reflected in the following section on design thinking. The innovation approach enables companies to release the creativity of teams through iterative steps and to use it profitably.

3.3.3   Design Thinking as a Common Language

3.3.3.1 Creativity as the Process of Social Interaction

What distinguishes humans—at least in 2021—from robots is their infinite creative potential and the ability to generate unpredictable, unforeseeable ideas. Humans come into the world with this potential. They move playfully during the first years of life. They use their creativity to discover the world and learn new things in an impressively short time. Through education and social conventions, this potential fades into the background over the years. Creativity and bottom-up ideas are often neglected later in professional life in favor of strictly predictable, conceptual top-down approaches. But this is about to change.

Creativity

The American brain researcher Nancy C. Andreasen explains creativity with the help of three essential components [36]:

1. Creativity leads to something new, e.g. new connections, new technical solutions (originality).
2. Creativity produces something useful (utility).
3. Creativity leads to the creation of an artifact (product).

According to Andreasen, the process of creativity itself consists of three components: person, process and product: creativity starts with a *person* who wants to solve a problem. During a creative *process*, he or she works on the task. When the process is finished, there is a result, a *product*. Andreasen considers the exact course of the creative process—how an idea arises from the brain—to be one of the most fascinating challenges of neuroscience.

The Hungarian-American psychologist Mihaly Csikszentmihalyi provides another view: He detaches the creative process from the mind of the individual and describes creativity rather as a social process of interaction between several individuals. "In this respect, creativity does not take place in the mind of the individual, but in the interaction between individual thinking and a socio-cultural context. It is a systemic rather than an individual phenomenon" [37].

Design thinking builds on such a systemic understanding of the creative process. The approach answers the question of how cross-disciplinary collaboration enables the generation of creative ideas in teams. It asks how companies can find completely new profitable products and solutions.

The approach to ideation underlying design thinking builds on the characteristics of creativity described by Andreasen, (1) originality, (2) utility, and (3) bringing forth an artifact. The focus is on *understanding* the user and his very own problem and observing him/her. Starting from the user's needs and the actual motive of his/her actions, the point of view is defined in a few steps, ideas for satisfying his/her needs are generated, prototypes are developed based on this and quickly tested with the user.

3.3.3.2 Design Thinking Changes Culture and Mindset

However, design thinking is more than just an approach to foster creativity. It is a *mindset*. Introducing design thinking offers you as a leader a chance to shift the corporate perspective back to the user *and to realign* the culture of collaboration within organizations for this. The mindset describes the attitude with which you approach the world. It is the logic that underlies our thoughts and actions, e.g. your fundamental attitude towards the importance collaboration. Successfully implementing design thinking requires leaders to embrace new ways of working. The design thinking approach to problem-solving is based on collaboration, team brainstorming and flat hierarchies. To work with this, leaders will need new facilitation skills and a different approach to their own role.

Anne Elisabeth Krueger, who is an expert for user driven innovation and user experience at the Fraunhofer Institute for Industrial Engineering IAO, emphasizes that a design thinking mindset has the power to transform a corporate culture with its clear focus on customers and users as well as on the following traits [38, 39]:

Fail Fast Culture Through Iterations

The design thinking process welcomes and benefits from failing fast. It revolves in time boxed, iterative steps around the user and his motivation to accept a possible offer. Only through iteration, when you pass through the different steps again and again, does a culture emerge in which "failure" is welcome. By quickly testing initial ideas with the user and directly receiving feedback at an early stage of the innovation process, what is perceived as failure becomes your friend. Critical feedback helps you to reach the ideal solution for the user faster.

Focus on People

At the same time, the approach focuses on the teams in the innovation process and the collaboration of people from different disciplines, fields and departments. This also helps to build an open, cross-disciplinary culture in companies.

Creative Self-Confidence

Design thinking reactivates the 'creative self-confidence' that we know from childhood. While children proudly show off their self-created works of art (pictures, lego buildings, etc.), many adults lose confidence in their own ideas. In the rarest cases, they reach for

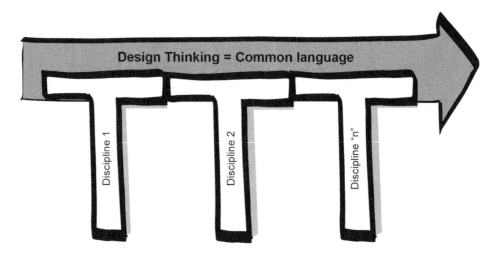

Fig. 3.8 Design thinking as a common language

paper and pencil and visualize an idea because they are afraid of the evaluation of others. And if it is once called for to sketch an idea, then comments such as "That didn't really turn out well now, ..." or "I can't draw, I'm not creative" quickly follow.

Visualization
Visualization connects people in the group and helps them to definitely talk about one and the same thing, despite their different professional backgrounds and respective languages. After all, who does not know the situation from everyday working life? We talk to each other, use the same words and yet mean different things by them. By visualizing their ideas, teams quickly speak a common language that everyone understands (Fig. 3.8).

Structured Process
After all, design thinking is a customer-centric, guided and highly structured process to orchestrate social interaction between individuals from different disciplines. The strict timing and working in short cycles require consistency and discipline. Because this is precisely what leads to results and thus success for the team in the shortest possible time.

"Fostering Creative Confidence"
Interview with Anne Elisabeth Krueger, expert for user experience at the Fraunhofer Institute for Industrial Engineering IAO in Stuttgart

(continued)

In your research, you analyze how companies can establish new digital business models and digital innovation processes that are more efficient. How can design thinking help?

Digitization opens up new market opportunities and new paths for companies. This is precisely why more and more start-ups are springing up. They develop business models that no longer necessarily require many years of technological development or investment. The starting point for larger companies is therefore, just like these start-ups, to no longer pursue an exclusively technology-centric perspective, but rather to proceed in a customer-centric way. Design thinking can help with this. It helps people access the customer perspective who have not thought from this perspective before.

What is the role of leaders in design thinking?

It is important that one person in the design thinking team—even if not explicitly—is in charge and moderates the process. If the process is structured and rules such as certain quality gates are set, idea generation in the team usually works much more efficiently.

At the same time, managers are needed as initiators and role models. If you want to introduce design thinking to engineers from scratch, it is important that someone exemplifies the mindset, thereby creating commitment and inspiring people for it. Only when the teams experience the success of design thinking and recognize the added value in real projects, will there be intrinsic motivation. In the introductory phase, I therefore see above all the leaders who support this and say: 'I provide you with rooms and spaces, I'll give you the backing to invest a little more time perhaps in the beginning in the discovery phase'. The leader can create freedom, provide space and introduce the design thinking methods.

You describe design thinking as a *mindset*. How can I as a leader feed this mindset?

When you introduce design thinking, appreciative communication is extremely important. You should not say 'Design thinking is now the big new thing and the way you worked before is not good'. Then the walls go up internally with the employees. But if I say, 'yes, what we've done so far is good, now we can expand our mindset by using design thinking in certain phases', then I am more likely to get people to accept the new way of working and integrate it sustainably.

How do you define the mindset of design thinking?

It is a special way in which I work: that I allow mistakes, that I dare to share my ideas, that I approach tasks playfully, create free spaces for spinning new ideas, which I then pursue again in a structured process. Design thinking promotes creative self-confidence and works in a visual, human-centric, interdisciplinary and structured way.

(continued)

Design thinking is also referred to as a cross-disciplinary common language. What does design thinking have to do with language and communication?

Design thinking brings together people from different backgrounds. Ideally, you have the so-called 'T-shaped people'. These are people who bring technical expertise, but who are also capable of empathy and communication. On the one hand, people who are capable of interdisciplinary work are beneficial for design thinking activities. But on the other hand, communication and interdisciplinary working is supported and promoted through design thinking.

By working visually (including early prototypes), the members of the design thinking team are guided to express their ideas in concrete terms and not just verbally. This avoids misunderstandings due to e.g. different technical languages and helps to find a common language. At the same time, it helps to structure thoughts and make implicit knowledge accessible.

Design thinking additionally permits a much more authentic communication. For example, there are warm-up techniques that are playful. This is how you get people to laugh with each other right at the beginning and break the so-called ice between them. This creates a completely different atmosphere for later collaboration, team spirit and also for communication.

Individual design thinking activities are extremely targeted and time boxed. E.g., there are 10 min to work on a topic. After that, each person has about 5 min to present their ideas and developed content etc. In this way, communication is consciously controlled. Time for speaking is distributed fairly. Shy people get a chance to speak and extroverted people are cleverly given a limiting framework.

Above all, however, design thinking simplifies communication with customers and users. For example, you create empathy and understanding for them by entering their world of experience and contexts of use and trying to empathize with and understand their experience. This combined with the consistent visualization of ideas and early prototypes as a basis for communication supports you to rapidly find a common language.

Anne Elisabeth Krueger, thank you very much for the interview!

3.3.3.3 The Steps in Design Thinking

The design thinking process is roughly divided into two phases, problem finding and solution finding. Before they start building and developing solutions, participants in design thinking teams take extensive time to adopt the user's perspective and understand the user's needs and problems. Only then do they begin to work out possible solutions and present approaches to solutions in prototypes. Iteration, the multiple going through the steps described in the following section, is a central feature of the design thinking process. Teams approach a solution in short steps and regular repetition of these steps. In doing so, they consistently wear the user's glasses. The five (or in German presentations often six) steps of the process are according to the definition of the School of Design Thinking of the Hasso Plattner Institute in Potsdam [40]:

1. Understand and observe the user (Empathize)
2. Synthesis and definition of the user's point of view (Define)
3. Develop ideas for solutions (Ideate)
4. Select ideas and create prototypes of them (Prototype)
5. Test the prototype at the user (Test)

1. Understand and Observe the User
The first two steps shown in Fig. 3.9, understanding and observing, are often summarized in English as "empathize". Understanding means finding the right problem and the right question. It is about understanding the user and what actually drives them. It is observing, asking and listening. Who is your user? What does she like to do? What drives her? How does she spend her free time? How does she work? What makes her tick? What inspires her? What problem does she have that you might be able to solve?

In order to complete the understanding and observation, this first step of design thinking immediately shifts the perspective to the user. You leave the internal view of your organization behind. You mentally leave your company and visit the user first and foremost. This first step sounds simple. However, it is often skipped in today's corporate world. We know what a customer needs!

Only that is often *not* the case. These first two steps will surprise you. Through active listening, interviewing, observing your potential customer, you find out what *actually* moves him. "Empathize" is the prevalent description of this first phase: You put yourself in your customer's shoes. "Oh, that's how she does it? I wouldn't have thought so" is a

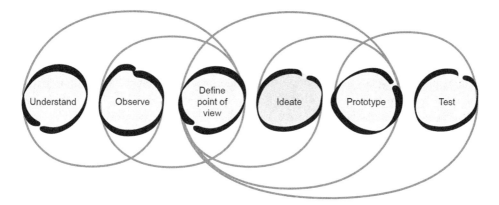

Fig. 3.9 Iterative design thinking process (source: own illustration based on HPI School of Design Thinking [40])

reaction often expressed by teams. The first two steps of the process provide a wealth of material. Nothing is assumed at first. All the information that can be gained is taken in. Really take in all the information you can find about your customer's problem. And let yourself be surprised.

2. Synthesis and Definition of the User's Point of View

This opening step is followed by a 'closing' second step: the synthesis of all the information gained. From the findings, you define the right problem, the actual need of your customer. Now you have to make the collected knowledge visible, get it out of your head and show it to the team. You work with pen and sticky notes. The problem goes on the wall. All the information from the first two steps is pasted up, painted on or written down. Then you can connect the dots. The point is to show the user's perspective. His or her 'point of view'. Tools such as storytelling or the use of customer journey maps are suitable for this. The latter observes the customer while using a particular product or solution and documents the ups and downs on her 'journey'.

Like in detective fiction where the *motive* is being searched for, in this step of the process you are on the hunt for the real *motive*: Why does a person want a vehicle? To get from A to B as quickly as possible? Or to play sports? To go shopping? To go on a trip with the family? To own a new status symbol? There are many reasons that can lead to very different solutions—from a rental car or car-sharing service to a high-tech electric sports car for private ownership. You might have offered an electrified sports car, possibly your user is looking for a ride-share. It is about finding the right motive of your customer and defining it.

3. Develop Ideas for Solutions

Only now do you leave the problem-finding phase behind and enter the solution space. Only now—in the third process step—do you start looking for a solution. Here you use tools such as brainstorming or mind mapping to generate a wealth of possible solutions that can satisfy the specific need of your user. It is important not to make any kind of evaluation at this step. You brainstorm without limiting the process.

4. Select Ideas and Create Prototypes of Them

By building prototypes, you get closer to finding a practical solution. To build an initial prototype, *select* from the plenty of ideas a small number that you would like to implement for the customer test. Whether you use 3D printing or cardboard, aluminum foil or paper—you need a wide variety of materials to build prototypes. The principle of early failure kicks in here, because building a prototype from affordable materials costs you little. Why is this step so important? In many cases, the production line is already in place when customers first come into contact with a product. Companies have made investments that cannot be easily thought away and can "weigh down" an innovation project for years. With a simple first prototype, you are allowed, even obliged, to make mistakes, because via the valuable feedback, you can find out more about the customer's need and save valuable time and money.

5. Test the Prototype

You get feedback when testing with the customer. The solution becomes tangible for the user through the prototype. You *show* what you have developed. The customer tries it out. You observe, learn and get feedback. What is fascinating about the design thinking approach is the iteration that now follows. It uses possible mistakes and user feedback to step-by-step develop a user-centric solution for a specific need of the customer. Like in monopoly, sometimes something drastic happens here: "Go back to start" or three spaces back and adjust the defined point of view. But it is precisely through these iterations that you increase the chance of market success.

▶   Design thinking is taught and researched at the Hasso Plattner Institute
     (HPI) in Potsdam in cooperation with Stanford University, among others.
     The website of the HPI School of Design Thinking provides numerous
     examples and further information:
         HPI School of Design Thinking: https://hpi.de/en/school-of-design-thinking.html
         Stanford d.school: https://dschool.stanford.edu/

3.3.3.4 Innovation and Play

A central feature of design thinking is the *playful* approach. It shapes the process and gives the participants freedom to think and act. It can often be observed that participants in design thinking workshops really have a sigh of relief. The approach causes different feelings than the usual everyday working life does.

In the search for the *reason why* this feeling is so different, a small booklet by Johan Huizinga (1872–1945) on the connection between culture and play from 1938 provides a conclusive answer [41]. In his work "Homo Ludens" (The Playing Man), the Dutch historian deals with the play element in culture. He defines formal characteristics for the human activity of play, which can also explain *why* design thinking is so successfully and enthusiastically adopted by teams [41].

1. Play is voluntary action
2. Play is intermezzo
3. Play is a self-contained action limited in time and space
4. Play is exciting

1. Play Is Voluntary

"In our consciousness, play stands in opposition to seriousness," [41] Huizinga explains. Play liberates through two essential characteristics: on the one hand, through the pure pleasure, the fun of playing, and on the other hand, through the mental stepping out of an actual, real world. It is precisely through this stepping out of the ordinary world that freedom in thought and action arises. This perceived *freedom* often enables participants in design thinking workshops to access creative new solutions that would otherwise often go unmentioned. Sometimes participants are coming up with ideas they "never thought" would contribute. But it is often the ideas that are "too crazy" or "not really feasible"—if they are thought through further and complemented—ultimately lead to the best solution for the user.

Moreover, you cannot force anyone to participate in such a process. That would simply be wasted time. Design thinking is *voluntary*. You voluntarily get yourself involved as a participant. "Commanded play is no longer play", describes Huizinga [41]. And this makes it clear why a hierarchical top-down management approach is not useful here.

2. Game Is *Intermezzo*

Huizinga speaks of areas where you wouldn't expect any elements of play, "namely those of economic production, of exchange, of state and legal life. Here, after all, compelling, bitter seriousness seems to prevail from the outset" [42]. "But," he questions, "this is not the only thing that comes into consideration" [42].

In this sense, the approach of design thinking breaks with the serious character often prevalent in organizations. It takes unfamiliar approaches that result in unexpected new solutions. "Play is not 'ordinary' or 'real' life. Rather, it is the stepping out of it into a temporary sphere" [42] of pleasure and fun.

3. Game Is Limited in Time and Space

"In the sphere of a game, the laws and customs of ordinary life have no validity. We 'are' 'different' and we 'do' it 'differently'." The cultural historian describes play as the "temporary suspension of the 'ordinary world'" [41]. Play is temporal, repeatable, it has a specific sequence, and eventually leads to the solution of a task. The five process steps of design thinking correspond to this. They are being repeated (iteration) until the best solution for the user is found.

At the same time, the game also runs spatially separated:

> The arena, the gaming table, the magic circle, the temple, the stage, the movie screen, the court of justice, they are all playgrounds in form and function, i.e. consecrated ground, segregated, fenced, sanctified territory where special rules apply. They are temporary worlds within the ordinary world, serving to perform a self-contained action [41].

New working worlds, co-working spaces, think tanks, co-creation labs—if you can provide such a space outside the ordinary world described by Johan Huizinga, that is the ideal space for innovation. But it is not the prerequisite. Because you can create this exceptional space anywhere and instantly repurpose any simple meeting room. Move tables to the side, use windows as whiteboards. All it takes is creativity and a bunch of materials to transform a conventional meeting into a creative workshop for generating fresh ideas. Design thinking spaces can be created anywhere in a very short time. Leaders can create and enliven these spaces.

Mobile Starter Kit

To transform any space, you need a mobile starter kit. Even with a small number of things and materials, a workshop can lead to unexpected solutions and a room can become a temporary "world outside the ordinary world". Basic equipment includes:

- A stopwatch / mobile timer for time-boxing
- Colored pencils
- Paper, e.g. sizes A4 and A3
- Whiteboard and whiteboard marker
- Sticky notes and moderation cards in different colors and shapes
- Box with LEGO
- Masking tape, scotch tape
- Alufoil
- Modeling clay
- Any material you like to work with
- Diverse design thinking templates [43]

4. Game Is Exciting

According to Huizinga, uncertainty and chance are key features of the play [41]. They are resolved in the course of the game. It is precisely this opportunity and the moving on uncertain, unknown terrain that is used in design thinking. Leaders and teams alike are given a chance to consciously approach the unknown and to use it for developing new solutions. Not knowing the outcome and being surprised at the end of the game always makes the activity exciting anew for the participants. "With a certain amount of tension, something must succeed," is the description from 1938 [41] that applies to design thinking just as well.

Conclusion: Play Shapes Culture of Innovation

Through play, a different kind of innovation culture unfolds—an idea that the American MIT innovation expert Michael Schrage already explored in depth in his 1999 book "Serious Play": The most important "raw material" of innovation is the interaction of different individuals and the expression of their ideas [44].

Schrage describes the prototyping step taken up in design thinking as "serious play", a serious game and an opportunity for communication and interaction: "Prototypes are a way to think out loud". Innovative prototypes inevitably lead to innovative exchanges between the participants and are the starting point for their further conversation, he says. Schrage sees the task for leaders in making this innovation, which arises in social interaction, possible [44].

Exercise: Setting the Stage with Lego® Serious Play®

Play in everyday corporate life—this is the approach taken by Lego® with its "Lego Serious Play" series [45]. For example: If you start a workshop with asking the participants to build prototypes for the round of introductions you will set the stage in a fundamentally different way. You can invite participants—even if they already know each other—to build themselves with Lego bricks in a few minutes and introduce the "prototypes" to each other afterwards. You will learn more than you would have expected in a professional workshop. This unusual information sets the stage for an unusual workshop day and, at best, provides valuable background information that can be used in generating ideas during the course of the day.

3.3.3.5 Leadership Shapes Corporate Mindset

It is now clear that design thinking requires a different mindset, a different attitude on our part. Now comes the next step: As a leader, you have the chance to change the mindset of an organization by inviting your environment to do so. For leaders, the added value of design thinking unfolds quickly when they actively use the method's potential to connect disciplines and apply it to solve problems.

This is of great value, especially in the case of complex problems, e.g. when new solution spaces have to be created for Industry 4.0 and digitalization. When hardware, software, and services merge in highly integrated intelligent products and systems. Or when new data-based business models are developed. The following insight into the practice of Bosch Power Tools shows that design thinking even has a positive effect on the spirit in the team.

"New Role for Leaders"

Interview with Andreas Leinfelder, Vice President Business Development at Bosch Power Tools GmbH

You have introduced design thinking throughout the company at Bosch Power Tools. What do you expect from this?

We are convinced that design thinking is more than just a method. For us, design thinking is a mindset that supports us in finding better solutions for our users, but also for internal issues, because they are optimized for the respective user. For this purpose, it is important that every employee has at least a basic understanding of design thinking. Ideally, however, as many employees as possible are able to use design thinking in their daily work.

What does design thinking have to do with communication?

From my point of view, design thinking facilitates communication in two different aspects: On the one hand, it strengthens the dialogue with the user, which is a key element in the iterative approach, and on the other hand, it improves the

(continued)

communication and networking within the team, as colleagues collaborate cross-functionally in all phases of the respective project and no longer disappear into their silos.

Does this approach improve communication?

In any case! Design thinking opens up new perspectives for everyone. It improves the common understanding of the user's problem to be solved as well as of the possible solutions and thus leads to better solutions in the end.

What role do your leaders play in an environment that is shaped by design thinking?

Leaders have a different role than before. Instead of proposing solutions to a problem, which are then implemented by the team, it is much more about accompanying and supporting the team, removing barriers and resistance and being an advisor. Leaders have to get used to this in many places. Teams notice very quickly whether the boss will 'know it better' in the end.

How do teams react to the new mindset?

Not only among the teams, but among all employees we find positive reactions to the new way of working and the changed mindset. Even if some colleagues were somewhat skeptical before the first practical contact with design thinking. The new mindset opens up new possibilities for everyone. At the same time, the market success of the solutions developed with design thinking shows that we are on the right track. This success naturally has a positive effect on the spirit in the respective team and thus in the entire company.

Thank you very much, Andreas Leinfelder!

As a leader, the new mindset in teams must be shaped, fostered, moderated, and seeded. The responsibility for finding solutions is handed over to the team and the collaborative process. Decision-making authority also rests with the team. Your role thus becomes a facilitating role. To introduce this new spirit, you can start working differently today, making everyday life more playful, visualizing and sketching your ideas. The sketch sheet (Fig. 3.10) is ready for use.

Visual Communication in Everyday Business

If you are still hesitating, the following book recommendation may help: The Dutch graphic and industrial designer Willemien Brand is convinced of the power of visual communication. With her manual *Visual Thinking—Empowering People & Organizations Through Visual Collaboration,* she has created a small masterpiece for everyday business [46]. The book is an inspiring practical guide for the simple creative design of the daily internal communication of leaders in a highly dynamic market and technology environment. When uncertainty and change become the "new normal," we need ways to quickly adapt to new circumstances and bring together diverse people and tasks. In this context,

For your notes

Fig. 3.10 Page for visualizing your ideas

Willemien Brand introduces *Visual Thinking* as a method to foster effective interdisciplinary collaboration that quickly leads to creative solutions. Pen to hand and let us start....

Summary: Design Thinking Can Be Used in Multiple Ways

If an innovation is viewed holistically, it consists not only of a technical solution, but additionally of numerous accompanying processes and elements: starting with IT infrastructure issues and up to the launch of a marketing campaign. Design thinking cannot be limited to product development, but can support all phases of the innovation process.

Wherever new ground is being broken, creative action can support—whether it is setting up a customer development center, developing a video campaign to launch a new product, building an IT infrastructure to sell software and services, or developing a trade show booth. There is no limit. You can go through the multi-stage process in a short session as well as a workshop day or in sprints lasting several weeks—the key is to apply the right mindset that underpins the thinking and action. Design thinking can be implemented today if leaders start with themselves and make the decision to create a new culture of innovation. ◄

3.4   Conclusion: Just Start

Kim and Mauborgne divide global markets into "blue and red oceans" [1]. Red oceans are characterized by saturated markets, commoditization and price wars among market participants. In the blue ocean, companies leave the competition behind. This is where digitization comes into play: digital technologies can significantly improve the cost structure *and* customer benefits.

Instead of managing a closed value chain, the future of leadership is in the management of open systems. We are encountering self-organized value creation ecosystems that deliver a desired performance in the form of products and services throughout the company and beyond its boundaries. This is a paradigm shift. Yet far too little attention is paid to the mechanisms of ecosystems in companies. Companies' processes are still geared to today's world. But how can companies play a role in dynamic business ecosystems if they do not adapt to such structures internally? If you want to be the keystone player in a market, you have to follow the new rules inside as well.

Communication Is the Linchpin
Innovation ecosystems, an agile operating system and processes that foster creativity—this chapter provided you with courses of action for everyday leadership in an innovative environment. These are approaches that have been tried and tested in everyday work life and that you can start with today. Because digital innovation needs different processes, a

corresponding mindset and an open corporate culture—because all elements have an impact on the result. And communication is the new linchpin in all areas.

In order for ecosystems to foster a new culture of innovation that enables the collaborative commercialization and marketing of digital innovations, leaders will have to provide *nurturing* connections. This is made possible with the help of various communication tools and the initiation of communication between ecosystem actors. Ecosystem management is communication management.

Consequences for the Entire Company

Once the decision has been made to build an innovation ecosystem, it has far-reaching consequences for the way companies have approached innovation processes to date. The seven steps of communication-based ecosystem management are a helpful guide for everyday work. Like the vision of a company, leadership must be rethought in a much larger frame of reference and across departmental, divisional and organizational boundaries. From the overarching vision to strategic action, ecosystem managers must continuously provide all relevant information in the open network. They must promote self-organization in interdisciplinary, cross-divisional teams, create communication platforms and implement an agile operating system with new working methods.

To work in an agile way, you do not need your teams work dogmatically according to the rules. Just the willingness to use a single element from the "method toolbox" improves communication and changes the mindset of a team. Wherever new ground is being broken, agile and creative approaches can support. Agile project management or design thinking can be introduced today if leaders start with themselves and make the decision to create a new culture of innovation.

People at the Heart of Digitalization

With this in mind, people are finally moving to the front of the digital transformation. Because *if* the process of creating digital innovations requires cross-functional teams to network, *if* the technical development of a networked system needs a culture of open doors, where ideas are exchanged in the corridors and across all hierarchical levels, *if* the development of digital platforms and the growth of ecosystems really means that more and more disciplines have to collaborate across company boundaries, then *communication becomes the central skill* of people in the innovation process.

This approach shakes the foundations of a hierarchical understanding of leadership. It describes a new communication-based leadership paradigm. Instead of making top-down announcements, managers consistently create an open culture of communication and networking. They provide the meaningful framework for action and open up spaces for interaction in the network. Through open communication, they provide the teams with a green field and encourage them to try out new ways.

Time Is Short

Because in many companies, the challenging task is to come up with new approaches and solutions for Industry 4.0 and digitalization in the shortest possible time. The competitive pressure increases exponentially. Organizations will only survive in a new digital ecosystem if they pick up speed, go to market quickly and produce innovations in close cooperation with the user.

Say goodbye to the model of the all-knowing manager and rather use a structuring, moderating approach. Build networks so that innovative solutions and associated ecosystems can emerge and grow. If you consciously adopt a new communication style, this can become the starting point for opening up the organization. This change in your behavior as a leader will be immediately noticed by the teams and will trigger a knock-on effect in your organization.

Minimal Effort

If you consciously change your communicative behavior as a leader, this does not require high investments. Nor will giant innovation budgets be needed for implementation. You will not need expensive consultants nor large-scale change projects. Because when you as a leader change, it will impact the entire system. If you consistently focus on the user, investment will follow and budgets will be allocated. You can create a new mindset, change the culture, and reach new territory with the people in your organization. However, you have to take the first step on your own and just start.

References

1. Kim, W. Chan; Mauborgne, Renée (2016). Der Blaue Ozean als Strategie. Wie man neue Märkte schafft, wo es keine Konkurrenz gibt. 2nd revised edition. München: Carl Hanser.
2. Kim, W. Chan; Mauborgne, Renée (2004): Blue Ocean Strategy. In: Harvard Business Review 82 (10), p. 76–84.
3. Pisano, G. P. (2015). Creating Organizational Capabilities to Innovate: R&D Management Conference, June 25, 2015. Pisa.
4. Porsche AG (2017): Wir setzen auf unsere Tradition und gestalten den Sportwagen der Zukunft. Interview mit dem Porsche-Vorstandsvorsitzenden Oliver Blume. Online: https://newsroom. porsche.com/dam/jcr:1a8f0416-531d-487f-a87b-12404dbdfa89/Porsche%20Geschaefts-% 20und%20Nachhaltigkeitsbericht%202016%20-%20Perspective.pdf [Accessed: 29.05.2020].
5. Porsche AG (2017): Digitale Transformation: Porsche investiert in Ökosystem. Pressemitteilung vom 22.06.2017. Online: https://newsroom.porsche.com/de/unternehmen/porsche-digital-noah-konferenz-investition-oekosystem-digitale-transformation-start-up-szene-berlin-13852.html [Accessed: 29.05.2020].
6. Iansiti, Marco; Levien, Roy (2004): Strategy as Ecology. In: Harvard Business Review, March 2004. Online: https://hbr.org/2004/03/strategy-as-ecology [Accessed: 29.05.2020].
7. Hoppe, Stefan; Fritz, Rüdiger (2016): Automatisierungspyramide – die Transformation beginnt. In: IEE Industrie Engineering Effizienz. 04/2016. p. 56–58. Online: https://www.beckhoff.com/ media/downloads/press/2016/german/iee_042016.pdf [Accessed: 29.05.2020].

8. Festo AG & Co. KG: Industrie 4.0. Auf dem Weg zur Produktion der Zukunft. Online: https://www.festo.com/group/de/cms/11903.htm [Accessed: 29.05.2020].

9. Plattform Industrie 4.0 (2016): Netzkommunikation für die Industrie 4.0. Diskussionspapier. Online: https://www.plattform-i40.de/I40/Redaktion/DE/Downloads/Publikation/netzkommunikation-i40.pdf?__blob=publicationFile&v=8 [Accessed: 29.05.2020].

10. Wiener, Norbert (1948): Cybernetics or Control and Communication in the Animal and the Machine. 2nd edition, Cambridge: MIT Press, 1961.

11. Duwe, Julia (2018): Ecosystem Leadership. Blog article, September 23, 2018. Online: https://www.ambidextrie.de/post/ecosystem-leadership [Accessed: 23.05.2020].

12. Osterwalder, Alexander; Pigneur, Yves (2011): Business Model Generation: Ein Handbuch für Visionäre, Spielveränderer und Herausforderer. Frankfurt/Main: Campus.

13. Duwe, Julia (2018): Führung im Ökosystem. In: Springer Professional, August 6, 2018. Online: https://www.springerprofessional.de/leadership/unternehmenskultur/fuehrung-im-oekosystem/15940648 [Accessed: 23.05.2020].

14. California Academy of Sciences: Ecosystems and Ecological Networks. Online: https://www.calacademy.org/explore-science/ecosystems-and-ecological-networks [Accessed: 29.05. 2020].

15. Heil, Sebastian, Enkel, Ellen (2014): Neue Geschäftsmodelle durch Innovationsökosysteme, in: Ili, S, Schmölders, M. (Hrsg.): Open Innovation in der Praxis – Erfahrungen, Fallbeispiele, Erfolgsmethoden. Düsseldorf: Symposion Publishing, p. 187–202.

16. Iansiti, Marco; Levien, Roy (2004): Creating Value in Your Business Ecosystem. Online: http://hbswk.hbs.edu/item/creating-value-in-your-business-ecosystem [Accessed: 29.05.2020].

17. Weinberg, Ulrich (2015): Network Thinking. Was kommt nach dem Brockhaus-Denken? Hamburg: Muhrmann Publishers.

18. Weinberg, Ulrich (2015): Network Thinking. Was kommt nach dem Brockhaus-Denken? Online: https://www.youtube.com/watch?v=BeBBaoLtw8o [Accessed: 29.05.2020].

19. Reeves, M.; Haanaes, K.; Sinha, J. (2015): Your Strategy Needs a Strategy: How to Choose and Execute the Right Approach. Boston: Harvard Business Review Press. Online: https://www.bcg.com/publications/collections/your-strategy-needs-strategy/shaping [Accessed 06.04.2021]

20. Scheerer, Martin (1963): Problem Solving. Scientific American, 208 (4), p. 118–128.

21. Najork, Rolf (2017): "Mut zu großen Schritten". Interview mit dem Vorstandsvorsitzenden von Bosch Rexroth. In: brand eins, Thema Innovation 4 (7), p. 58–61. Online: https://www.brandeins.de/magazine/brand-eins-thema/innovation-2017-laeuft/mut-zu-grossen-schritten   [Accessed: 29.05.2020].

22. Jansen, Slinger; Cusumano, Michael A.; Brinkkemper, Sjaak (2014): Software Ecosystems. Analyzing and Managing Business Networks in the Software Industry. Northampton, Massachusetts: Edward Elgar.

23. Brand eins (2017): Loslassen. Ausgabe 08/2017. Online: https://www.brandeins.de/archiv/2017/loslassen/ [Accessed: 29.05.2020].

24. Kotter, P. John (2014): Accelerate: Building Strategic Agility for a Faster-Moving World. Boston: Harvard Business Review Press.

25. Kotter, John (2016): "Ein völlig neues Spiel". Interview mit John Kotter, June 23, 2017. In: Haufe.de. Online: https://www.haufe.de/personal/hr-management/john-kotter-ueber-agilitaet-unternehmen-brauchen-2-betriebssystem_80_362438.html [Accessed: 29.05.2020].

26. Cunningham, W. (2001): Manifest für Agile Softwareentwicklung. Online: https://agilemanifesto.org/iso/de/principles.html [Accessed: 29.05.2020].

27. Festo AG & Co. KG (2017): Festo Motion Terminal. Online: www.festo.com/motionterminal [Accessed: 29.05.2020].

28. IBM (2017): Globaler IBM Watson IoT Hauptsitz in München öffnet seine Türen – IBM startet weltweites Ökosystem für Innovation. Press release, February 16, 2017. Online: https://www.

pressebox.de/pressemitteilung/ibm-deutschland-gmbh-ehningen/Globaler-IBM-Watson-IoT-Hauptsitz-in-Muenchen-oeffnet-seine-Tueren-IBM-startet-weltweites-Oekosystem-fuer-Innovation/boxid/838354 [Accessed: 29.05.2020].

29. Twitters gefährlicher Strategiewechsel. In: Sueddeutsche Zeitung, July 3, 2017. Online: http://www.sueddeutsche.de/digital/-zeichen-netzwerk-twitters-gefaehrlicher-strategiewechsel-1.1399088-2 [Accessed: 29.05.2020].

30. Twitter-Aktie steigt rasant nach Quartalszahlen. In: Finanzen.net vom 26.04.2017. Online: http://www.finanzen.net/nachricht/aktien/erwartungen-uebertroffen-twitter-aktie-steigt-rasant-nach-quartalszahlen-5381880 [Accessed: 29.05.2020].

31. Twitter (2020): Q1 2020 – Letter to Shareholders. Online: https://s22.q4cdn.com/826641620/files/doc_financials/2020/q1/Q1-2020-Shareholder-Letter.pdf [Accessed: 24.05.2020].

32. "Twitter-Umsatz knackt erstmals die Milliardenmarke". Handelsblatt vom 06.02.2020. Online: https://www.handelsblatt.com/technik/it-internet/kurznachrichtendienst-twitter-umsatz-knackt-erstmals-die-milliardenmarke/25518682.html [Accessed: 24.05.2020].

33. F&E Manager (2014): AGIL. In: F&E Manager, 01/2014. München: AS&P.

34. Huffington Post: Contributer – Terms of Use and User Agreement. Online: https://www.huffingtonpost.co.uk/p/contributor-terms-of-use-and-agreement [Accessed 24.05.2020].

35. Buchholz, Ulrike; Knorre, Susanne (2017): Interne Kommunikation in agilen Unternehmen. Eine Einführung. Wiesbaden: Springer Gabler (essentials).

36. Andreasen, Nancy C. (2005): The Creating Brain: The Neuroscience of Genius. New York: Dana Press.

37. Csikszentmihalyi, Mihaly (1997). Kreativität. Wie Sie das Unmögliche schaffen und Ihre Grenzen überwinden. Stuttgart: Klett-Cotta.

38. Krüger, Anne Elisabeth (2017): Building Ideas. mit Design Thinking und User Experience zu Innovationen. Seminar und Workshop des Fraunhofer Instituts für Arbeitswirtschaft und Organisation IAO in Stuttgart, May 16. /17., 2017.

39. Krüger, Anne Elisabeth; Fronemann, N.; Peissner, M. (2015): Das kreative Potential der Ingenieure. Menschzentrierte Ingenieurskunst. In: Stuttgarter Symposium für Produktentwicklung (SSP). Entwicklung smarter Produkte für die Zukunft, H. Binz, B. Bertsche, W. Bauer und D. Roth, Hrsg., Stuttgart, 40.

40. HPI Academy: Was ist Design Thinking? Online: https://hpi-academy.de/design-thinking/was-ist-design-thinking.html [Accessed: 24.05.2020].

41. Huizinga, Johan (1938): Homo Ludens. Vom Ursprung der Kultur im Spiel. 24. edition, 2015. Reinbeck: Rowohlt.

42. Huizinga, Johan (2014): Das Spielelement der Kultur. Berlin: Matthes & Seitz.

43. Design Kit by IDEO.ORG. Online: http://www.designkit.org/ [Accessed: 24.05.2020].

44. Schrage, Michael (1999): Serious Play: How the World's Best Companies Simulate to Innovate. Boston: Harvard Business School Press.

45. Lego Serious Play: Online: https://www.lego.com/de-de/seriousplay [Accessed: 24.05.2020].

46. Brand, Willemien (2017): Visual Thinking. Empowering People & Organizations Through Visual Collaboration. Amsterdam: BIS Publishers.

Improving Your Current Business

4

Abstract

Beyond artificial intelligence and the digital transformation, the corporate world continues to revolve around your core business. Is your business profitable? Do global price wars increase? Do we need to undercut competitors' prices? Must we improve our process efficiency and reduce our costs? Then we have to redirect our attention now. Because this world is about efficiency instead of innovative new solutions. It is about top-down management and clear announcements in the organizational hierarchy. From the top, to the staff.

This chapter summarizes the most important means and ways of distributing information in organizations. They are standard in large corporations for implementing strategies effectively and rolling them out across the organization. You already know this world. It has stood the test of time and gives us a sense of comfort. But even though we are at home in the management world of the red ocean, we take far too little advantage of the opportunities that communication in the hierarchy offers. For leaders, communication is often a tool that can run alongside the day-to-day management. A wasted potential...

This chapter describes how internal communication of managers increases efficiency. It is about how your projects speed up, accelerate, reach and maintain top speed and finally hit the market. Your communication will be an important management tool in the red ocean. It just appears in a different nature than in the environment of revolutionary change. It pursues the goal of reducing reaction times and bringing people in companies to a common denominator in the shortest possible time: One company, one voice.

4.1   In the Red Ocean

4.1.1   Beat the Competition

To win over the competition is the key goal in the red ocean. While in blue oceans you have reached an almost uncompetitive state, in the red ocean competition is the top priority. Markets are globalized and saturated, technologies are mature. And as your products become commoditized, prices plummet to all-time lows, and you struggle with your cost structure, your only chance is to attack your opponent. It is a matter of taking advantage of every open flank he offers you. There is a war going on in the red ocean.

This struggle will cost enormous amounts of energy. Because in order to be able to shape the future *at all* in the long term (see Chap. 3), companies must *first* master the present. Customer wishes must be fulfilled, the company must be in the black, sales growth must be achieved and salaries must be paid. After all, only those who operate successfully in the here and now will have sufficient resources to finance the great leap into the future. Evolution must pay for the revolution.

Exploitation

To survive the battle in the red ocean, speed and efficiency are the top priorities. Instead of sophisticated engineering, the aim is to offer good-enough products at the lowest possible prices and to drastically reduce your product variants. The focus is on volume business and volume markets as well as investments in automation and increased productivity. The goal is to radically reduce manufacturing costs and achieve economies of scale. Manufacturing companies must optimize existing processes in the red ocean and extract the greatest possible performance from their own organizations. The answer to the red ocean is exploitation.

What does exploitation mean? The American experts for ambidexterity Charles O'Reilly and Michael Tushman describe the path of exploitation as an approach consistently focused on costs and profit [1]. Stanford professor James March—mastermind behind the Exploration/Exploitation Trade-Off—explains, how exploitation creates value from existing resources and represents continuous improvement, efficiency, and speed [2]. In the formal, hierarchical, mechanistic organizational structure for exploitation, a rather authoritarian top-down management style prevails. Margin and productivity take hold as metrics of a strategy- and revenue-driven management control. Tight planning, efficient decision-making processes, the targeted implementation of strategic measures and a policy of stability and continuity are at the heart of corporate management in exploitation settings [1] (see Sect. 2.1).

You already know this world from the past. It has proven itself over decades and provides us with comfort. Because in contrast to radical breaks and erratic market changes, that we have described in Chaps. 2 and 3, here the known world is continuously optimized. While technological discontinuity [3] describes a development in which an existing technology is replaced by a new technology with substitute potential (see Fig. 2.1), continuity means that we remain on the S-curve [4] of a proven technology and continue to pursue it continuously. For the improvement of existing products, it is sufficient to use your familiar competencies, resources, routines and processes. You draw on the existing stock and strengthen your position in a consolidated market.

4.1.2 Shaping Times of Transition

4.1.2.1 The Intermediate State

In such a red ocean environment [5], organizational structures and leadership approaches have successfully evolved over the years. These structures support companies in optimizing processes and becoming even more efficient. Managers are granted the central responsibility and decision-making competencies in this environment. They steer the organization at various hierarchical levels and have the knowledge of *what* needs to be done. They provide the organization with orientation and set the direction. They decide which steps to take and which not to take.

Danger: Rigid Structures

What at first glance seems determined and conveys a pleasant sense of security and stability can, however, also lead to teams relying on the fact that the decision has already been made 'upstairs'. The workforce 'executes' delegated tasks. They receive the tasks from their direct manager—who in turn listens to the announcements coming from the next higher manager, and so on. The result of such processes is often entrenched structures in which no one wants to take responsibility for making a decision until, finally, an issue finds its way to the board. In the worst case, strictly hierarchical organizations become highly rigid rather than efficient entities.

It is therefore easy to understand that more and more studies and management guides forecast a move away from traditional hierarchical models in companies. A well-known representative of the organization as a living organism is the Belgian author Frederic Laloux [6]. In his widely translated book *Reinventing Organizations*, the former McKinsey consultant runs through the various organizational paradigms of the past. He builds on this a new comprehensive 'integral' model of organization that focuses on self-determined human action. Hierarchies are not abolished in the process. Rather, power and decision-making processes are detached from a predefined role of the manager and decentralized broadly across the organization. Hierarchy is not established by assigning positional authority to people, but emerges in a natural process of self-leadership based on the skills of the people who contribute to a task. But this is a state that we have not yet reached in most cases.

More Responsibility *and* Clear Instructions

So back to the traditional organizational hierarchy: Here, a study by the HR consultancy Kienbaum and the career portal StepStone on the organizational structures in German companies reveals an interesting development: Employees are indeed in favor of more organic management models and decentralized decision-making processes. At the same time, it is *the employees* in companies who do not always want the increased responsibility this entails. The participants in the study—among them specialists and managers from German companies in various industries—rated companies with few hierarchical levels as more innovative than companies with a strong hierarchical structure [7]. At the same time, the surveys show that employees still welcome a top-down management style [8]: Four out of five professionals in Germany would like to work in companies with flat hierarchies. At the same time, however, they do not want to do that without clear guidelines from the top. According to the study, employees in organizations want more responsibility. But they still want managers who give clear instructions and who know what needs to be done. In other words, they want *everything*.

Welcome dear reader to the *intermediate state*. In theology, the term *intermediate state* describes the state of a person between death and resurrection. It is also a suitable metaphor for the change that people in organizations are going through right now. They are in the intermediate state between today and tomorrow. They oscillate between organizational paradigms. And *you*, as a leader, must be able to switch from one moment to the next. Because long before your organization is swimming unrivaled in the blue ocean, you as a leader need to shape the transition. Creating the bridge between the new and the old is the task at hand.

This book takes a closer look at this interim state between the worlds. It considers the point of time when companies shift from one organizational paradigm to the other (see Chaps. 2 and 3). It provides answers for stability and for change in organizations and recommends using strategies from both worlds: for tapping into the blue ocean and for surviving in the red ocean.

4.1.2.2 Celebrating the Past

When companies decide that they need to transform, the future state is usually glorified. The new ways of working, the digital technologies and solutions will bring 'salvation'. Once we get there, everything will be better.

But what exactly does the period of time actually look like *before* we reach the future? If we do not plan and design the journey from A to B precisely, we may never arrive at our destination. Nevertheless, dealing intensively with the mindset and strategies for the phase of transition is often neglected, even though this period can drag on for a long time. Building a bridge across the 'gap' between today and tomorrow, continuously moving between the worlds, is not just a necessary evil that we need to overcome as quickly as possible. It is an important period of transition, that we have to consciously shape in order to pave our way to the future.

Shaping the Transition Space

Times of transition are of utmost importance when it comes to human self-development, explains media scientist Claudia Duwe in her research on transition spaces in the personality development of children [9]: "In earlier societies, there were many more social rituals to appreciate the significance of beginnings, endings and transitions in our lives. Each entry into a new phase of life was celebrated, and it also symbolized the end of the previous one." The author points out, that in times of rapid technological change, in which necessary transitional periods become shorter and shorter and beginnings and endings tend to coincide, it is ever more important to *consciously* shape these transitional spaces.

Just as important as this is for the development of the human personality, it is for the development of entire organizations. Consciously perceiving and shaping change is a core competence that companies urgently need in order to move from one world to a new one. It becomes the core skill of leaders who must balance the tensions within their organizations until the time is right for them to successfully leap into a new world. So how do we get started?

Stability: Building on Today's Foundation

If you meet your employees and teams where they are today, if you address them with familiar leadership approaches and at the same time familiarize them with new ways of thinking and acting, then the chances are good that the change will succeed. After all, inspiring organizations build upon a future *and* a past with tradition. Ideally, they offer structures and processes that are geared towards efficiency. They have valuable knowledge and resources on board that have developed over decades. Ambidextrous leaders know that they have to exploit what is available and proven. Because there is a reason your organization is successful today. With all the enthusiasm for the future, they do not forget to celebrate the best of the past!

Because questioning everything would mean that you do not use the previous strengths and in the worst case alienate your team. With the message "The way you are doing it today is wrong, do it differently" you will lose the commitment of the people. But you will urgently need them to move into the future (see Interview with Wilhelm Bauer Chap. 2). And you weaken the self-confidence of the team. Celebrating the recipes for success of the past and *at the same time* welcoming the trends and innovations of the future will give you sufficient scope (and money) for the future.

And it is not just your existing business that needs to be improved in efficiency and speed. At some point, even the newest and most innovative solution will need routines: Put yourself for a moment in the shoes of a future Michelin star chef planning to cook his first star: Bringing forth a completely new menu, a revolution in cuisine, will require extensive creativity. Flavors will be combined, ingredients tried out, preparation methods rethought and completely new procedures tested. It is about breaking new ground, differentiation, standing out from the crowd of first-class restaurants and chefs.

At the same time, to achieve his goal, the chef will rely on routines that the team can master blindfolded. Whether peeling potatoes or grating carrots—when it comes to serving the fragrant menu quickly and perfectly, there will be steps that do not require creativity but efficiency and routine. This is where hierarchy takes hold, where instructions are given and carried out. Command and control.

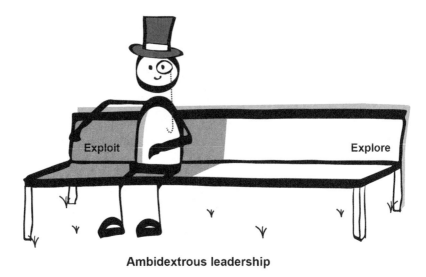

Ambidextrous leadership

Fig. 4.1 Exploitation as a strategy in the red ocean

Not only your current business needs methods to increase efficiency. They are also helpful for innovation and for opening up new territory. Even a star menu needs a creative process *and, later on,* steps for the efficient preparation of each course. At the very latest, when you launch your product in the market (or serve the menu to your guests), you will find it easier to access existing processes and infrastructures that are based on hierarchies, top-down approaches and experiences that have grown over decades. So why not leverage the best of both worlds?

In this chapter, we look in detail at the existing strength of your enterprise—the left half of the bench in Fig 4.1. We'll find out what elements of this foundation can be used to consciously shape the transition space.

Summary: Addressing People in Today's Business

When companies talk about digital transformation, in most cases they glorify the future. Only by implementing new ways of working, and new technologies and solutions, the customer will get the highest value in the future. At the same time, we will reduce our costs as well. Once we get there, everything will be better. While in such a blue ocean of optimal cost and benefit, there is a non-competitive state, in the red ocean competition is paramount [5]. Markets are globalized and saturated, technologies are mature. And as products become commoditized, the only chance is to attack the competitor. To do this, processes are systematically optimized and the greatest possible performance is extracted from one's own organization. The answer to the red ocean is exploitation. It is accompanied by a corporate culture of tight planning, efficient decision-making, targeted implementation of strategic actions and a policy of stability and continuity.

Organizational structures and management approaches that have been tried and tested over decades help companies optimize processes and become even more efficient.

In the worst case, however, strictly hierarchic organizations become highly rigid instead. It is therefore easy to understand that more and more studies and management consultants are forecasting that companies move away from traditional hierarchical models. Against this background, many employees in organizations ask for more responsibility. At the same time, they still want managers who give clear instructions and who know what needs to be done. They want it all. Welcome, dear leader, to the *intermediate state* of shifting consciousness between today's and tomorrow's business.

Against this backdrop, consciously shaping the digital transformation means to use the best of both worlds: Celebrate the future and celebrate the present! If you pick up your employees and teams where they are today, address them with familiar leadership approaches and at the same time familiarize them with new ways of thinking and acting, then the change efforts will succeed. After all, large organizations ideally offer valuable knowledge, resources and infrastructures built up over decades; they have a future *and* a past with tradition. It is therefore important to exploit what is available and proven. ◀

4.2   Using the Organizational Hierarchy

4.2.1   Hierarchy as Opportunity for Efficiency

Hierarchies are powerful means to increase the efficiency of an organization. This is shown by the fact that hierarchical organizational structures have been established and developed over decades in the industrialized world. In these hierarchy-based structures, a form of communication has emerged that corresponds to the patterns of top-down management and centralized decision-making. In the exploitation context, there are numerous ways to communicate in order to optimize processes and align a team towards a common big goal.

Whether you choose articles on the intranet, videos, podcasts or an employee event—in order to execute a strategy in the organization, controlled communication from the top is the method of choice in the hierarchical world. Communication serves to convey strategic content, creates clarity around goals, and can push a team and key stakeholders to action. However, there are conditions that need to be met for a hierarchy-centric communication style.

Managerial Expertise
A prerequisite for centrally organized communication to work is that managers in a central position *know* what they are doing. This path requires expertise from the leaders. In order to issue clear instructions for action, they must know the right path. They need to know the road to success. This is usually the case in a rather stable environment of continuous improvement, existing products and processes and a deep knowledge base. It is most likely

to happen when the answers to problems are already available and when it is "only" a matter of execution.

In such a top-down environment, the processes and responsibilities are clearly defined right from the start. One boss pulls the strings. She has the power to make decisions and can make them quickly. If she is convinced that she is taking the right path, the team is also more easily motivated to follow.

"Efficiency Through Hierarchy"
Interview with Prof. Dr. Manfred Aigner, since 1998 Director of the Institute of Combustion Technology at the German Aerospace Center (Deutsches Zentrum für Luft- und Raumfahrt, DLR) in Stuttgart, formerly Vice President for Gas Turbine Development at the Swiss power plant manufacturer ABB.

Professor Aigner, you have been the head of a large DLR research institute. What do you think of flat organizations and working in networks?

I believe in the flattest possible hierarchies and a culture of open doors. Because such a culture serves innovation and promotes networking and creativity among all people involved. Scientific research institutions often work this way. However, this is usually not an approach *with or without* hierarchy, but a combination of both.

Hierarchies should not be eliminated then?

No, that would not be helpful. Because it always depends on what you want to achieve. E.g. are the solutions for a problem already available or do we have to take completely new paths? According to this, most successful companies pursue combinations of different approaches. In the research department of a firm they might be more creative and networked, while in the production site work is more efficient and hierarchy-oriented. In the areas in between, you have to take the individual case into account: If a project or product is very young, creativity will matter more. If a product is very mature, efficiency becomes more important.

What do you recommend to leaders?

As someone with leadership responsibility you should always ask yourself how much innovation and how much efficiency you need for a task. This is completely different in a research setting, where new approaches to solutions are constantly being sought, than in a car manufacturing environment. There, it is all about speed, competition and cost-cutting. This means that I have to achieve as much efficiency as possible.

Methods for promoting creativity are very suitable when you are looking for an innovative solution, i.e. when no one in the world has yet mastered the problem at hand or has not yet solved it in *this way*. Then I bring together as many minds as possible and also lateral thinkers who can freely discuss and inspire each other. I need a lot of time for this, but I also get the most creative solution through this more

(continued)

interactive communication. In contrast, I get the *fastest solution* from a strictly hierarchical organization. You therefore have to ask yourself what is appropriate for a certain task. If I want to increase efficiency and speed up, then clear announcements are the best way.

How do you proceed then?

When it comes to efficiency, I usually rely on top-down communication to the team. In my experience, clear announcements are particularly necessary and useful when you, as the boss, know exactly what the solution is and the aim is to implement something as effectively as possible in the shortest possible time. Then I direct and 'order'.

How do you get away with that?

I provide a reason *why* something has to be this way now, e.g. due to deadline pressure or complaints from an important customer. It is important to motivate and explain your way so that the team is not puzzled about why they are receiving top-down announcements. Imagine a typical situation in everyday industry: A company sold something that was not finished. Penalties are looming, we have to take action as the 'fire department' and save the company. Then it is important to get everyone on board as quickly as possible. I then give a motivational speech and provide a reason why everyone must now accept to simply follow the instructions.

As the boss, you know exactly what to do then?

That is the basic requirement. The hierarchical approach goes absolutely wrong if I as the boss do not know what to do. The condition for top-down announcements is that I have the competence to really make the decision. However, if I do have it and really know the solution, then that is the most effective way.

How does that work with a team of several hundred people?

It works the same way, but with an intermediate structure. I create teams and groups with team and department leaders. Finally, I build a hierarchy as flat as possible. Then there are clear announcements that are passed on from the respective level below. Hierarchies have evolved because they are efficient. Hierarchies are not innovative; they may not always be fair. But they are efficient.

Thank you very much Professor Aigner!

In the interview it becomes clear once again that top-down communication does not work in every environment. It presupposes a certain stability, i.e. that know-how is available and existing routines, structures and processes are in place.

Prerequisites that must be met for top-down communication:

- The manager has a high level of expertise and knows the solution and how to get there.
- The manager has a valid rationale for a course of action.

- The approaches to solving the problem do not have to be developed from scratch, but are available in the organization and accessible to the teams.
- Teams can access existing structures and processes and use existing resources and routines of the organization to solve problems.

Once these minimum requirements are met, you can use various top-down communication tools and options to achieve commitment, efficiency and speed in the organization.

4.2.2   Communication for the Efficient Organization

How exactly does communication in hierarchical structures work? Which basic types should you know as a leader?

In his standard work on the administrative behavior of organizations, first published in 1947, the American organizational theorist Herbert Simon defines communication as a constitutive element of organizations: For him it was obvious **that no organization can exist without communication,** since there is no possibility for the group to influence the individual [10]. Simon describes communication as a process of transferring decisions from one organizational member to another. Decisions can be centralized or decentralized, transmitted through formal or informal channels, and carried from the top down, bottom up, or across the organization. This simple distinction into three basic manifestations is still relevant and helpful today if you, as a leader, want to shape your own communication in a hierarchy-centric environment.

So first look at your communication activities in terms of

1. The direction of information transfer (bottom-up / top-down),
2. The degree of formalization (formal / informal), and
3. The underlying management model (centralized / decentralized).

Transmitter-Receiver Model
If we want to explain the nature of communication for an efficient, rapid distribution of information in a hierarchy-centered environment, a look at the rather technical linear *sender-receiver model* helps. *The* American mathematician Claude Shannon, who was employed by a telephone company, first presented the communication model, which is still widely cited today, in 1948 to describe the exchange of information between two systems in a communications environment [11].

The linear model describes the idea of a central sender that has information to be transmitted and uses a transmission channel—in Shannon's case, preferably a corded telephone—to transmit it to a receiver.

If we apply this model to the corporate context, the process of information transfer is more or less a one-way street of communication from the upper levels of the hierarchy to the employees. Neglected here are effects that can arise through social interaction between people and that, for example, lead to the fact that content can change, new content can be added. This approach also neglects the fact that emotions and sensitivities often play an essential role in the communication process. This approach mainly focuses on the transmission of information and is rather dominant in strictly hierarchical organizations.

According to the model, communication has three facets:

1. Top-down distribution of information
2. Formal, official communication activities
3. Hierarchical communication with centralized control

1. Top-Down Distribution of Information

Top-down communication refers to the direction of information distribution. Information is not carried from the bottom to the top or across the company, but is distributed from the top to the employees in a controlled manner. Top management derives the content to be communicated from a strategy and identifies the essential messages and courses of action. The information is distributed, e.g. by the board of directors or the managers, directly and or indirectly *downwards* to the employees via the channels of corporate communication. According to their hierarchical level and depending on the topic, managers are involved in defining the content or in passing on strategic information from the level above them.

As a manager, you can use this method of communication to present a clear framework for a project, to distribute information, to synchronize knowledge and to bring your internal stakeholders up to speed. Top-down communication serves to integrate all stakeholders and legitimize a project. When a message comes from 'above', all employees in the company understand that the management is behind it (Fig. 4.2).

2. Centralized Communication

In addition to the direction of information distribution—from top to bottom—it is crucial for the success of information distribution where the threads come together. People ascribe power to this central hub. Communication is directed from a central point with decision-making power to a larger group of recipients to all employees. If a message comes from a central point, i.e. from central influential authorities such as the management, the board or senior executives, it is perceived by the recipients as particularly significant. And you can take advantage of that.

If you do have that formal authority and choose this path, you can derive the content from your strategy and pass the relevant information to your employees. Alternatively, find a decision-maker in the higher levels who agrees to communicate your strategic content. The content is then carried through the hierarchy levels to the staff with the help of various communication channels. This transmitting communication either runs through campaigns, media and channels of corporate communications or is communicated directly by senior management, for example at major town hall meetings. Centralized communication uses communication cascades down to the individual employee.

Fig. 4.2 Top-down communication: top down at full speed

3. Formal Communication

Communication that is broadcast top-down and centrally from the board or senior management is in most cases highly formal, well-planned and strategically relevant. The official
channels of internal corporate communications are usually used to pass on important
information. Communication is thoroughly organized, the group of recipients meticulously
defined. Coincidence and informal communication are disturbing factors in this process
and should be eliminated as far as possible. Formal communication is mostly nonpersonal
from a few people to the masses. Depending on the size of the group of recipients,
information is transmitted via different types of media. Examples of formal communication
are messages from the board of directors in the intranet, official employee events such as
town hall meetings or articles in the employee magazine. Formal communication also
describes communication in the everyday life of a company, e.g. minutes of steering
committees or project meetings or official reporting. Formalized means *well-planned*,
intended and *recognizable* as official communication of the company (not office
grapevine!).

You Create Facts

For the matter of *office grapevine*: Beyond the centralized, formalized top-down approach
described here, far more extensive (perhaps also far more important) informal communication *naturally takes* place at all levels of your company. Grapevine talk becomes more and
more prevalent the less open and transparent you communicate. However, by formally
communicating important strategic messages, in time and as transparent as possible, you
can control and shape this informal process. With your official communication you can
ensure that information is carried quickly through the organization including the appropriate context. You can communicate goals quickly and achieve efficiency and speed of

implementation among the addressed target groups. And you can ensure that a previously unknown topic gains official importance in the shortest possible time.

If you use this official way, however, it involves an extensive preparation and coordination process. Because only when all relevant stakeholders have given their OK, when all decision-makers have really been met and agreed, can you start the communication process. The more important a message is and the higher up in the hierarchy a topic is, the more elaborate the preparation for the transmission of information into the organization.

Whereas you can send informal messages through the office within just a few seconds, you should plan several days up to weeks for the coordination of an official message from the board. In return, you then also create facts—as opposed to an unconfirmed rumor.

Summary: Top-Down, Formal and Centralized

Hierarchies can be a purposeful means of increasing efficiency. This is shown by the fact that hierarchies have developed successfully over decades. In hierarchy-centered structures, a specific communication and leadership style has also developed. It corresponds to the patterns of the sender-receiver model of communication, of top-down management and centralized decision-making.

Whether it is articles on the intranet, blog posts from the board or all hands meetings—in order to execute a strategy in an efficient way, centralized communication controlled by upper management is the method of choice. It serves to communicate strategic content, creates clarity, and can enable your team to move. Provided that the managers understand the company's strategy.

For successful hierarchical communication, leaders need to know what they are doing. They are able to explain the chosen path and provide resources, competencies, infrastructures and processes that the teams can access to solve assigned tasks. If these conditions are met, information can be distributed quickly and efficiently to employees through the hierarchy levels according to the linear sender-receiver model. To design communication in a hierarchy-centric environment, it is helpful to distinguish three basic forms: First, communication occurs as a top-down distribution of information. Second, it is formally and officially planned and, third, it is controlled by a central authority. ◄

4.3   Courses of Action

4.3.1   The Common Denominator

What will you achieve when you take the path of official, formal communication? What intentions can you pursue? The hierarchy-centered style described here looks at the members of a company against the background of their common goal. The aim is to successfully achieve a common performance of all people involved. This style of communication becomes essential, especially in times of crisis, when you have to quickly provide the entire organization with the same information, realign it, and move it to synchronized action in the shortest possible time (see Chap. 6). So let us take a closer look at what you can achieve with a well-planned, well-organized and centralized top-down communication.

Winning Stakeholders for Your Strategy

If your intention is to take your stakeholders with you on your journey, to gain their commitment, to motivate them and to win them over for the implementation of a strategy, then consciously managed, well-organized communication will help you. As the key opinion maker of your corporate environment, you have direct influence. You connect the hierarchy levels and you are broker and translator of content and meaning [12].

Centralized communication first serves to convey important information. It must create absolute **clarity** about a plan in order to get a team or stakeholders in the company to implement it. If you want to lead a large project to success, where you need many people, leaders must communicate a clear framework and context for a strategy, synchronize knowledge levels and explain what the contribution of the individual to the strategy is.

This communication starts from the top. It takes formal, planned and organized forms. When you want to address all employees, this can be an all-hands meeting, articles on the intranet or in employee magazines. There is little room for dialogue and feedback channels. This is *airtime* now.

Homogeneity Instead of Heterogeneity

While creative processes build upon the diversity of voices and opinions in a group (see Chap. 3), with top-down communication you want to keep your employees aligned to reach strategic goals: *one company, one voice*. In order to be able to align your stakeholders towards a common goal, it is important to use centralized formal communication. Only if you leave no questions unanswered, can you bring teams and employees to a common denominator [13]. You can inform, win them over to a cause and rally them to an appropriate course of action. Through your communications, you can provide a rationale for a course of action and gain understanding from your audience. You can do this by highlighting the contribution of each individual employee and explaining how much their efforts will contribute to the success of the cause.

Legitimation

If you want a project to be perceived as a top priority and to set the organization in motion, **consensus** in your leadership team is an important message. If everyone knows that management is united behind a cause this creates trust and legitimizes your project: "If management is behind this project, there must be something to it." It is so important that you rally management behind your plan as much as possible for all to see. Your project will gain legitimacy.

Do not underestimate the impact of a board member who is absent for no reason at an all hands meeting where all other board members are present. How should the staff and teams in his/her division behave? What is the message? Does she really stand behind it? You achieve legitimacy through presence and unity. This must be a central pillar of your communication strategy.

Trust and Understanding

Yet, even if you have all decision makers involved in your communication plan, this is not enough. To "follow" and really actively support an endeavor, teams need to understand *why* something is being done. As simple and clear as this sounds, people often forget to provide a **reason why** and a **clear vision** for something. If this is forgotten, you are sure to lose the team. If you want to get people to follow your ideas, you must explain *why* something needs to be done and what the goal behind a plan is. When *every single person* understands the intention, you can count on their support.

Commitment

You achieve understanding when you try to put yourself in the position of the teams and people involved and when you highlight their respective contributions. This motivates and makes a big plan suddenly tangible for everyone. When you clearly derive from your strategy what the individual contribution is, this is at the same time an **appreciation of everyone involved**. Your communication will lead to success if people can find themselves in it in some way and can be enthusiastic about it.

Increase Efficiency and Gain Resources

Through your communication, you not achieve commitment and motivation within a team. You can also bring the interests of *all* stakeholders to a common denominator. Communication is crucial for success in gaining additional resources for a project and will contribute to the prioritization of your topic at different points in the company. With top-down communication, you can **promote** the company's actions**, educate and generate enthusiasm for a cause.** You can increase the willingness of people to support a project. After all, the more people you win, the greater the chance that your plan will succeed. At the level of single strategic actions, top-down communication can help to synchronize all efforts. Sources of error are eliminated by passing on information at an early stage. And the whole course of action will be optimized through communication. In times of crisis, centralized communication controlled by top management will be essential for survival.

4.3.2 Reaching Your Goal at High Speed: Communication Is Planned Carefully

Once the strategic goals and actions have been defined and your intention is clear as to *why* you want to communicate, the next step is to address the right target groups. Depending on who you want to reach in the company—all employees, a project team, the executives, all sales companies—different media and channels of communication are suitable. The focus is now on the careful planning and organization of communication and the appropriate cascades of information transfer. In most companies you will find well-established communication processes and routines. The following section describes the top five most effective tools and practices for gaining commitment from relevant stakeholder groups.

The top five internal communication practices and tools:

1. All hands meetings / town hall meetings/ employee events (physical / virtual)
2. Intranet articles / video messages / articles in the employee magazine
3. Classic print media / flyers
4. Social media: podcasts, blog posts, posts in communities
5. Official reporting/ steering committee meetings with minutes

To successfully use these top five tools, you must make sure that your stakeholders have access to the internal communication channels. If this is the case, you are well supplied with the five most important communication practices in everyday life. To achieve sustainability in your communication (and since one-time messages usually get lost in the shuffle), you will use a combination of the actions described below and repeatedly send your message.

4.3.2.1 Town Hall Meetings

Internal events are most suitable if you want to reach as many people as possible at once and at the same time convey a personal atmosphere. If you are the speaker or even the host at such an event, you should focus on winning the audience for your mission.

What sounds feasible, however, is not so easy in reality: Because these all-hands meetings often take far too long for employees (exhausting). Or they take place at too late an hour or in a far too conventional format. In other words, one power point presentation follows the other. It is broadcast time. After the twelfth presentation at the latest, the audience is tired. Information has already been distributed in abundance. In the worst case, you are now the last speaker just before the opening of the buffet or the first speaker right after the lunch break. Whether they already had enough or still are hungry, their will hardly be any attention left.

Enthusiasm as a Common Thread

Now it is your task to get the attention of your listeners back for a few minutes and to inspire them. And you will inspire them when you are enthusiastic about your topic yourself. When preparing a speech for employees—no matter how boring the topic—it is recommendable that you first ask yourself what excites you personally about the topic.

The Preparatory Question

What motivates you to stand up for this cause? What do you find remarkable about it? Why are you passionate about this topic of all things? You will always find an answer to this question. From experience, there is something remarkable about any project.

If you have clarified this first question, you have already done 50% of the preparation work. Because it is exactly this passion that you will (implicitly) radiate. Second, the question helps you to uncover your core message. The thing that excites you should become the common thread.

Figuring out your own enthusiasm and motivation is easy when it is an exciting new topic or strategy. It is sometimes desperately difficult when you find yourself in a crisis situation. If you cannot motivate yourself now, how should your employees? Look for your motive to keep going now. A crisis situation in particular can bring people together. An anticipated success or victory can now be essential to get your audience on your side. There is always an aspect that will excite you. It is as simple as that: if you are enthusiastic, your listeners will be. By doing so, you activate your listeners to participate. The enthusiasm and motivation you send out will return to you in any case.

Setting the Stage
If you are not only one of the speakers but the initiator of an event, you'll have to take effort. But the effect of a town hall meeting will be even more in your hands. What essence, what character will your event have? Will it tire the participants or set them on fire? Will a wave of enthusiasm go through the room? Do you want to create sparks, even perhaps a fighting spirit? Do you want to rally your guests to a cause? Yes, your *guests,* because you are their *host.* As with any party at home, it is all about "Setting the Stage." Hosts set the stage. Hosts are responsible for setting the atmosphere at an event.

Hosts can influence the mood in which people will leave a room. Organizers of all hands meetings are often not fully aware of this responsibility. But this is exactly the *second 50%* of your effort. If you want commitment from your employees, the 50–150 min (or more) of an event is about making the audience feel good. That they can 'refuel' and that they are sworn in to your common goal. Do not skimp on this event. And if you do not have the budget, even small details will do. Just do not skimp on attention for your audience. Invest. If the guests notice that they are important to you, then you can calmly send your message and you will also receive commitment afterwards. If a town-hall meeting was surprisingly good, this will spread like wildfire.

There is a simple basic rule in press relations. A press conference (and here we are broadcasting!) does not start without taking care of the participants and making them feel comfortable. It is a short but important onboarding time. Whether it is with pretzels, coffee or finger food—lightly satiated and happy, your guests will be in a different mood. Just take care of them, 'nurture' them. In the best case, this can be a small reception with snacks. If you are on a tight budget, it can also be words of welcome. If your customer is king in your business relations, then your employee should be king at a town hall meeting.

How Do Your Guests Feel?
If you plan the agenda in such a way that you treat the employee as your guest, whom you want to win over, then you'll have the other 50%. A former CEO of a large bank once said in an interview, "People never remember what you tell them. They always remember how

you made them feel". This is the mantra for organizing your event. If you keep this phrase in mind, you will attract people to your cause more easily. If you set the stage like this, then you can "broadcast" your message. And you will see it works.

You Are Throwing the Party

Unfortunately, the importance of being a real good host is often neglected in everyday business life. A 3 h town hall meeting begins without this short 'welcoming ceremony' of making your guests feel good. And after just a few minutes it is already clear that you will lose your audience quickly. Hundreds of power point slides have been prepared for nothing. Shannon's [11] simple sender-receiver model of communication means that you also need to take care of the *receiver*. If it is not set up correctly, all the effort is for nothing.

That is tough, but it is exactly the effect that many internal events achieve. If your event implicitly sends the message that it is 'just internal and not that important', then you should better save the effort and costs. Do the math on what a 3-h event (including prep time for endless power point presentations) with your senior leadership team will cost. Let us assume there are 50 executives, plus board members and senior managers. This simple arithmetic exercise MUST encourage an organization (that has been calibrated for cost efficiency and market leadership!) to get the best of those 3 h.

Forms of events are

- Town hall meetings with board and top management to communicate the strategy
- Information events/marketplaces
- Kick-off events, e.g. for large projects or innovation projects
- Milestone events when you have reached an interim goal
- The opening ceremony, e.g. when you inaugurate a new location
- *Swearing-in* ceremony: e.g. before a big fair or an important event

If the most important features of events should be summarized, then it is firstly the common thread of enthusiasm and motivation. Then, second, it is taking on the role of the host. And third, it is the focus on the well-being of the guests. Events are the best way to reach larger groups of people. They are well suited to communicate the vision, mission, strategy of an organization or a project and to get everyone involved to work towards a common goal. The personal attendance of top executives gives weight to an event and a message. What is sent here radiates beyond. After all, once events are over, they can continue to have an effect for weeks and months. Provided that you help along a little...

4.3.2.2 Intranet Articles/Video Messages/Articles in the Employee Magazine

The report on the intranet about a major town hall meeting can have a crucial spin and impact on the perception on the event. Such a coverage is quite elaborate. You have to find an author, capture statements and impressions, order a photographer or maybe even write the report yourself. Depending on the number and 'importance' of those involved, you will need enough time for the approval for your report. But this time is well spent. After all, the good vibes transported by your positive coverage will support you to promote your project. Support that you may urgently need to push your topic.

Posts on the intranet are usually spread globally and in real time. You can positively charge topics and ensure that the same message is available in all subsidiaries of your organization. Intranet articles or video messages to the staff are suitable both as one-off information and as part of an information campaign. One-off information would be: "Person X, Y is taking on a new function Z", "National company A celebrates its 50th birthday". You can report recurrently on the progress in your project: "Long awaited: A-Team opens new future lab". Or you communicate over a period of time, e.g. during acute exceptional situations such as crises (see Chap. 6) with regular personal messages from the top-management.

This Message Is Important

The effort to create such posts is worthwhile for another very simple reason: What appears on the intranet is official information. Everyone knows that the messages published here went through the official processes of corporate communications. What can be read here is legitimized and accepted (from now on) as official. Depending on the channel you choose, you will achieve different effects on the audience. An official message from the board, a notice or a short news item may be suitable for the mere distribution of information. But when you want to address the emotions of your audience, you'll be better of with a video or an extensively illustrated article in the employee magazine. Choose consciously.

If you want to reach the target group of 'all employees' or 'the entire company', articles on the intranet or official announcements are effective. In this way, you spread information widely and can ensure that the company as a whole receives the same information.

Reports in the classic employee magazine of companies are also suitable for this purpose. An article in the official internal publication of a company, whether in the print or online edition, is perceived by employees as an official statement of the company. If you get one of the rare pages of the print edition, this is the 'accolade' of internal communications. Because what is written here is officially recognized. In large companies, it is even translated into x languages and distributed worldwide. It can no longer be erased from the company's consciousness. In case of doubt, a magazine also makes its way beyond the company's borders. The information published here is therefore coordinated several times and approved for publication by a central body, often the management board itself.

To appear in the employee magazine, you work closely with corporate communications. Here you can seek advice and hope for the expertise of in-house PR specialists and their agencies. Such a contribution is an elaborate process, but highly recommendable to give importance to a topic, to push it and to generate support from many sides.

Compared to glossy brochures, employee magazines are usually distributed all over the world or country. Here you really reach 'everyone' even your stakeholders beyond the company boundaries. Accordingly, the messages must be neutral enough and not contain any strictly confidential company internals.

4.3.2.3 Classic Print Media

Classic print media are threatened with extinction. Everything is now online. However, when a magazine, brochure or flyer *does* appear, they somehow again gain weight in today's world. Why not use this old-fashioned channel for differentiation while everyone else is online? A well-designed printed magazine stands out. Even if it may seem outdated at first glance: If your flyer is available in the staff canteen, people are quick to pick it up while eating. If a project is presented in a glossy brochure, this adds value.

Flyers, brochures, magazines, books: printing on paper is an expensive business... Information in print products has a long preparation time. The content has to 'last' over a long period of time. It has been coordinated and read through umpteen times, approved umpteen times, printed in high quality, perhaps with elaborate photographs. If a company spends this money, a topic *must be* important. You can *also* use this effect to enhance your project.

With regard to the target group, however, you are limited here. High-quality print publications are usually only made available to a limited target group. You therefore need to define in advance exactly who you want to reach.

4.3.2.4 Social Media and Communities

Just as Instagram, WhatsApp and Co. dominate our private lives, it is also important to shift your communications to digital channels and platforms at work. If you decide to launch new communities or use existing digital channels, however, you have to show presence and stay tuned. Because this is where visibility and continuity count. Once a dialogue with a target group has been opened, it must be maintained.

Depending on where they appear, short posts on social networks are often perceived as less "official" than, e.g., a messages from the board on the intranet or in an official mail to all managers. Nevertheless, you can reach a high frequency via this channel and connect with your target group in real time. The higher the benefit for the target group, the more successful you will be with your topic. Whether Slack, Teams, Yammer or other connect communities—depending on the channel you choose, it will help you to understand the culture in the respective community.

4.3.2.5 Official Reporting: The Meeting Minutes

Finally, there is a fifth, more traditional but promising means of communication, which, although it may sound marginal, is worth mentioning. Because while you establish virtual communication platforms and online news in your communication and post regularly in communities, the familiar rules of the game of classic reporting still apply in your organization.

This is about hard facts, decisions and resolutions instead of news and emotion. And these can be found in the official reporting that still is part of the management of companies in many areas. After all, is a post on an online platform actually perceived by employees as a call to action? Presumably, it is simply consumed.

In contrast, the most important points are decided and necessary actions are recorded in numerous committees and meetings. This is where the exchange of official decisions takes place. The target groups of the minutes and the participants of the committee meetings are usually precisely defined and mentioned by name. You can hardly communicate more target group specific.

Make sure that your project also appears regularly in the minutes of the committees that are most important to you. Depending on the size and scope of the project, you will increasingly need the official commitment of the entire company. If you finally make it into the board minutes, you can be sure that all areas of the company will be informed about your project and will give your topic a little more attention next time. When it comes to communication, do not neglect the power of traditional committees and meeting minutes.

4.3.2.6 The Campaign

Once is not enough. Just as you want to be in touch with your customers as often as possible and become a permanent partner to them, sustainability makes the difference in your internal communications as well. Only by 'keeping up', i.e. by the recurring communication of your messages on different channels, people are moved to action.

So think of your communication activities as a campaign. As in an election campaign, the aim is to shape the public opinion over a long period of time. Of course, there are topics that are better suited for a one-time announcement—e.g., a personnel matter or a company acquisition. But do you need to implement a strategic change of direction or initiate a change in behavior? Do you need to attract resources and support for a long-term project? Then a campaign that runs over a longer period of time is the right way to go.

Designing and implementing campaigns means continuously sending, receiving, processing, sending again, etc. information on a topic. To do this, it makes sense to use a range of media, digital channels and formats. Because one-off communication will get lost in the shuffle. In the best case, therefore, you combine different the channels and types of communication to achieve long lasting attention in the organization.

4.3.3   Excursus: Communication for Innovation

Back to the field of innovation. We are in the chapter on exploitation and top-down communication management. Can this kind of communication also be applied in the context of radical innovation projects? In any case, it can.

With their principle: "No innovation without communication", the communication researchers Zerfass, Sandhu and Huck emphasize [14] *how important* the systematic communication of innovations is and what contribution communication makes to value creation. After all, the mere process of new product development does not lead to the achievement of sales targets.

Explaining Innovation and Communicating It in an Understandable Way

The mediating nature of communication is therefore not only useful for driving your existing business forward. *At a certain point,* communication can be extremely helpful for large-scale information transfer in the context of radical innovations. Top-down management might not be helpful for the initial generation of new ideas. But when it comes to the market launch and to *explaining* the complex innovation to your stakeholders, carefully organized communication will help your audience understand and accept the innovation.

As introduced in Chap. 2, we are now talking about the situation when 'innovation' describes an already existing result, i.e. when new products, ideas or technologies already exist and have to be positioned in the company and beyond the company boundaries. If a newly developed, promising *artefact* (see Fig. 2.6) already exists, you should think about informing the world about the innovation. With the right messages, you can win over the first users, supporters, fans and sponsors.

Because just like the core business, innovative new solutions or entire business areas must at some point be firmly anchored in the company. The proven methods and processes of top-down communication are then also suitable for the latest products. Simply use the best approaches of communication of the existing world for this!

Innovation Threatens Status Quo

The communication of innovation is so important and necessary because new topics threaten the status quo. They always take place "in the area of tension between different stakeholder interests" [14]. Due to the lack of experience with a new solution and a high uncertainty about the potential benefits, communicating the value of the 'new' is critical to its success. The communication of innovation is therefore highlighted in the scientific community as a central management task. It is defined as follows:

> Communication of innovation is the systematically planned, executed and evaluated communication of new products, services, technologies, processes, concepts and ideas with the aim of creating an understanding for it and trust in the innovation and of positioning the organization behind the new solution as an innovator [15].

Communication of innovation pursues the goal of winning people over to an innovation, explaining complex topics and generating a common understanding of an innovation among all relevant target groups via different media and channels. By repeatedly explaining innovations and demonstrating their importance for the company, you can legitimize an innovation project within the organization. You can create trust, achieve a high level of commitment among those involved, and ultimately gain the necessary resources for your project.

Example: Winning Stakeholders for an Innovation

During the early research phase of an intelligent technology platform for the Industry 4.0 market, a small group of participants from the R+D division of company A is initially involved. The research project is then launched. When it is later decided to start an official product development project and to bring the technology to market maturity, additional resources from different company divisions are needed. The approval of an ever larger group of stakeholders in company A becomes necessary.

The management in charge of this development task now makes communication a central task to gain commitment and support from the relevant stakeholders. In addition to the technology itself, market potentials, customer benefits, and even potential sales targets are presented. The communication target here is *not to generate* a diversity of voices and opinions, but rather to create a widely accepted understanding of the innovation among all stakeholders. Starting from a central point, the project management, all relevant stakeholders are brought to a common denominator via different media and channels of project and corporate communication. The goal is to legitimize the innovation project in this way and to obtain the necessary resources to finance and finally implement the project.

At the same time, the acceptance of a new solution within the own ranks up to the sales department is of utmost importance if you want to win customers on global markets. For this reason, communication with stakeholders also plays a central role in the further course of the development project. The communication and positioning of the technology is coordinated and controlled centrally: At regular milestone events, the executive board and its management team motivate the ever-growing group of people directly involved in the innovation project. All of the company's employees worldwide are getting prepared for the launch of the innovation through reports in the employee magazine. The global sales companies are trained in regular training sessions. Finally, at the time of the market launch, external market and customer communication starts, based on the internal messages. In company A, a coherent overall picture is created in internal and external communication through the communication of innovation that was started early. ◄

As in the example presented here, managers can use various instruments of official, centrally controlled corporate communications to disseminate an innovation within their own organization. The use of hierarchies can be a helpful way to legitimize an innovation project. The patterns of action described in this chapter for the exploitation environment can also be used for explorative projects at the moment when the innovation is about to be launched and you need support, resources, and acceptance from the whole company. Whether this is all hands meetings with participation from the board of management, articles on the intranet, or via blogs and posts—when it comes to anchoring an innovation throughout the company, the means of centrally controlled top-down communication are just as suitable for revolutionary innovations.

Summary: Communication Equals an Election Campaign

What do I want to achieve with my communication? And how do I implement communication in my day-to-day business? The hierarchy-centered communication style described here considers the members of a company against the background of their common goal. It supports the intention to involve stakeholders, to obtain commitment, to motivate and to win people over for the implementation of a strategy (or an innovation) or also for coordinated rapid action in exceptional situations (see Chap. 6). Whereas in creative processes it is precisely the *diversity* of voices and opinions in a group that is promoted with the help of communication tools, top-down communication aims to achieve absolute *unanimity*: One company, one voice. And this unanimity starts at the top. In order to give a project an official character and really get the organization moving, consensus in your management team is an important message. Only if you send out a clear message from the top will you create trust and legitimize your project. If you have all decision-makers on board, this alone is not enough. To really actively support an endeavor, teams need to understand *why* something should be done. As simple and clear as this sounds, people often forget to provide a solid rationale for a plan.

Once the strategic goals and measures have been defined and your intention is clear as to why you want to communicate, the next step is to provide the right target groups in the company with the right strategic messages. Now the focus is on the 'streamlined' planning and organization of communication cascades. Communication tools include events (physical or virtual), intranet articles, video messages, classic print media, articles in employee magazines, posts, blog contributions and dialogues in communities, official reporting in steering committee meetings with minutes. Understand that your communication activities are a campaign. As in an election campaign, you are shaping the public opinion over a long period of time. ◄

4.4   Conclusion: Communication Is Value Creation

Why all the fuss about communicating? Especially in the environment of technologists, researchers, developers and engineers, it is all about facts and engineering. Why invest a large part of your time in processes and activities that do not *directly* contribute to value creation? Why invest your time in planning and orchestrating communication? Doesn't it cost vast amounts of time and money?

The answer is: communication is essential for business survival. Maybe not for you as a person directly, but for the issue you stand for. For the survival of your division and for the survival of your organization. Communication *is* leadership. It *is* value creation. Because to survive in the red ocean, speed, efficiency and attention are paramount.

Efficiency

Although we know how important it is to increase efficiency in the company, we still make too little use of the potential offered by communication. For managers, communication is often a tool that can run 'alongside' everyday management. But in times of a dynamic market and technology environments, communication must be the *first* management tool to shorten reaction times of the organization. Communication tools, used consciously and effectively, can bring the organization to a common denominator in the shortest possible time.

If you want to get to the customer quickly with solutions, your team must act with absolute unanimity. Ambiguities must be cleared up, room for interpretation eliminated. It is all about acting quickly, purposefully and cost-efficiently. If you want to get your team on a common path, the only way to do this is through top-down communication. Clear announcements, clear implementation. You need to know where things are headed and communicate this clearly.

Attention

In addition to this competition for speed and efficiency, you also have to fight for scarce resources for your project. Your competitor is not only outside in the market. There is also an internal fight for budgets, for people, and for attention. Your mission is to drive one issue forward, while X other teams and departments are receiving similar missions and pursuing completely different goals. It is true that an overall strategy helps you to prioritize your tasks. But in order to push a project through in the long term, only the means of communication will help you. This is because management levels are replaced, organizations are restructured, topics are regularly scrutinized in a completely new way, strategies are changed. Therefore, you have to continuously account for why an investment is worthwhile. For this, the performance must be *visible*. The objective must be clear and the benefit for the company unmistakable. Without visibility and a continuous spotlight, your topic will be lost, because you are competing for resources throughout the company.

While the development of completely new business models and digital innovations requires the heterogeneity and diversity of voices in ecosystems and you as a leader step into a moderating role, you need clarity, competence and power in the red ocean. In the team, you need homogeneity. You need to get the best possible support from your organization. If everything is clear from the beginning, it your plan is 'only' about implementing tasks quickly and efficiently, then you communicate top-down. This will bring power to your team in the shortest possible time. Whether through events, intranet articles, blogposts or minutes, a mix of communication media and channels with clear messages and clearly stated information will help you address the different stakeholders. This type of communication is based on sending information. You deliver the message from the top to the staff in a formal, official way.

Innovation Also Needs Top-Down Communication

And it is not just your existing business that needs to be aligned on efficiency and speed by communicative actions. At some point, even the newest and most innovative solution will become a 'grateful recipient' of existing company routines: What is crucial about the form of communication described here in exploitation is that you can always use it in the exploratory innovation environment as well. And this is always the case when already created content is to be spread across the organization and innovations are to be disseminated.

References

1. O'Reilly, C. A. & Tushman, M. L. (2004): The Ambidextrous Organization. Harvard Business Review, 82 (4), p. 74–81.
2. March, James G. (1991): Exploration and Exploitation in Organizational Learning. Organization Science, 2 (1), p. 71–87.
3. Schilling, Melissa A. (2013): Strategic Management of Technological Innovation. 4th edition. New York, NY: McGraw-Hill.
4. S-Kurven-Konzept. In: Gabler Wirtschaftslexikon. Online: http://wirtschaftslexikon.gabler.de/Definition/s-kurven-konzept.html [Accessed: 29.05.2020].
5. Kim, W. Chan; Mauborgne, Renée (2016): Der Blaue Ozean als Strategie. Wie man neue Märkte schafft, wo es keine Konkurrenz gibt. 2nd revised edition. München: Carl Hanser.
6. Laloux, Frederic (2015): Reinventing Organizations: Ein Leitfaden zur Gestaltung sinnstiftender Formen der Zusammenarbeit. München: Vahlen.
7. Je flacher die Hierarchie, desto innovativer das Unternehmen. Wirtschaftswoche, July 3, 2017. Online: https://www.wiwo.de/erfolg/management/mittelstand-je-flacher-die-hierarchien-desto-innovativer-das-unternehmen/20002628.html [Accessed: 29.05.2020].
8. Kienbaum, Stepstone (2017): Organigramm deutscher Unternehmen. Studie von Kienbaum und Stepstone zu den Organisationsstrukturen in deutschen Unternehmen. Online: http://assets.kienbaum.com/downloads/Hierarchie-Organisation-Fuehrung_Fuehrungskraefte_Kienbaum-Stepstone-Studie_2017.pdf [Accessed: 29.05.2020].
9. Duwe, Claudia (2004): Zeit der Begegnung – Begegnung mit der Zeit: Zeitliche Aspekte literarischen Lesens. Wiesbaden: Deutscher Universitäts-Verlag.
10. Simon, Herbert. A. (1947): Administrative Behavior: A Study of Decision-Making Processes in Administrative Organizations. 4th edition, 1997.
11. Shannon, Claude E. (1948): A Mathematical Theory of Communication. Bell System Technical Journal, 27 (3), p. 379–423.
12. Mast, Claudia (2014): Interne Unternehmenskommunikation: Mitarbeiter führen und motivieren. In A. Zerfass & M. Piwinger (Hrsg.), Handbuch Unternehmenskommunikation (p. 1121–1140). Wiesbaden: Springer Fachmedien.
13. Zerfass, Ansgar (2014): Unternehmenskommunikation und Kommunikationsmanagement: Strategie, Management und Controlling. In: Manfred Piwinger und Ansgar Zerfass (Hrsg.), Handbuch Unternehmenskommunikation. Wiesbaden: Springer Fachmedien. p. 21–79.

14. Zerfass, Ansgar, Sandhu, S.; Huck, Simone (2004): Innovationskommunikation: Strategisches Handlungsfeld für Corporate Communications. In P. M. &. S. G. Bentele G. (ed.), Kommunikationsmanagement (Loseblattsammlung) (Bd. 1.24). Neuwied: Luchterhand. p. 1–30.
15. Zerfass, Ansgar; Huck, Simone (2007): Innovationskommunikation: Neue Produkte, Ideen und Technologien erfolgreich positionieren. In: Manfred Piwinger und Ansgar Zerfass (ed.): Handbuch Unternehmenskommunikation. Wiesbaden: Springer Fachmedien. p. 847–858.

Connecting the Two Worlds

5

Abstract

How do you turn a difficult trade-off into an elegant balancing act? How can leaders introduce new ways of thinking and working into a company and at the same time prioritize the existing business? How can they simultaneously lead innovation projects with contradictory forces? And what mindset do they need for the balance?

While Chaps. 3 and 4 present courses of action for *either* exploitation *or* exploration, this section lays the groundwork for *both*. Ambidextrous leadership requires more than the ability to move confidently in one environment *or* the other. Simultaneity is required of senior leaders: a connective, balancing approach between the worlds is needed. On top, you need a strong, all-connecting vision that puts the current business in the context of the long-term future outlook. That is why we are leaving the 'red and blue oceans' behind and head into space in this chapter. Ambidexterity requires a view of the overall system from above.

This chapter uses case studies, interviews and possible courses of action to show how you as a leader can navigate yourself and your teams through two worlds. At the same time, the question of mindset is answered—how do ambidextrous leaders think and act? All findings are based on research and case studies in the German mechanical engineering industry and can be applied to other sectors and industries. The scientifically based communication model of ambidextrous leadership presented in Chap. 2 forms the basis of the following section.

© Springer-Verlag GmbH Germany, part of Springer Nature 2022   137
J. Duwe, *Ambidextrous Leadership*,
https://doi.org/10.1007/978-3-662-64032-6_5

5.1   In Another Universe

Whether incubators, innovation hubs, co-creation spaces or digital labs—numerous special units of large companies have sprung up in recent years aside from existing processes and organizational structures. They have been established to generate new ideas and solutions for the parent company, usually in the immediate vicinity of a thriving start-up scene. In the young, highly interdisciplinary innovation teams, very specific rules apply.

Old-fashioned processes are being thrown overboard. People think out of the box and work in an agile, networked and self-organized way. Just as the office furniture and the fashion of the people, the agile mindset in the hubs and labs differs heavily from the familiar one of large corporations. This intended break-up allows companies to challenge their status quo and bring forth radical, revolutionary ideas, Ideas that shake up today's world.

But while the step of breaking away happens easily at first, simply splitting off does not propel companies into the future: "The results of separate corporate worlds are disillusioning," observes John P. Kotter, Harvard professor of leadership and change management [1]. The common practice of companies to separate the existing business (exploitation) and the innovation units (exploration) regarding organization and structures does not lead to the desired success.

Conflicting Interests

"The relationship between the 'old world' and the 'new world' must be put to the test" as one can read in press articles on the relationship between corporate start-ups and parent companies [2]. The German magazine *Wirtschaftswoche* [3] reports on "irresolvable conflicts of interest", "PR shows", "initial withdrawals, distress sales and bankruptcies". "Only about half of the companies actually succeed in effectively and purposefully integrating the digital units and sustainably creating innovations and new products," the business magazine *Capital* [4] sums up. "The digital spin-offs have one major shortcoming: no one has really made any money yet, not even those that have been around for a while" [4]. Finally, the magazine *t3n* demands: "Kill your innovation labs!" The sustainable alternative would be the comprehensive internal restructuring [5].

Increasingly, the cooperation between parent companies and their start-up units is being tested. The different interests, processes and cultures are being criticized. As easy and smooth as the separation is, the integration of the new digital world into the corporate structures and balance sheets of the large parent companies is proving difficult. The existing processes, the culture, the speed are not made for the new operating system. At the same time, the existing structures, hierarchies, and the middle and top management layers [6] are far too strong and powerful in many places to really dare to shake the foundations.

Ambidextrous leadership

Fig. 5.1 Ambidextrous leadership through communication

Dual Operating System

But this is where the work of ambidextrous leaders begins (see Fig. 5.1). Because the two worlds do not connect by themselves. The clear signal, the commitment to change, must come from the very top. And the green light from a visionary CEO is rarely enough. He needs his management team. In this transformation process, expensive contracts with digital consultants will not go far enough. The *mindset* must come from within.

In order to avoid the problem of separate worlds and instead draw profit from the conscious balance and connection of the two, John Kotter recommends a "dual operating system" [7]: "In a truly reliable, efficient, agile and fast enterprise, the network meshes with the more traditional structure". In such a *dual operating system*, described in this book as "contextual ambidexterity" (see Sect. 2.1), different rules and approaches coexist *within* one organizational unit and are not separated. Stability and agility run in parallel and are closely intertwined. In many places, this calls into question the traditional management style and confronts the managers with a mammoth task that can only be solved by looking at the system as a whole.

The View from Above

To look at the system as a whole, we now leave the world of the oceans and get to know another universe: the two-world space. We do not know how big it is. Imagine that it is very, very big. In this space, not only the present takes place, but also the future. The present and the future are not separated in time, space, organization, structure, culture. They exist simultaneously. They are intertwined. Now, before you read on, why don't you linger in this space for a few minutes...?

- What does the two-world space look like?
- How does it feel?
- Where does the present stand?
- Where is the future?
- Do you see any limits?
- Are there any boundaries at all?

From this perspective from above, the field of action of contextual ambidexterity becomes tangible. While companies often structurally separate current and future businesses because they want to avoid possible tensions and sources of conflict between the worlds, the approach of *contextual ambidexterity* (two-world space) relies on the *synergetic effects* of the tradition and the future: The two worlds coexist peacefully within one company, and there is a balance between driving the existing business forward and promoting new approaches and solutions for the future.

▶   **Balancing the Two Worlds Is a Central Leadership Task** In their essay "Building ambidexterity into an organization", Christina Gibson and Julian Birkinshaw, who are experts on contextual ambidexterity, describe the shaping of this very large space as a central leadership task [8]. Whereas leaders can confidently retreat into their respective oceans in times of separate worlds, their balancing behaviors come into focus in a world where *both* approaches are taken. They must orchestrate, balance, create connections. Because if they do not balance carefully and instead neglect one world or the other, a company can lose out in no time: "Focus too much on alignment and the short-term results will look good, but changes in the industry will blindside you sooner or later," [9].

Ambidextrous leaders manage to skillfully move back and forth between the red and blue oceans. "Balancing the needs of core businesses and innovation efforts is a central leadership task," emphasizes Michael L. Tushman, organizational theorist and expert on ambidexterity [10]. You can only achieve balance, however, if you first take a brief leave from the earth. You have to get out and take in the view from above.

Of course, a flight into space requires courage. But only from here can you create a context in which the worlds flow into each other, in which each individual can decide in his day-to-day business which activities to push forward and when. Ambidextrous leadership, then, means building an environment where each individual knows how to act. Gibson and

Birkinshaw additionally convey an understanding of leadership, which is not necessarily linked to the role of the leader. Contextual ambidexterity brings forth leadership at all levels and from within the organization [9]—provided that you reopen the space for it and push the boundaries far outwards. So let us take off in this chapter....

Summary: Flight into Space

Increasingly, innovation units of large enterprises have sprouted from the ground in recent years. The step of splitting off is easy at first. But change expert John P. Kotter speaks of a sobering outcome: The spin-off alone does not propel companies into the future. Rather, it is the sustainable cooperation of both worlds that should lead to the goal. Experts therefore recommend a "dual operating system" in which agile networks are intertwined with traditional structures. But in many places the structures are too rigid for such a dual operating system to be easily implemented. Connecting the two worlds thus becomes a difficult management task. To better understand this task, we first leave the oceans and travel into the two-world space of contextual ambidexterity. This space relies less on the trade-off of exploitation and exploration, and more on the synergistic effects of tradition and the future. Whereas leaders could confidently retreat into their respective oceans when worlds were separate, their balancing behavior comes into focus in a world where both approaches are pursued. They must orchestrate, balance, and create connections with the goal of having two worlds coexist profitably within a company: the core business and the future business. ◀

5.2   The Flyover

We are now travelling in the two-world space, an interplay of pyramid, network and ecosystem. In this transitional space, your context of action can change every hour (or even in shorter cycles). Here, however, you as a senior leader, as a CEO, as a managing director, have a unique opportunity to shape and design the context of action for the people in your organization. You can enable your teams to choose existing or future business depending on what a situation in the market requires.

In the sales environment, for example, employees may ask themselves whether they need the quick win or invest in long-term customer loyalty with innovation. As a leader, you can empower your teams to consider for themselves which direction is appropriate, and when a combination of the present and the future will lead to the greatest success. We will stay in sales for now and look at an example from the industrial automation environment.

Case Study: Ambidexterity in Sales

One example of how conventional and network-based approaches coexist within a company is demonstrated by the Dutch sales company of the German supplier of automation technology Festo. The sales company, based in Delft, has switched to a dual operating system in 2016. Network structures and a self-organizing team coexist alongside traditional processes. Initiated by the management, the Dutch leadership team had previously analyzed the existing processes and methods of sales management within the company and established a new organizational model for a young business unit in the midst of traditional structures and processes.

Together with the management team, the sales targets were defined for a team of sales engineers, and a "green field" was created for implementation and target achievement. The team was authorized to separate from conventional ways of thinking and processes and was called upon to autonomous, self-responsible control. This approach was implemented amidst the existing organization that had grown over the years. Success was not long in coming. The targets were achieved—and exceeded—in a very short time.

"It is a Self-Directed Team"
Interview with Dennis van Beers, Managing Director Cluster Benelux of Festo, Delft
Dennis van Beers, how did you explain to your team that you had to follow two completely different paths?
At the end of 2015, when we discussed the sales figures for our latest product family in electric drive technology, we saw that they did not meet expectations. We had not managed to convince new customers, nor did we keep the existing customer base. Our process-centric organization was obviously not on the right track to enter new fields of applications and customers.

With our management team, we studied the market and found that customers needed a different level of support and response time. Our organization had adapted to mature markets and their customers. It was not open anymore to new applications and technologies for existing and new customers. This was a completely different game. In addition, we found that our younger generation of engineers, despite being highly motivated, did not feel comfortable in the existing project management structures. They did not have enough space and time to try out new things and explore the limits of our new technologies. Here, we did not tap the full potential of the team.

What happened next?
We installed a team, called it the "EASi^3" team and gave them two big tasks. First, put in place the best possible highly responsive support to dramatically increase customer retention with our existing customers. It is significantly cheaper to keep existing customers loyal than to acquire new ones. Second, we gave them the task of acquiring new applications and customers in order to sell our latest technologies in electrical drive engineering. This is where our existing team had the greatest difficulties. In addition, we communicated to the team that speed was the key success factor. We permanently provided two company cars for the team members. We also

(continued)

empowered them to make their own decisions without involving management. I expected my direct managers to support, not to manage this multidisciplinary team.

How did you support the team?

Although the team is self-directed and has no formal reporting line with a manager, two managers from the overall organization's management team are part of the team to coach and help make the right decisions and set priorities. One member of the team is the coordinator of day-to-day ongoing activities. The team knows that if a problem arises, they can call in the management team or the CEO directly.

How does the EASi^{3}Team work? What does the team do differently from the other teams?

The team has no formal manager. The team works with different functional roles and informal leadership. For this, it is extremely important to choose the right people. They communicate through apps instead of official reports. They are very receptive to and respond quickly to opportunities that arise with the client. Since activities are posted instantly and shared with a highly flexible pool of people, it is always possible to respond to customer requests immediately. Team members know each other's activities and are able to jump into a process at any time. Sharing resources in a pool guarantees us almost 100% instant response to customer inquiries.

This is completely different from a process-oriented organization where work packages are passed from one department to the next and from one desk to the next. Most meetings in a process-centric organization are about adjustments and improvements between departments with minimal results. The EASI^3 team has a half-hour meeting every week to discuss opportunities and define what needs to be done to take immediate action on them. In an overview they monitor all current and new activities: pre-sales, sales and post-sales activities.

How do you communicate the need for an ambidextrous leadership style to your direct management team?

Twice a year we have town hall meetings. There, I try to communicate to all employees the need for us to change the organization in the direction of an ambidextrous organization. An organization driven by an outside-in perspective of a rapidly changing market and in need of change in its own structures. Instead of the word "ambidextrous" I use the metaphor of "two hands".

Describe your role as CEO in the implementation of an ambidextrous strategy.

It is important and critical to success that the CEO personally believes in ambidextrous leadership and continually carries it into the organization. This process changes a company and many forces within an organization can hold back change due to numerous reasons. For example, executives feel responsible for their own

(continued)

departments and are less likely to like it when their people move to other teams. They like to "manage" because that means they have control.

However, this is not the way to successfully evolve into an ambidextrous organization. The CEO must also keep an eye on this. He needs to guide and support the leaders so that they can adapt to and embrace the changed leadership situation. From a 'command and control' approach, we are changing to 'empower and support' of the teams. For this to happen, it is very important that the CEO gets personally involved and openly shows his commitment to the change.

Thank you very much Dennis van Beers!

The case study of Festo's Dutch sales company illustrates that several prerequisites must be met if firms want to benefit from ambidextrous leadership. The five most important lessons learned and recommendations for action from this case study are:

1. Ambidexterity requires commitment from the CEO and top management.
2. Leaders act in changing roles.
3. Exchange of experience connects both worlds.
4. The structure of the new operating system is customer-centric.
5. Leadership develops naturally and informally.

1. Ambidexterity Requires Commitment from CEO *and* Top Management
The CEO and the management team must stand behind the two different approaches. This is where the change process begins. The CEO's first task in the example described here was to convince his management team of the change. For managers, ambidexterity means starting with a new, different leadership culture next to the familiar, learned ways of doing things. On the one hand, they control less and empower more, while on the other hand, existing routines continue in the *known world*. The openness to such a balancing act and the willingness to enter the "transitional space" demands openness, courage and a willingness to take risks from the management team. The support of the CEO alone is not enough for innovative projects. In their day-to-day business innovation teams also need the support of the senior management [10].

2. Leaders Act in Changing Roles
The example described here shows how this balancing act can be mastered when managers become real leaders and take on an additional second role to drive change. While they act as traditional managers in "World 1", they take a place as team members in "World 2". They exercise *one* role or the other depending on the context in which they operate. This new culture of everyday flexibility requires real leadership and a different mentality and way of thinking and acting.

3. Exchange of Experience Connects Both Worlds

By mixing the teams, e.g. when managers from conventional operations participate as team members in the innovation team, the exchange of experience between the worlds is also ensured. Both worlds can learn from each other. The innovation team can tap into the best of "world 1". At the same time, the experience of new ways of working can be helpful for the existing business. Through this permeability of the boundaries between the worlds can you achieve synergies. But it does not come about on its own. It must be deliberately built in, e.g. through the planned exchange of people.

4. The Structure of the New Operating System Is Customer-Centric

Existing processes and routines that work for familiar products often do not work for new customers, new markets or new technologies. This was shown by the figures of the Dutch sales company. The new business brought its own rules of the game, which were not compatible with the conventional routines. The EASi[3] team therefore derived its structures, processes, and behaviors 100% from the market and the customer and designed them anew within the team (see "Customer Obsession" Chap. 7).

5. Leadership Develops Naturally and Informally

In the case study, the formal role of the "manager" with positional authority has been eliminated. Nevertheless, the team does not work without leadership. It emerges naturally in the network, based on the competencies and know-how of the team members. At the same time, the team has the support of the CEO, who in his function and role does not control, but who empowers and supports and ensures that there is a balance in the overall organization.

Summary: Creating the Context

In the two-world space described here, the context of action for you as a leader can change hourly—which is a challenging field of action. At the same time, it is precisely here that you have the unique opportunity to profitably shape the context of action for the people in your organization. You can enable your teams to decide for the existing or the future business, depending on what a situation in the market requires.

For this reason, Festo in Holland has an equally successful small ecosystem in the midst of proven hierarchical structures. To achieve this, the sales approach was radically broken up and the sales team interlocked with the customer and the market. This example shows how completely different philosophies take effect depending on the requirements of the technology and the rules of the market. The context for such a change and the co-existence of both approaches to become possible has been created by the top management. Because such an initiative will fail if it is only bottom-up. Teams need the backing, the protection and space from above to try out something new. ◄

5.3 Courses of Action

5.3.1 Writing Exercise

Have you ever tried to write a text with your non-dominant hand? If you are curious to find out, then feel free to do it right now. Get blank paper and a pen and write a few sentences. If you are right-handed, first write a sentence with your right hand, then the same sentence with your left hand—or vice versa. If there is no paper to hand, there is a blank sketch page in Chap. 3 (Fig. 3.10) to try. Try it for a few minutes (Fig. 5.2).

. . .

Now, before you read on, reflect briefly:

What do the two handwritings look like? Which letters or words did you find particularly difficult? Are you proud? Or rather embarrassed? How did your hands feel? What does the text look like? What thoughts and feelings did you have while writing?

. . .

Usually, when I do this little exercise in workshops, every participant now is invited to show his or her 'handwriting artworks' to the group and describe the personal experience and feelings. As there are rarely any ambidextrous participants, most often the comments are like this:

- "Transferred back to the classroom"
- "I was terribly slow"
- "It was really frustrating"
- "A strange experience"

Fig. 5.2 Exercise: Writing with your right and with your left hand

- "The opposite of a sense of accomplishment..."
- "Something I used to be able to do doesn't work anymore"
- "Irritating"
- "I was bitten by the bug, though..."
- "Like a rookie..."
- "I'm surprised that somehow it does work out"

With this exercise in mind, now put yourself in the shoes of your organization. Imagine a large enterprise with numerous people, routines, processes, with a vision, mission, strategy, a control center, divisions, departments, teams, production facilities, logistics centers, etc.

Imagine that you now turn this company to the left (or to the non-dominant side).

You might have an idea now of *what it feels like* for the organization, for the teams and finally for the individual leaders, employees to change from the dominant, familiar side to the non-dominant side. And now you know what we have in mind in this chapter....

It Is New Territory! Beginner's Mind!

Interestingly enough, after the writing exercise there is never the feedback that it does *not* work at all. On the contrary, each time it becomes visible that the participants, despite all frustration or irritation, are surprised that they put something on paper at all. For some it is real fun! For a moment, sometimes even the 'beginner's spirit' [11] springs to life. It is the spirit that is so valuable for finding new territory (see Chap. 7). So there is some hope!

Just as there are plenty of tools for left- and right-handed people—scissors, fountain pens, computer mouses or keyboards—that make life easier with one hand or the other, people in organizations also need tools that make it easier to navigate one world or the other, or both at the same time. And *communication* is one such tool, which we will now look at in more detail.

5.3.2   The Innovation Context

Let's enter the enterprise. It's Monday morning, your day is starting. As an ambidextrous leader it is your task to create a context in which teams and employees can move freely in and between worlds. So first of all, you must grasp for yourself what context you are in at any given time. In order to shape an environment, the first step is to determine where you are and where you want to be.

Let us take an everyday life example of senior manager *Mr. A.* (*Mr. Ambidextrous*). He attends different meetings and goes through different situations during a regular day in the office. Different topics, projects, strategies are waiting to be heard and discussed. On the hour, *Mr. A.* meets different teams and tasks. If there was a reset button now, it would be helpful to use it. Because after each encounter and context, *Mr. A.*, as an ambidextrous leader, acts differently and approaches situations in a different way. And he does so with regard to the innovation context exploitation/exploration.

"Reset" After Each Meeting

Mr. A. asks himself again and again in every new situation: In which context am I now? Is it a meeting about innovative solutions for our future digital business? Does he meet a highly interdisciplinary team that knows best what the solution is and just wants to pick up some advice from him? Or is it about routine activities? What does the team need now? Is his expertise needed? Is it clear top-down-announcements or do they need space for generating new ideas?

Figure 5.3 shows the path through either an ambidextrous or a non-ambidextrous organization. In order to decide which are the right courses of action for the respective context, *Mr. A.* must first clarify whether the specific context requires ambidexterity. Is he dealing with *both the* current core business *and* the future business? Or is he in a setting where he can focus on one *or* the other without interference? The answer to these questions leads to *different* behaviors and respective results.

Ambidextrous Leadership: Finding Your Position Is Elementary

Determining your own position in the innovation context and the respective goals is the first step towards ambidextrous leadership. This takes a short moment of your attention: In every new situation you consider the people, the innovation context and the objective (explore/exploit). Only *then do* you align your actions.

This first step is based on the ability to observe situations, to listen to people, and to recognize the state of the organization or the team. *Only then* can you assess what kind of leadership is needed here. And this depends on whether you are dealing with familiar technologies, complex new digital business models, or with *both worlds simultaneously.*

> Ambidextrous leadership involves the crucial step of briefly determining your position and goal *before* you begin to interact.

The right side of Fig. 5.3 shows a non-ambidextrous context. If you are working in an exploratory field, e.g. in basic research for a new technology or in the incubator of a company, and your objective is to discover new territory, then you follow the path of "no ambidexterity". You focus on finding new solutions. The same applies to working in a strictly exploitative environment, e.g. with a focus on volume business and process efficiency. Here you need to roll out defined strategic measures efficiently. If you are *either* into exploration *or* into exploitation with a stable environment, you can stay in the appropriate leadership mode.

However, if you switch between the extremes from hour to hour, from conversation to conversation, and your job is to drive *both,* then the ability to act ambidextrously is required. Then it's about striking the balance between exploitation and exploration and creating a context where both work for you and for the teams.

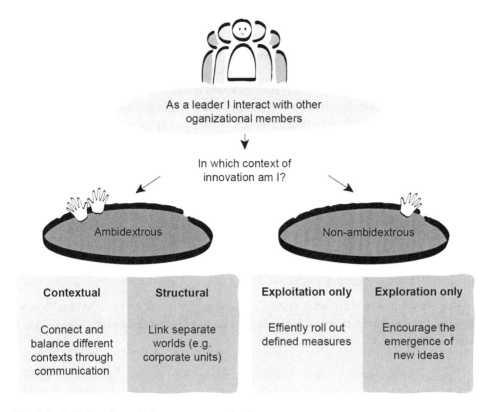

Fig. 5.3 Guideline for ambidextrous communication

In Top Management, Ambidexterity Is Daily Business

Everyday corporate life shows that leaders at the upper levels usually operate in ambidextrous settings. The higher up in the hierarchy and the more far-reaching a leader's influence is, the more likely will she be responsible for multiple innovation projects and approaches.

Even if you have established *separate* worlds within your organization, e.g. separate business units, for the existing and the future business, at the top level you need to orchestrate both. At the very top, in the place where you oversee the present and the future, ambidexterity is *always* contextual in nature. You are confronted with both *every single day*.

But ambidexterity is also important at mid-enterprise levels. Even within a project or an organizational unit that is clearly oriented towards exploration *or* exploitation, it often becomes apparent that skills from both worlds are required: Depending on the progress of a project or the maturity of a technology you will need skills for idea generation as well as skills for top down management. Mutual acceptance, learning and exchange is beneficial for both sides.

We will concentrate in the next few minutes on the left side of Fig. 5.3, which is *ambidexterity*. In this environment, you need a range of different action patterns that you can use depending on the situation and context.

The Three Basic Patterns of Ambidextrous Leadership
The 2016 study on ambidexterity among managers in the German mechanical engineering industry [12] found that simply combining action patterns from exploration and exploitation is not sufficient to reach ambidexterity. Ambidextrous leaders additionally use a further action pattern that is tailor-made for an ambidextrous setting. This makes a total of *three* different basic patterns that you will have in your backpack to promote ambidexterity in the company. The three together will help you lead safely through the ambidextrous organization:

1. Communication for exploration (Chap. 3)
2. Communication for exploitation (Chap. 4)
3. Ambidextrous communication (Chap. 5)

You may wonder whether it makes any difference at all if the individual leader changes her communication style. Perhaps you object that communication is just a drop in the ocean...?

   ...

The answer is simple. Transformation requires a cultural change. This cultural change starts with the mindset of every individual. With mine, with yours, with everyone's in the organization. It begins in our thoughts and actions. And both, thoughts and actions, are revealed in our communication.

The culture of an organization arises from the collective thoughts and actions of the people who live and work in it. The spirit, the very special spirit of an organization, grows out of the individual mindset of the individual employees and their team spirit. Each individual decides what contribution he or she will make to it. So if you are a leader and want to change something, the decision is easy. If your mindset does not change, your organization will not change. But if your mindset does move, then suddenly interesting things will happen....

▶ **Let Us Simply Start and Try** Without extra costs, without expensive consultants. We simply change our own habits. It is a conscious steering of one's own communication and a conscious purposeful steering of the communication in the network.

   If leaders take their communication seriously and consciously work with it they will turn the big wheel. They'll be turning the culture.

1. Communication for Exploration

We briefly summarize again the most important points from Chap. 3. Exploration requires a communication-based leadership style that is completely detached from today's organizational paradigm of the pyramid. In order to arrive at new solutions in the environment of digitalization, we must take responsibility and decision-making power from the top-management floor and share it with the teams. This is where the know-how is located. Here you'll find the numerous competencies and disciplines that you need to create complex technology platforms and digital services.

If you want to design and orchestrate digital ecosystems, you need to change your understanding of leadership. You'll have to place communication at the very center of your action. Because the more a digital solution for your customer is itself characterized by communication and networking features, the more these human skills must be activated in your teams along the innovation process. Because your process will shape your product.

Ecosystem management requires that you decentralize communication. You'll leave the pyramid and work in the network instead. You build networks and communities across divisions and companies and "feed" them with useful information and participants so that a self-organizing system can emerge and grow. Communication in the ecosystem runs bottom-up and across and outside your organization. Hierarchy in the traditional sense fades to the back. Instead leadership that is independent from positional authority takes place at the points where decisions can be made based on capabilities and knowledge.

While fewer announcements from above are required, formal and informal communication increasingly takes place at all levels of the enterprise. It creates transparency and supports self-organization and customer-centric approaches such as design thinking and other agile working methods.

Conclusion: The focus of your actions as a leader is on orchestrating ecosystems and shaping an agile mindset for innovation. The goal is to generate—and seize—new knowledge and opportunities for new business models through communication and networking.

2. Communication for Exploitation

In the environment of exploitation you'll find sufficient information and knowledge about your running business. Managers usually know the right path (or at least think they do) and they are empowered to make top-down decisions (Chap. 4). A hierarchical top-down communication style in the organizational pyramid assumes that the top-management knows more than the workforce (e.g. on strategy, market developments etc.). To achieve strategic alignment in the organization, they give clear directions to their employees.

In order to gain traction and get decisions through the organization quickly, it is important to centralize your communication efforts and tightly organize the process of information transfer. There is one control center of communication, from where information is directed through the different communication channels. Whether as an event, an article in the employee magazine or intranet, a blog post, a brochure, or an entry in the minutes of a meeting—in order to achieve unanimity and clarity within the company, the message must be right on target and the media and channels must be selected in a targeted manner. Dialogue with employees is kept as controlled and small as possible, because the decisions have already been made. Now it is a matter of execution. For efficiency and speed, tap into existing processes and structures, do not reinvent the wheel. Clear announcements. Command and control is the basic principle. From the top to the bottom you inform about vision, mission, strategy or action plan and you explain the *reason why* something has to be done. The goal of your communication is to achieve homogeneity. You bring the organization to a common denominator.

Conclusion: The focus of your activities as a manager is on centrally controlled communication and top-down transmission of information for executing a strategy. The goal is to create a common understanding of a certain topic, to optimize efficiency in the processes and to accelerate the execution of tasks from your action plan.

3. Ambidextrous Communication

Ambidextrous leadership goes beyond combining the approaches of exploitation and exploration. Ambidexterity requires additional, further leadership behaviors. Because if you want to ensure that activities for the present *and* for the future move forward successfully in your organization, you need to balance the two worlds. As soon as the ambidextrous organization is out of balance, one or the other will be at risk.

The following analogy was brought in by a seminar participant during a workshop on ambidexterity. He compared leadership to being a parent in everyday family life. He explained that ambidexterity requires far more than the leadership competence in two individual areas:

Let us therefore take look at *Mr. A.* again, who, in addition to his professional life as a senior manager, is also an enthusiastic father of two children. He has a very individual relationship with each child. With his son he plays football and tennis. With his daughter he discusses tricky math problems. In doing so, Mr. A. must always make sure that neither of the two children feels disadvantaged. If a child feels that he or she is not getting enough attention, domestic row is inevitable. This must be avoided at all costs. And *Mr. A.* also knows that a lack of attention, even if it is only a subconsciously experienced lack, does no good to a child.

Mr. A. therefore distributes his attention fairly. In addition, he ensures that there is a lively exchange *between the two children,* that they not only accept each other's existence, but understand the advantage of learning from each other or helping each other and doing things together.

Exploitation and exploration projects in the transition space need exactly this. It does not mean that you have to promote and support every start-up idea that sprouts up in your organization. It means that you make the fundamental decision for two different directions of innovation and open up a space where both co-exist.

Conclusion: The focus of your activities as an ambidextrous leader is to balance both worlds. Through your communication, you appropriately direct the organization's attention to exploration and exploitation initiatives. You strike the right tone in both environments, and create a context in which employees can operate in both worlds. The goal is to

Table 5.1 The three basic patterns of communication for ambidextrous leadership

Communication for exploration	Communication for exploitation	Ambidextrous communication
Organization and leadership Ecosystem/ agile mindset Heterogeneity, diversity of voices New knowledge emerges Natural leadership emerging from the teams	*Organization and leadership* Hierarchy/ pyramid Homogeneity, common denominator Use existing knowledge base Management by positional authority	*Organization and leadership* Pyramid/ Network/ Ecosystem Balance and connection between the worlds Leadership by positional authority and natural leadership in teams co-exist at eye level
Communication Decentralize communication Build networks and communities, enable bottom-up communication Avoid management-centered top-down communication, let natural hierarchies emerge	*Communication* Centralize communication, organize it and cascade it top-down (you "send") Clear announcements Avoid communication that opens the discussion	*Communication* Communicative context management: Creating an environment in which exploitation and exploration co-exist and complement each other
Content Communicate a strong vision, thereby set framework, do not dictate action Allow content (ideas, solutions) to emerge Promote greenfield mindset	*Content* Inform about vision, strategy, action plan Give clear directions for action	*Content* Communicate a two-world vision that puts the present in the context of the future business Communicate the need for a balanced innovation and business portfolio for long-term survival
Formats / methods Use customer-centric approaches to innovation such as Design Thinking Support self-organization through agile working methods, agile project management	*Formats / methods* Use official media channels and formats such as town hall meetings, articles in employee magazines, intranet, video messages, committees, and minutes	*Formats / methods* Use official formats such as town hall meetings to communicate the vision. Otherwise give room for top-down *and* bottom-up and network communication

strengthen *both innovation approaches* and to create an environment in which both can develop successfully (Table 5.1).

5.3.3 The Communication Tools for Ambidexterity

You will see it in the thoughts and actions of the leaders whether an organization is truly ambidextrous. Ambidexterity requires the ability to consciously shape the period of change in an organization. It requires a sense of successfully leading a current state while learning and practicing the behaviors, routines, processes, methods of a new state [12]. While you are successful with known procedures in the existing business, it is at the same time necessary to recompose and reconfigure your knowledge base, disciplines, skills that exist company-wide and beyond the borders.

You provide stability and at the same time you upset things with other activities. Through the appropriate use of your communication, you can relax this situation and achieve **synergetic effects.** Then, what exactly does this communication look like?

Essentially, **four** balancing core elements can be observed in the behavior of ambidextrous leaders. Through their mindset and their actions, they create a context in which ambidexterity can emerge as peaceful coexistence and interaction of two worlds in one organization.

1. **Vision:** You convey a comprehensive vision of the future.
2. **Strategy:** You continuously communicate the strategy for both worlds.
3. **Integration:** You connect both worlds through communication.
4. **Reconfiguration:** You create profitable *new* organizational connections.

With the help of these four elements it becomes possible to put the principles of ambidextrous leaders proposed by Tushman and colleagues (Chap. 2) into action. The ambidexterity experts call for senior leaders to develop a larger identity, locate and endure tensions, and embrace contradictions [10]. To achieve this and bring the principles to life, we recommend to implement the four core elements presented here into your communicative actions.

1. **Vision**

    If you want to create a context that enables organizational members to work and make decisions in a field of extreme tensions, begin with building a vision that addresses *both*: The vision puts today's business in the context of future. By showing important technological trends and medium to long-term developments in the market and the role you are going to play, you connect today's business to the future business of your company. By repeatedly communicating the vision of the two-world space that leaves no room for doubt, you create the overall framework for an ambidextrous organization [13].

2. **Strategy**

    This goes hand in hand with the communication of the strategic actions and intentions of both worlds. Because exploring and exploiting at the same time means that both are reflected in the action plan of your strategy. When activities in both directions have finally been launched, then the real balancing act begins. Because now it is about the integration of two contrasting approaches, organizational paradigms, ways of acting and thinking within your organization.

3. **Integration**

    Integration of both worlds means that teams from one and the other side do not feel disadvantaged, but find a solid position in the overall direction of the company.

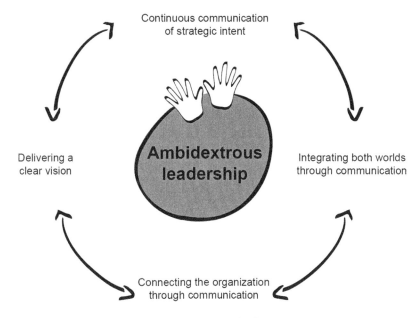

Fig. 5.4 Four core activities of ambidextrous communication

Activities for today and for tomorrow take place on an equal footing and are equally valued. It also means that you promote exchange between the teams and ensure that the different experiences are shared [14].

4. **Reconfiguration**

And finally, it is your job to create new organizational connections that enable resources from both worlds to be reconnected through communication across the organization, thereby generating value for the future.

Figure 5.4 illustrates the four key activities you can use to promote ambidexterity. If you want to build your company's future business today, even though the present core business is still bringing in the returns, then you need persistence and perseverance at this point. Because acting once is not enough here. These patterns of action will stay with you in the future. They need to be applied continuously and repeatedly if you want to bring about real change in your organization. So let us delve deeper into the courses of action.

5.3.3.1 Communicating the Vision of the Future

The vision is a binding guiding principle for the members of an organization. In an ambidextrous enterprise, the vision puts the current and future direction of the company into a large context. It conveys a picture in which evolutionary improvement and revolutionary realignment are balanced and coherently intertwined. Evolution prepares the revolution—the connection must become visible here so that every individual in the organization understands why activities for the future are already being launched today.

Why this or that initiative now? We are doing well! The vision explains why stability and increased efficiency in the existing business are necessary for survival. At the same time, it shows how today's business will pave the financial way to reach the future and not miss technological leaps.

▶ The vision is a binding and inspiring statement for the members of an organization. In an ambidextrous organization, the vision puts the current and future directions of the organization into a full context. The vision of an ambidextrous organization breaks through existing boundaries, inspires and tears down thought barriers. It spans the vast two-world space between the here and now and a desirable, exciting future.

But any vision, no matter how promising, is worthless if no one knows about it. A powerful vision must inspire and carry away the broad mass of the workforce. And for that you need *communication*. In the portfolio of instruments and methods, a conventional means of top-down communication is suitable for communicating the vision (Chap. 4): the town hall meeting. You want to reach *all* employees. You do not just want to convey facts, but create an experience. The vision should charge and inspire the team. Inspire and connect. It makes visible how much all those involved, regardless of whether they are working for exploitation or exploration, depend on each other. Because one cannot exist permanently without the other. This is how you weld your teams together.

With an enthralling vision event about the future direction you can make it clear why a company cannot afford to drown in day-to-day business. At the same time, it shows how exciting and encouraging a view of the big picture can be. It ignites your company's energy.

As a CEO, board member, managing director, senior manager, project manager, you have a duty and a role to *communicate* this vision and *explain* how far a company needs to think beyond today's boundaries. You can instigate your teams and employees to do the same. The vision of an ambidextrous organization breaks through existing boundaries and tears down thought barriers. That is the opportunity. And it is the first step toward an organizational context where ambidexterity can emerge.

"The Art of Finding the Right Balance"
Interview with Prof. Dr. Hans Müller-Steinhagen, former Rector of the Technische Universität Dresden (TUD), 2010–2020
You've headed one of Germany's largest technical universities. The CHE Centre for Higher Education calls you a "visionary with your feet on the ground" [15]. How important is the vision of the future for you?
A university as large as TU Dresden can be compared to a tanker on the high seas. If you do not know your destination, you cannot steer and hold your course, but are

(continued)

simply drifting through the seas. Navigation without knowing your destination would be impossible. But in order to be able to formulate goals and strategies and determine a course, you first need a vision. In my eyes, a vision is a kind of guiding idea, binding for all employees and students.

My vision for TU Dresden is reflected in our institutional strategy, with which we were successful in the German Excellence Initiative in 2012 as one of eleven German universities. And the upward trend has continued since 2019 with the confirmation of our status of excellence: TU Dresden is an internationally leading, highly innovative university. This is thanks to its ability to cooperate synergistically, i.e. across disciplines and institutions, and due to its willingness to continuously rethink and optimize its structures and processes. At the same time, we establish a culture of responsibility across all areas: for the fulfilment of our tasks and duties in research, teaching and transfer, in the management of our resources and in our collaboration with all university members.

From your point of view, how important is it to communicate a strong vision? How do you do that?

A vision that only exists in your thoughts is a lost vision. The more people you can inspire for a vision, the greater the chance to implement it. Everyone prefers to get involved in things that are important and meaningful to them. Only by getting everyone involved can I get everyone in the university walk in the same direction. That does not mean that we always have to agree on everything! But we must know and support the vision and goals of the university.

Without communication, this is impossible. For this reason, one of my first decisions after being elected Rector of TU Dresden was to relocate the communications department into the rector's office and to set up a strategy department. Together we develop strategies and action plans on how to get the entire university involved in decision-making processes.

As Rector, I use personal conversations as well as large town halls to communicate TU Dresden's goals and plans internally and externally. There is hardly a day when I do not inform people about TU Dresden and solicit support for our university at various events. These include, for example, regular meetings with representatives of the different groups of our university—starting with the students and ending with the university professors. It is also the participation in meetings with politicians from the city council and state parliamentary groups or the active participation in numerous committees at the federal level.

In all of this listening is particularly important. Fears and worries are sometimes brought to me in conversations. Always having an open ear and taking these fears seriously is an important prerequisite for cooperation in change processes.

(continued)

In your innovation management you cooperate closely with the industry. Companies are often stuck in their day-to-day business. Why should they nevertheless look far into the future?

If you don't keep an eye on the big and long-term developments, you will make the wrong decisions. It is just as important for companies as it is for universities not to get lost in everyday business, but to always keep an eye on the big picture. Companies that do not only focus on the present, but continuously explore future scenarios, gain decisive competitive advantages. The further you look into the future, the greater the chance of not missing out on technological leaps. The earlier you can also initiate changes in your own corporate policy, which usually takes time to implement. German industry has a global reputation for outstanding quality and optimization, but has also missed out on a number of disruptive innovations in recent decades.

What role does 'innovative capacity' play for a globally recognized university of excellence like the Technische Universität Dresden?

Without the ability to innovate both in teaching and in research as well as in administrative and support processes, a university cannot compete internationally. For many years, TU Dresden has committed itself to the goal of helping to solve the mega-problems of humanity with its research and the education of highly qualified graduates.

As one of eleven universities of excellence nationwide, we have proven that innovation and vision are an integral part of our DNA. Last but not least, in 2016 we were rated as one of the 20 most innovative universities in Europe by the Reuters agency. More than any other institution a university must stay in motion and be able to reinvent itself again and again.

In 2014, the German magazine DIE ZEIT and the Centre for Higher Education selected you as the university manager of the year with the title "The Motivator". How do you motivate your employees to keep opening up new territory for the university, while at the same time the existing day-to-day business has to keep running?

It is the 'art' of finding the right balance between creativity and new ideas, the creation of free spaces and autonomy on the one hand and detailed requirements and sometimes also clear announcements of the running business on the other hand. We have to create a framework for our employees, just as we do for our students, that opens the space for new ideas and visions and for their implementation. This also includes building an appropriate climate or culture. We must have the courage to put old structures and routines into question.

While we have to meet growing demands as a university of excellence, it is also important to set priorities and to avoid overloading one's own resources and, above

(continued)

all, the employees. A constant "faster, higher, further" in all areas at the same time leads to wear and tear in the long run. At first glance, it is often tempting to constantly initiate new activities for the TU Dresden. But as a leader I also have to keep an eye on this: Anyone who permanently operates at the limits will not be able to be successful in the long term. This applies to the university as a whole as well as to each individual employee and to me as rector.

Thank you very much Professor Müller-Steinhagen!

The interview concludes with a key insight for communication: if the vision overburdens your organization by asking too much of it, there is a risk that you will lose your audience. The image of the "visionary that is down-to-earth" [15] answers this very question. Stretch the space to experience the journey from today to the future and take the organizational members along for the ride. A vision that contains both worlds, that celebrates the best of the past and describes an intriguing future, creates a unifying transition space in which all its stakeholders will find their way.

Communication task for manager:

- Conveying the vision of the future with a down-to-earth mentality that creates identity as well as inspiring and igniting enthusiasm
- Making visible the inseparable connections between evolution and revolution
- Create commitment through your communication

5.3.3.2 Communication of the Strategy

Once the vision has been communicated and accepted by the organization, the next step is to communicate and implement the action plan to achieve the goal. And evolution and revolution must both be reflected in this action plan. As a manager, first make sure that the two aspects of the vision are also anchored in the strategic planning. Because this is often where you fall back into your running business. Sales targets, financial ratios, "the future costs money, we have to survive in the here and now" are objections that managers tend to prefer [10].

If the future is not reflected in the action planning, you can bury the ambidextrous organization now. Because it is essential for the success of an innovation project that you can communicate and prove that it is part of the strategy. Mere bottom-up activities do not have enough power in the long run.

If both directions are anchored in the strategy and the CEO as well as his management team stands behind the ambidextrous strategy, the usual communication mechanisms of corporate communication take effect. Information packages are put together and cascaded top-down. At the same time, it is important for managers to repeatedly underline and emphasize the importance of individual actions of one world and the other. If both are to happen in an organization, no team, no team must feel disadvantaged.

This is about distributing and directing attention within the organization. Whether with the help of employee events, articles in the employee magazine, newsletters or blog posts— setting spotlights now works best with the proven means of top-down communication (Chap. 4). How good that we can access the best of both worlds...

Communication task for manager:

- Communicate the ambidextrous strategy and promote acceptance
- Highlight an action plan for evolution *and* for revolution
- Continuously spotlight, direct and "fairly" distribute the organization's attention through your communications.
- Use top-down communication tools and channels

In the following interview Prof. Volker Nestle, Head of Product Development LifeTech at FESTO, describes the role of ambidexterity during the strategic goal-setting process. Already as early as in this process leaders have to balance conflicting interests and objectives and get their employees involved at the earliest possible stage.

"Ambidexterity Is Everyday Business"
Interview with Prof. Dr. Volker Nestle, Chairman of the Board of Hahn-Schickard-Gesellschaft fuer angewandte Forschung e. V. and Head of Product Development LifeTech at Festo SE & Co. KG

What is the role of ambidexterity in your everyday business?

This is quite simple: Ambidexterity *is* everyday business. The main driver of ambidexterity is the competitive environment of a company. Volatile markets in the regional, national and international environment, faster technological changes as well as ever shorter product life cycles force companies to be more flexible and to accelerate their innovation cycles. At the same time, companies need stability and must be profitable with their running business. To achieve this, existing competencies have to be exploited in the best possible way and products and services must be turned into value as efficiently as possible: Without liquidity, the game will be over soon.

What is the biggest problem in this area of tension?

Companies increasingly find themselves in the situation of competing investments in innovation vs. investments in efficiency enhancement. The associated payback periods differ severely and this is a major problem. Actions to increase a company's efficiency usually show their effect in the operative business quite quickly, while innovation projects are a risky investment into the future.

Incidentally, the statistics show that the majority of companies have developed a preference for short-term amortization and optimization of existing products and services. This is easy to understand for the reasons I just mentioned. The optimization

(continued)

of the existing portfolio is often driven by a company's existing knowledge base and successful products. On the one hand, this is good news for the running business, but on the other hand, it bears the risk of lock-in effects, which can quickly become problematic when competitive conditions change.

How do you react to this as a leader? How do you prevent it?

Since no company can escape these tensions, managers must prepare themselves for the challenges that the topic of ambidexterity brings. This already starts in the goal-setting process for the corporate strategy. In this process cost optimization and profitability goals have to be balanced with innovation and growth goals. It is extremely important to get the employees involved in this process and to carefully explain and discuss the ambidextrous strategy. Because when you implement an ambidextrous strategy, the processes and approaches to be applied differ dramatically depending on the strategic direction: from formalistic/mechanistic routines and processes to agile/transformative approaches. The methods and processes used are extremely important, as the leaps in innovation are directly related to them. As a leader, you must make sure that the entire organization knows your vision and mission and understands the importance of an ambidextrous strategy.

How does ambidexterity manifest itself in your processes?

In general, product optimizations in the core business are driven by incremental innovations. Here we use the same process landscape as for the original product for reasons of efficiency. However, completely new products and solutions often require a radically new perspective on products and markets. As they put a radical focus on customer needs they follow different processes. For this reason, more and more new product development projects are being set up in an agile environment and context. The new solutions are developed starting with a small set of specifications. They are optimized in iterative recursions towards the customer needs. In this way, employees are gradually and methodically introduced to innovative topics.

Does this also have an impact on culture?

Yes, of course! Over time, the corporate culture changes, experimentation and creativity become more important again in everyday life, and speed and flexibility in the innovation process increase. However, the new understanding of roles in agile projects also calls established hierarchy levels into question. The extent of this organizational revolution, the possible effects on the organizational structures and also the opportunities cannot be predicted yet.

What tools do you use to implement and promote ambidexterity in your organization?

There are tools that can be used in top-down management and communication and tools that promote interaction between employees along the more project-based business. For formal communication of the strategy that has to be controlled from

(continued)

the top, employee information, e.g. in town hall meetings, is a good choice. In this way, information on the current situation, strategy, or on important areas of the company's core business can be distributed quickly and efficiently. These events are also important from a psychological point of view because they build trust and promote the feeling among the employees that they are well informed. In addition, personal speeches by the top management—live or via video stream—can be used for strategic topics. Of course, top-down communication still works excellently in writing, e.g. in newsletters on the inter- or intranet, Facebook, Twitter or XING and LinkedIn. And personal one-on-ones with your employees are of course particularly important, because here you can talk not only about the content, but also about how people feel. However, communication from the top to the workforce is always more of a sending of information. In order to generate new knowledge, innovation and progress, there must be a second kind of communication which is organized in the teams.

How do you do that?

I then tend to moderate and network communication in the team. In our day-to-day R+D business there is more lateral and bottom-up communication. In these discussions and meetings reality is "constructed", so to speak. In addition, there are project planning tools, for example, that provide a framework for formal communication among the R+D staff. Requirement specifications and functional specifications are an ultimate part of this. In the official committees along the innovation development process, communication is strongly product-related.

For new ideas, you should carefully consider internal, open forums on future topics, whether with a physical presence or supported with appropriate web tools for idea management. Unfortunately, the acceptance and success of online tools is still low because the critical mass of participants is not reached. In my experience, conferences and onsite workshops on previously specified and communicated innovation topics are most suitable for idea generation.

Thank you very much Prof. Nestle!

5.3.3.3 Integration of the Two Worlds Through Communication

Your vision and strategy have now been communicated top-down. Acceptance has been widely solicited. Now, at the latest, all members of the organization know that there will be activities for today's core business as well as for future business areas. Up to this point, the communication task has been comparatively easy. It is a familiar game. You have broadcast from the top down. However, that does not mean that the two worlds are now compatible. Nor does it mean that there is a healthy balance and synergy. You must now convey the added value that mutual toleration and perhaps even cooperation (!) possess.

Unfortunately, this task is often underestimated and this results in worries and fears of people in the ambidextrous organizational environment:

The Fear of Being Less Important
The public opinion among employees that an initiative of exploitation might be less innovative only gains weight because there are initiatives of exploration within an organization that carry the radiance of innovation around them. "After all, we're *just* doing the old standard business. The exciting new things, the digital business, is happening on the other side." You can see the danger that those working on existing lines of business will feel left behind when they see the new, seemingly more exciting issues that they are not involved in.

The same fear of being disadvantaged can be observed in the highly innovative environment: Those involved in innovation projects react anxiously when everyone is looking at the short-term success of the high-revenue core business. While the innovation teams quietly build new competences, others get applause for sales and profits in the core business. They deliver. The others apparently don't. And even though long-term competence building generates value, it doesn't show up on any balance sheet in the short term.

In an interview, organizational researcher Wilhelm Bauer, Director of the Fraunhofer Institute for Industrial Engineering IAO in Stuttgart, highlights this potential for tension and emphasizes the importance of equal appreciation and recognition of both poles: "We have to carefully avoid the impression that there are important and less important divisions of the company" (Chap. 2). As a leader, it is therefore imperative that you resolve this tension and convey to all employees that it is only through the existence of both directions that they can look forward to a secure and promising future. The mediation between the worlds is a major communication task.

The Opportunity to Exchange Experiences
In the case study in mechanical engineering, in which a contextual setting of ambidexterity was investigated, exploitation and exploration took place within the same organization [12]. It became repeatedly visible how strongly initiatives of exploitation and exploration can cross-fertilize each other. After all, in everyday business life it becomes clear that hardly any project is fully exploitative or explorative in nature.

If you as a leader (hardly anyone else will feel responsible for this) promote networking and communication between the worlds, whether in the form of experience exchange or the mutual use of knowledge or infrastructures, you can ensure that acceptance gradually increases and useful connections emerge. For example, a design thinking workshop in an exploitation environment can help in finding a quick solution to an efficiency problem. The experience gained from manufacturing can help in the design of a smart product-service-system. Learning from each other and using existing knowledge and experience from the other world can optimize processes and significantly accelerate the change (for which you are responsible as an ambidextrous leader).

While the classic top-down instruments of internal corporate communication are sufficient for the mere communication of vision and strategy, you now have to take a different path. You are a **systems integrator, networker, mediator, connector**. As a manager with "authority", you can lend weight to the exchange of experiences in a top-down manner and eliminate doubts. But for the exchange to be successful, you must then provide the space for communication between the worlds and place yourself in the moderating role.

The Chance of Joint Marketing Efforts

In practice, there is another beneficial effect when you combine both worlds. The communicative linking of exploration and exploitation is not only important for the internal acceptance and commitment of the employees. Especially in external communication with customers, offering a balanced innovation portfolio proves to be extremely helpful. Evolution and revolution can be marketed to the outside world in a wonderful "set". They do not 'bite' but complement each other ideally. While you may struggle to find a balance and mutual understanding within the organization, the global sales force will jump on the duo of commodity and high-end solution and thank you as an innovator for offering both. That is because the sales force now has both on offer: volume products for mass markets *and* innovative solutions for the future. The combination makes the difference. It conveys a value that you cannot convey with one offering alone.

> **Communication task for manager:**

- Mediate between the worlds as a systems integrator and dissolve employees' fears
- Establish and moderate exchange of experience between the worlds
- Use the profitable connections of both in your customer communication

5.3.3.4 Reconfiguration Through Communication

By creating new connections between both worlds and by coordinating and designing these new connections, you can generate value and drive change in the future. This is now no longer about systems integration as in the previous step, but about *reconfiguration*. It is about operational intervention.

Reconfiguration includes moving away from routines of today's business and from established structures and methods. Redistribution or change of resource compositions can take place between worlds, when knowledge and people are shifted to the respective other context. In the process of reconfiguring, you will notice that some people are employed in a world that is unfavorable to them and that they could be much more effective in the other environment. This assumes that the culture is open and that there are leaders who recognize and take advantage of this potential. In case you have any doubts now: This role is also part of ambidextrous leadership! Because you do not let any opportunity slip through your fingers. In the first step, in addition to observation skills, you need your communication.

Here, the hierarchical top-down communication of broadcasting alone will have little effect. Because it is about breaking through silos and the flexible use of knowledge and skills. The communication task here is to make contact and establish links, because mutual knowledge of each other is the starting point of the process of shifting and reconfiguring people and resources.

Communication task for manager:

- Search for required knowledge and skills in both worlds and connect them
- Prepare resource shift between worlds through communicative networking of people and departments
- Accompany reconfiguration (exchanges and shifts) through communication

Ambidexterity Is Part of Everyday Business

With these four options for action—the communication of your vision, the communication of your strategy, systems integration and reconfiguration—you can implement an ambidextrous leadership style in your everyday life. You can start testing it right away tomorrow, because if you listen to the statements of the interview with Volker Nestle: No company can escape from ambidexterity.

Summary: "Turned Inside Out"

When we try to do things in everyday life with the untrained, non-dominant hand, everything suddenly becomes slow and difficult. Applied to entire organizations, we can hardly imagine what it means to turn a company *inside out*. In the best case, the beginner's mind sets in. In order to elicit this spirit and facilitate the challenging situation, this chapter offers communication-based courses for ambidextrous leadership. The first prerequisite for communication-based navigation through everyday life is that leaders briefly determine their position and goals in each situation. Depending on the innovation context, fundamentally different approaches to communication will help them achieve the company's goals.

   The reality of everyday corporate life shows: It is in particular the managers at the upper levels who operate in an ambidextrous setting. The higher up in the hierarchy, the greater more likely that several innovation approaches have to be orchestrated in the same system. Three different basic patterns of communication can then be used by managers to help: Communication for exploration contexts (ecosystem management), communication for exploitation contexts (top-down communication), and ambidextrous communication. The latter requires that you create a context in which both worlds can develop successfully. For this context you need to promote a comprehensive vision of the future (1), communicate a dual strategy with actions for both directions (2). You'll have to balance and orchestrate both worlds (3) and you will benefit from reconfiguring and recomposing the resource base according to the more suitable context (4). ◄

5.4   Conclusion: Ambidexterity Needs Courage

Ambidexterity is more than the mere ability to navigate exploitation and exploration. When organizations and leaders are ambidextrous, they *connect* both worlds and achieve a state of balance between activities for the present and for the future. Building on the model of communication-based ambidextrous leadership, this chapter has highlighted different patterns of action in leadership communication: from communicating the two-world vision up to intervening in the allocation of resources of the two worlds.

More than others, ambidextrous leaders shape the corporate culture and mindset through their actions. Only through transformative communication efforts can they create a context for both worlds to coexist, to cooperate, and for the boundaries to eventually blur. Just as there are tools for left-handed and right-handed people to make it easier to perform different activities, everyday leaders need tools to navigate their company through a highly dynamic technological and market environment and increasingly complex organizational structures. The tools presented can be used directly in everyday life.

If you, as a leader, operate in a field of tension between evolution and revolution and have to deal with the challenges of both worlds, your personal communication will support you. Depending on the context in which you operate, you can access different types of communication and use them consciously to promote exploration *or* exploitation *or* both worlds.

Courage!

You must then also set a good example of the interplay between the present and the future and bring both worlds together. The most important ingredient for this is courage. The example of the Dutch sales company of FESTO shows that the CEO's commitment is the first step but not enough to transform the organization. Only the intensive dialogue between him and his management team forms the basis for implementing new ways of thinking and working. These new ways of working on collaboration, communication and networking. As a manager, it is important to facilitate this within the team and to encourage self-organization.

The exercise of writing with both hands gives a first idea of what it means for organizations to change. It is about understanding how people in organizations may feel when they go through this transformation process. Experiences range from frustration to curiosity. And the full range is what you're dealing with as a leader in an ambidextrous organization.

Initiating the Transformation Process

Three different basic patterns ultimately help you to address people in each world of your company. In your toolbox are actions for exploitation, for exploration and for orchestrating both worlds. While Chaps. 3 and 4 address the types of communication in *either* one *or* the other environment, Chap. 5 delves into the communication of ambidexterity. It is about balancing and connecting both worlds and finally trigger the fundamental transformation in which the boundaries gradually blur and the organization aligns itself with the future.

The third type of communication for both worlds builds on four core elements: communication of your vision, communication of your dual strategy, balancing of both worlds, and reconfiguring to align your resource base towards the future.

First of all, it is important to open up the large space from the present to the future in your vision. This space looks at current activities against the backdrop of a future position of the company. The vision touches the activities of everyone involved so that everyone can find themselves in it. The metaphor of the 'down-to-earth-visionary' helps to understand that a vision must not overwhelm but integrate. With this picture you leave the world of the red and blue oceans and look at both in an overall sense: the two-world space. This image must be communicated. Typical forms of top-down communication such as town-hall meetings or articles in the employee magazine are suitable for this. A vision is not just a factual picture. It is also an attitude towards life, a unifying purpose that you want to shape in the organization. You transport this purpose with the help of communication. Because everyone needs to know and experience it.

Once the vision has been established, strategic planning and implementation also follow the principle of ambidexterity. Actions from both worlds must be reflected in this and also communicated. Because only if activities are of strategic relevance, will they be recognized as important in the company and prioritized by the teams. The importance of both worlds in a dual strategy of a company must be communicated continuously. Again, you can access top-down approaches. The point is to keep shining the spotlight on both worlds of your organization.

In order to prevent silos from forming between the present and the future, it is your task to connect the two worlds and to enable the best of both worlds to be exchanged. Skills and experiences from one world can provide the decisive impetus for achieving the respective goal in the other—whether in increasing efficiency or in generating ideas. At the same time, teams in both worlds must notice that all areas of the organization are important and that the firm cannot survive in the long term without the other.

Blurring Boundaries

Finally, you blur the boundaries between the worlds by reconfiguring and recomposing your resource base through communication and networking. Disciplines, skills, fields of competence from "World 1" and "World 2" need to be connected in the long term, in order to still break new ground with tight budgets and limited resources. Reconfiguration starts with communication and exchange. Through this you integrate new knowledge from other areas and trigger a shift in resources. If people and teams know about each other and understand the added value of collaboration it will make it easier for you to recompose the organization and prepare the leap into the future.

After reading this chapter, you now know the basic three communication types of ambidexterity and it is best to start with them now. From now on, ambidexterity will support you in your everyday business.

References

1. Kotter, John (2016): "Ein völlig neues Spiel". Interview mit John Kotter vom 23.06.2017. In: Haufe.de. Online: https://www.haufe.de/personal/hr-management/john-kotter-ueber-agilitaet-unternehmen-brauchen-2-betriebssystem_80_362438.html [Accessed: 30.05.2020].
2. Fünf Punkte für den Erfolg von Corporate Startup Initiativen. In: Computerwoche.de vom 14.06.2017. Online: https://www.computerwoche.de/a/fuenf-punkte-fuer-den-erfolg-von-corpo rate-startup-initiativen,3330920 [Accessed: 30.05.2020].
3. Warum Konzerne als Gründungshelfer oft scheitern. In: Wirtschaftswoche Online vom 5. April 2015. Online: http://www.wiwo.de/erfolg/gruender/inkubatoren-als-pr-show-warum-konzerne-als-gruendungshelfer-oft-scheitern/11532078.html [Accessed: 30.05.2020].
4. Deutschlands beste Digilabs. In: Capital vom 22. Juni 2017. Online: http://www.capital.de/dasmagazin/ranking-digitalisierung-deutschlands-beste-digital-labore-lufthansa-daimler-man-9067.html [Accessed: 14.07.2017].
5. Killt eure Innovation Labs! t3n vom 30.11.2019. Online: https://t3n.de/news/killt-innovation-labs-1228358/ [Accessed: 24.05.2020].
6. "Mein Leben in der Lehmschicht". In: Capital vom 18.12.2013. Online: http://www.capital.de/meinungen/mein-leben-in-der-lehmschicht.html [Accessed: 30.05.2020].
7. Kotter, P. John (2015): Accelerate: Strategischen Herausforderungen schnell, agil und kreativ begegnen. München: Vahlen.
8. Gibson, C. B. & Birkinshaw, J. (2004): The Antecedents, Consequences, and Mediating Role of Organizational Ambidexterity. In: Academy of Management Journal, 47 (2), p. 209–226.
9. Gibson, C. B. & Birkinshaw, J. (2004): Building Ambidexterity into an Organization. In: MIT Sloan Management Review. Online: http://sloanreview.mit.edu/article/building-ambidexterity-into-an-organization/ [Accessed: 30.05.2020].
10. Tushman, Michael L; Smith, Wendy K.; Binns, Andy (2011): The Ambidextrous CEO. In: Harvard Business Review. Juni 2011, 89 (6), p. 74–80.
11. Suzuki, Shunryu (2012): Zen-Geist, Anfänger-Geist. Unterweisungen in Zen-Meditation. 3. ed. Freiburg, Basel, Wien: Herder.
12. Duwe, Julia (2016): Ambidextrie, Führung und Kommunikation. Interne Kommunikation im Innovationsmanagement ambidextrer Technologieunternehmen. Heidelberg: Springer Gabler.
13. O'Reilly, C. A. & Tushman, M. L. (2008): Ambidexterity as a Dynamic Capability: Resolving the Innovator's Dilemma. In: Research in Organizational Behavior, 28, p. 185–206.
14. Taylor, A. & Helfat, C. E. (2009): Organizational Linkages for Surviving Technological Change: Complementary Assets, Middle Management, and Ambidexterity. In: Organization Science, 20 (4), p. 718–739.
15. Schmidt, Marion (2014): Der Motivator. Hans Müller-Steinhagen hat die TU Dresden zur Exzellenzuniversität gemacht. In: Die ZEIT, No. 48/2014, November 20, 2014. Online: http://www.zeit.de/2014/48/tu-dresden-che-ranking-exzellenz-universitaet [Accessed: 30.05.2020].

Ambidextrous Leadership in Times of Crisis

6

Abstract

This chapter is the result of an interview study on the question of how leadership drives people and companies to come out stronger from the crisis. It documents the exceptional circumstances of the first months in 2020 in six interviews with representatives of the German corporate landscape. Between March and May, they shared their perspectives with *Ambidextrous Leadership*.

The finding: "Double ambidexterity" increases the resilience of companies in times of crisis. Navigating ambidextrously is the key to an adaptable and flexible organization that withstands the crisis. The chapter shows in practical examples how ambidextrous leadership works in the crisis.

6.1 Does the Virus Eat Up Leadership?

In spring 2020, the world looks spellbound at the Corona pandemic, at its extent and at the consequences of the shutdown of public life [1]. Since March 23, 2020, contact restrictions are applied in public and private spaces in Germany [2]. As the virus grows from a health crisis to a global financial and economic crisis, the lockdown forces companies to hit the brakes and threatens numerous livelihoods. Airports operate in emergency mode. Businesses are closed. Global stock markets drop. By mid-April 2020, about 50% of the German economy is at a temporary standstill [3]. Inside companies, the virus is turning everyday working life upside down. It is an ultimate leadership test for managers at different levels. People are cautious in moving forward.

"Virus eats fundamental rights". With this headline from March 28, 2020, the Sueddeutsche Zeitung emphasizes the serious consequences that became apparent after just a few days of the Germany-wide lockdown [4]: This crisis was not just health,

© Springer-Verlag GmbH Germany, part of Springer Nature 2022
J. Duwe, *Ambidextrous Leadership*,
https://doi.org/10.1007/978-3-662-64032-6_6

financial and economic crisis. It had severe social impacts, up to the restriction of the fundamental rights and civil liberties of individual citizens [5]. As the coronavirus continued to spread globally and to affect our everyday life, it was forcing companies around the world to hit the brakes. Inside companies, the virus was turning everyday working life upside down and managers across the globe were severely tested. The balancing act between personal concern and professional responsibility affected all leaders equally. What was important in this exceptional situation? What was the right way to lead through the crisis?

According to an employee survey in Germany conducted by Gallup between March 19 and 24, 2020, only 33% of the employees were convinced that their employer communicated a clear plan of action in response to the coronavirus [6]. Crisis management could be improved, headlines the German newspaper FAZ [7]. At the same time, there were doubts in many places about the modern leadership approaches of the digital transformation. Agile leadership, digital leadership, leadership in the ecosystem: in the first-moment shock and faced with an unpredictable situation, there seemed to be no recipe for success (see Fig. 6.1). Did the coronavirus now also undermine good leadership?

COVID 19 Crisis: A Time of Tensions

Despite the uncertainty about the future course of the pandemic, the crisis demanded consistency and clarity of action, top-down management and simple instructions to follow. Decisions had to be made as quickly as possible: to protect employees, to reduce capacity, to introduce short-time work, to implement drastic cost-cutting measures.

At the *same time,* empathy with people's concerns was required. This was about personal fates, about fears and worries of the employees and their relatives.

In order to secure business operations during the lockdown, it was a core task—and at the same time a major challenge for many managers—to maintain cooperation and cohesion in the teams—now at a distance, digitally, in a virtual world. It was a matter of testing and trying out new ways of collaboration and shaping the new digital space together.

And it was about dealing openly with uncertainty—with regard to the crisis, but also to the new everyday working life. Leadership now meant transferring a lot of responsibility to the people in the home offices and *really* trusting them.

After all, it was the task of the executives, in the midst of putting out fires in the operative business to keep alive current innovation projects and to build up a *new* strong vision of the company: For the new future of the organization *after* Corona they had to identify entirely new fields of business. Leading through such extreme areas of tension in a very short time was new—at least in this intensity.

Interview Study

This chapter is the result of an interview study in the spring 2020. It revolves around the question of whether and how effective leadership helps people and companies navigate

Fig. 6.1 Does the virus eat leadership?

through the crisis and emerge stronger from it. What helps best in the crisis situation? What makes companies more resilient? How should firms change after the coronavirus crisis? Are they prepared if something like this happens again? How does a new vision emerge from the crisis that connects people and organizations and keeps them moving forward?

This chapter documents the exceptional situation of the first months of 2020 in six interviews with leaders from the German corporate landscape. Between March and May, they shared their perspectives with *Ambidextrous Leadership.*

The first interview with Constanze Holzwarth, psychologist and top management consultant, looks at the level of the individual manager. This is followed by the practical view of Wiltrud Pekarek, member of the board of management of the private health insurer HALLESCHE. The interview with Thomas Fischer, chairman of the supervisory board of the family-owned company MANN+HUMMEL, delves into the importance of empathetic leadership in a crisis. We learn what makes leaders resilient in an interview with Karin Pahl, an expert on resilience in the corporate environment. We meet Frank Riemensperger from Accenture and his view on the international management consultancy and its clients. And finally, we dive into the ambidextrous leadership of a global IT company in the interview with Gregor Pillen from IBM.

The chapter intentionally moves away from theory and delves into individual leadership experiences during the weeks of the Corona lockdown. It presents personal insights on successful crisis management.

▶ **The Finding** In a crisis, "double ambidexterity" increases the resilience of companies (see Sects. 6.3 and 6.8). In order to build a robust, resilient organization through leadership, managers need a high degree of flexibility in dealing with contradictions and tensions. They strengthen the resilience of their organization by starting to rebuild the corporate vision early on in the crisis.

6.2 Interview 1: Constanze Holzwarth, Top Management Consultant

The first days of the Corona crisis are characterized by quick decisions, quick reactions, ensuring safe conditions for the health of all employees, securing the day-to-day business. From 1 day to the next, the mode of business operations changes for the company management and executives at all levels.

How managers best deal with the challenges of the first days and weeks of a crisis is described by Constanze Holzwarth for *Ambidextrous Leadership*. She holds a doctorate in psychology and has been working for more than 20 years with top managers and management teams of large corporations and leading medium-sized companies in major transformation and innovation processes [8]. The conversation about leadership in a crisis situation took place shortly after the first Corona lockdown in Germany began.

> **"Now Is the Time to Be Visible"**
> A conversation about areas of tension with Dr. Constanze Holzwarth, psychologist, top management consultant and expert for leadership.
>
> **Constanze Holzwarth, you advise top managers in large corporations on leadership in complex global environments. What do you recommend to managers now in the time of the Corona crisis?**
>
> I recommend that managers are visible now and not dive into problem-solving. This is important with regard to all stakeholders: their customers, suppliers and, above all, their employees. Now is the time to be visible and to address not only the business-relevant issues but also the emotional aspects, the concerns and needs of the staff.

(continued)

How can you be visible and approachable while leading at a distance?

Visibility is especially difficult in this moment of contact restrictions. This is precisely why it is so important to stay in touch. All employees must be able to see that the management is available. In a virtual workplace, there are just as many ways to be seen and to be heard, for example via the intranet or communication platforms.

Does this only apply to management?

It is important for all management levels to be visible. We cannot send people to the home offices and then leave them alone. If you do not meet in the office, regular meetings are even more important to get in touch with people, whether this is in team meetings or one-on-ones.

You raised a second point at the beginning: The danger of diving into problem-solving too early. What do you mean by that?

In an emergency, managers should not focus only on problem solving and 'managing' things—whether this is what the short-time work regulation looks like or the technical equipment in the home office. Just as important, they need to be open for the individual situation of the employees. Some have to reconcile work and childcare. Others are on their own without any social contacts. In addition, there is carrier anxiety. People are wondering what's next for the company. In this crisis, it is important for leaders to communicate.

Please define good communication.

Communication must be fast and frequent! We currently receive information updates in the news on a daily basis. We receive daily news from the Robert Koch Institute and the German government. The fact that the situation is constantly changing has a severe impact on companies. Firms have to communicate just as quickly and often: The more often you communicate the better. Even if you just let everyone know what the current political developments mean for your own company. It is imperative that this communication takes place across all hierarchical levels and that is not filtered through management levels. Everyone needs the same information from management at the same time. It is about reaching all employees and, above all, about dialogue and offering opportunities to discuss topics and answer questions.

Middle managers in particular, who work closest to the people, are torn between rational action and the fears and emotions of affected employees. How do you manage the balancing act?

In many companies, we currently can observe that the frontline managers are overwhelmed with this situation. In the best case, companies support their managers and let them know that they do not have to solve the situation alone. For example, tasks can be distributed among teams that are in close communication with each other, one team takes care of operational issues, another team takes care of the

(continued)

communication issues. It is also important to provide managers with a point of contact, e.g. regular online meetings to exchange ideas on how to deal with this difficult situation. However, these supportive steps have to be taken by the top management of the company.

What can individual managers do?

At the level of the individual manager, self-management is now required. And this is a big challenge when you are constantly exposed to unexpected events. It is about becoming aware of one's own fears and insecurities. If I am aware of these, it is easier for me to respond to the employees. Managers must now set boundaries and take good care of themselves. If necessary, they can explain: 'I need this time slot to keep myself capable of managing the situation'.

This is the first area of tension: self-protection vs. presence and visibility.

And it is an extremely important one: Only when I am mentally healthy and strong, I can manage to help others. If I skip this step of self-care, I will have a problem. The caring professions also face this challenge—let's take health care workers, psychologists, doctors. You face the suffering of others every day. You have to be empathetic, but then you have to go home and care about yourself. That's the job. If you can't do that, you burn out after a short time.

And in a crisis like we face it now?

When you are faced with an extreme pressure in a short period of time, this kind of self-management is even more important. Additionally, leaders must also be aware of the fact that moods and emotions are contagious. This is especially true top-down because people take their emotional cues from the top. Therefore, in a crisis, it is of particular importance to manage your own emotions as a leader. If I am on the move with negative emotions or with fear, this is transmitted to those around me. You could also say that moods and emotions are virulent. However, I don't have to suppress my own emotions—I can certainly talk about how I feel. But it becomes dangerous when this self-reflection is missing and when I spread my emotions unconsciously. And precisely for this reason, we need to take care of ourselves in the crisis.

Let us move on to the second area of tension: how do you find the right balance between clear decisions and a high level of empathy—especially when everything happens at the same time?

On the one hand, it is important to make offers to talk to people and to be open to them. However, it is advisable to think carefully beforehand about what you can really offer in an extreme situation. I speak from my own voluntary and therapeutic experience. In my early days, I experienced what it was like to offer one's help and then suddenly feel completely overrun and overwhelmed. This is where you have to be careful! This is not part of the leadership trainings. If you offer 'You can call me

(continued)

anytime', you risk of the phone ringing in the middle of the night. So really only offer what you can honestly do.

Despite the need for empathy, the same rules apply as on the plane? In an emergency, put on the oxygen mask first and then help the others?

Exactly. That is a suitable comparison. When everyone is affected by the emergency situation, one's own ability to act must first be ensured in order to be able to help others at all.

The balance between the rational management and the emotional leadership arises...?

...by separating the two aspects if possible. This can be solved, for example, by clear time slots: 'I'll take an hour at X o'clock and talk to the employees about their personal situation.' This can also be achieved by starting a conversation: 'I have a lot of information now, I would like to talk it through with you. I know that this might trigger a lot of things for you, but let us first discuss the factual situation. Following that, we will take time to discuss your questions, objections, and personal issues.' When everything comes at the same time, it helps to create structured time slots for the different demands that allow you as a leader to consciously switch from a rational to an empathic mode.

It is not part of the curriculum of standard management trainings how to act in a sudden crisis situation that cannot be planned and that happens ad hoc...

... and in addition, many leaders are affected themselves. This is an exceptional situation. In an emergency it is important, for example, to take very short breaks and to think about: What are my options now? Everyone has experienced suddenly having their back to the wall. What were the strategies to win back your power? What strategies did I have in this situation? It is about stepping back from the situation for a few minutes, taking a breath and applying your own strategies. Actually, a crisis like this is something that leaders should be prepared for. Now we know that navigating crises must become an essential part of future leadership trainings.

On the one hand there is the pressure to act clearly and at the same time there are many fears and worries... Isn't it all very contradictory?

The crisis requires ambidextrous leadership to an extreme degree: On the one hand, there is this completely rational way of acting, an approach that is completely guided by reason. And on the other hand, you encounter irrational action and strong emotions. And these are two totally different things. This is particularly difficult for executives and managers. They are often people who are used to taking action, who, when they fall, immediately get up again, look for solutions, move forward proactively. That is their way of dealing with problems and crises. And then to be confronted with exactly the opposite—with people who have fears, who also give

(continued)

in to these fears, who see no perspective—that requires a completely different perspective.

What can individual managers do now?

They should listen. This also requires extreme ambidexterity. Listening is exactly the opposite of active crisis management. Listening and just knowing I do not have to do anything right now. It is really all about listening. Extreme emotion often sounds like an appeal to the listener. But you should not take it as an appeal. You do not have to make a suggestion, you do not have to solve the issue, it is just about the honest signal: 'What you say resonates with me'.

How can the company support?

A crisis is a massive burden for managers. On the side of the company, it is important to offer contact points, to provide communication channels for the employees and to support the management team by assigning tasks of the crisis management to other groups than the proactively acting management.

If we take a look at the future, at the time after that the crisis, we have a third area of tension. On the one hand, we need to organize the present and at the same time we have to anticipate the time after...

You can achieve a lot if you keep in touch during the crisis. If you openly communicate the uncertainties: 'We have to do things now that we don't want to do. But what we really don't want is to lose you.' It is important to prepare now for the time afterwards. Here it is very important to stay in touch with the employees.

I would like to add a fourth area of tension: Today we have the stressful situation of the Corona crisis with its extensive contact restrictions. From 1 day to the next, companies were forced to work digitally. This is not easy for traditional managers...

This time also shows a lot about the flexibility of the management team, i.e. their ability to try out new things and move into unfamiliar territory.

How can executives who are not familiar with the digital workplace deal with the abrupt change?

I recommend that all leaders quickly face reality and find someone to support them. From reverse mentoring to being mentored by your own employees, there are many options. Many board members have trainees and young employees coaching them. In many cases, employees are much more proficient at working digitally than executives.

Some may worry about losing their reputation if they ask for help....

This is exactly where a mindset change is needed! I have to change as a leader and allow the change that we 'up there' are not the ones who always know everything and can therefore make all the decisions. On the contrary, we are dependent on the input of others.

(continued)

How do the employees think when the boss asks for help?

Employees notice quickly when a boss is not capable of doing something. The boss tends to lose face if he rejects new things or does not admit his ignorance. Instead, he wins if he is open about it and asks for support. It is about admitting insecurities. Now is the ideal time for this mindset change because we can see it everywhere—even in politics. Uncertainties are admitted: 'We are cautious in moving forward, because we do not know any better at the moment'.

Moving forward cautiously still sounds competent. But if I have to admit to my employees, e.g., that I am not familiar with digital tools, I am much more likely to be embarrassed—in the worst case, I cannot lead a virtual team at all....

It is simple—right now you can really say, 'If you don't keep up with the times, you will quit over time.' If I do not ask for help now, I'll have an issue! I cannot keep up in a crisis like this. I appear much more confident if I say, 'Up to now I've gone without your help, but now I really want to learn. Please understand that I have to get familiar with this first.' That makes you human. And it emphasizes your new mindset: 'I say what I can't do and I get educated!'. There is no better time than this moment to try new things. This is not the time for perfectionism anymore.

Thank you very much Constanze Holzwarth!

The interview with Constanze Holzwarth emphasizes that the crisis is a massive burden for managers in companies. Numerous areas of tension are described in which leaders find themselves in the emergency. As a first step, it helps to become aware of these tensions. Table 6.1 shows eight selected areas of tension derived from the interview.

The finding: The ability to change modes helps leaders to navigate robustly through the crisis. The Key is to quickly recognize the areas of tension, to consciously organize time slots for the different requirements and to balance both sides.

Consciously Switching Between the Modes

Especially in a crisis, the preferred, well-known routines quickly take effect, while under pressure the less practiced new behaviors are less likely to take effect. However, in order to lead robustly through the crisis over a longer period of time, balance is imperative. For example, one contradiction in the day-to-day crisis is to stay in touch with your colleagues and employees and be visible while simultaneously reducing contact during the lockdown. Another tension lies in admitting uncertainties as a leader and yet moving confidently forward. It is a matter of consciously applying contradictory behaviors that will help you navigate the crisis precisely *because of their contradictory nature.*

Dealing with Crises as Part of Leadership Trainings

To ensure that those who work close to people navigate the crisis well, it helps if companies protect, strengthen and support their leaders in times of crisis. "Now we

Table 6.1 In crisis mode: ambidexterity in leadership

	Mode 1	Mode 2
1	Focus on rational problem solving	Being visible, communicating a lot
2	Managing business issues; clear, common sense approach	Consideration of irrational, emotional aspects, concerns / needs in the workforce
3	Organizing contact restrictions	Staying in touch, strengthening relationships with employees
4	Managing at a distance, working remotely, only being able to communicate virtually	Showing presence, being 'seen' by the employees
5	Deciding and communicating quickly and top-down	Listening, creating space for dialogue and questions
6	Using familiar management tools	Moving in unfamiliar, e.g., digital terrain, quickly adapting to new things
7	Acting confidently, giving answers	Admitting uncertainties, trying out new things together with the team
8	Being empathetic, offering to talk, providing support, responding to employees' insecurities.	Self-protection, setting boundaries, becoming aware of one's own insecurities, taking time for reflection

know that navigating crises must become an essential part of future leadership trainings," recommends Constanze Holzwarth. At the same time, it is important for each individual not to rely solely on support from the company. The most important leadership decision during a crisis is "to choose self-compassion", as one also reads in an Harvard Business Review article at the end of April 2020 [9]. One's own ability to recharge must be ensured.

6.3   Interview 2: Wiltrud Pekarek, HALLESCHE Krankenversicherung

In week 3 of the lockdown, just before Easter 2020, Wiltrud Pekarek, a board member of a company that is systemically important in the Corona crisis, reports: The crisis has accelerated digital transformation. Boundaries have been overcome in a very short time in the past few days.

HALLESCHE Krankenversicherung is a German private health insurance company with headquarters in Stuttgart [10]. Board member Wiltrud Pekarek emphasizes how crucial it is for the organization to start early in the crisis to build up a new picture of the future. After the duty of care for the employees and the safeguarding of ongoing business operations in the exceptional situation, it is a matter of quickly *looking ahead to* the time after the crisis and designing a new picture of the future.

What does the future look like after the crisis? Where will our company be then? In Wiltrud Pekarek's view, there will be no return to the time before the crisis, to the workplace and leadership that existed before.

"We Need Double Ambidexterity Now"

Interview with Wiltrud Pekarek, mathematician and Member of the Management Board of HALLESCHE Krankenversicherung aG

Wiltrud Pekarek, you have been a member of the board of a private health insurer for many years. Tell me about your experience with the current crisis.

The outcome of the current situation is a health crisis that affects all people in this world equally and almost simultaneously. No one is protected from Covid-19. There are only different starting points. This can be a certain age, or the belonging to a risk group or the state of your immune system. Yet, Covid-19 affects everyone at the very core. At the same time, the policies and restrictions to combat the epidemic and to protect our health are leading to a global economic and financial crisis. The Corona crisis is an expression of a highly interconnected world, both in the way the virus spreads and in the way we combat its effects. This is different than any crisis before.

How did you and your colleagues lead the company through the situation?

The first step was to ensure the safety and health of the employees in the company and to provide guidance as quickly as possible. That was the basis—the duty of care. Almost at the same time, we began to define which functions in the company were essential for emergency operations and thus for protecting our core business operations. For example, as a health insurer, it was very important for us to guarantee our customer service and be available for our customers. Working from home was made possible for an increasing number of employees in a very short time. The people's trust in the actions of the management board grew accordingly. The third step was to look ahead to the time after Corona and to communicate our vision of the future and the associated goals to the employees: What does our future look like after the crisis? Where will our company be then? What goals are we pursuing? . . .

What was different during the crisis?

The new home office situation inevitably shifted responsibility to the employees. Managers had to lead differently from 1 day to the next: at a distance without losing contact, online, via digital tools. They had to 'drive on sight', act cautiously at the beginning of the crisis, with sensitivity for the unpredictable. And they had to empower, support and encourage their employees to take responsibility. Sometimes the managers simply had to trust that it would work. Because they no longer had control of everything.

(continued)

And the result?

Despite all the challenges, the ownership taken by the employees and our common goal of doing well during the Coronavirus pandemic released so much energy and creativity. Suddenly new ideas for collaboration emerged and were shared and further developed in our company chat. Solidarity and cooperation have grown. Everyone continued to work on their topics in a highly focused and efficient manner. They supported each other and made decisions on their own. The letting go of control of the managers was a critical factor here. What was known so far in the context of digital transformation and new business models was now demanded from every manager.

Can you explain that in more detail?

Up to now, we have been busy transforming our successful core business to the digital world and corresponding digital business models. The challenge was and still is to balance both equally well over a long period of time: the core business and the new digital business. In the current crisis, this ambidexterity has suddenly become even more important and is proving its worth.

We used to have about 20% of our employees in the home office, now it is 80%. The long discussions about whether working from home is promising at all are obsolete. Managers must now provide extremely clear and decisive guidance, set a clear framework and provide sufficient and timely information—this in close collaboration and dialogue with their employees. At the same time, letting go, trusting and giving freedom are more important than ever. I have observed this shift towards ambidexterity in leadership in recent years, especially in the environment of digital transformation. Due to the rush of the crisis, many things had to be improvised. A complete return to the collaboration and leadership methods of before the crisis will not happen and will not be possible anymore. Corona has accelerated the transformation.

How did your own leadership style change in the last few weeks?

An open and appreciative communication has always been of great importance to me. It is communication that pays attention to a wide variety of situations, topics and employees. And I notice now that in this exceptional situation I invest even more of my time in communicating with the employees and in trying to support and stay in touch with them. There is no such thing as too much empathy and too few occasions to engage in conversation! Video conferencing is currently the communication tool of choice. Whether it is to participate in division or group meetings or to talk to employees instead of replying by e-mail. I always ask them how they are doing in the home office and how they are coping with the situation. I consciously try to get a good sense of how people feel in our organization. The content is usually not the main focus at any given moment. For me, it's more about conveying and

(continued)

strengthening emotional security and creating the mental space in which people can work well now.

How exactly do you create this space?

When looking to the future, I often use the idea of a *tunnel* in which we are currently moving. There is light, we do recognize the path, as a society, as a company and as individuals. The tunnel will come to an end. And I would like us to find a green meadow at the end of the tunnel. This is where we sow and reap. And that is what we are working towards. I do not know if we are harvesting spring flowers or if summer blooms are already here—no one can predict the course of the pandemic. We know that in our society right now many people are experiencing great suffering, either because they have sick or deceased people in their environment or because they face financial hardship. Out of this awareness and the discussion of the future after the Corona pandemic, the common goal arises to emerge strengthened from the crisis and to take opportunities in a positive sense.

Isn't this time in the tunnel an adversary of shaping the future?

During this time, it is particularly important that the working conditions are safe and suitable for everyone. Our teams very quickly had the opportunity to work from home and take responsibility for our customers. This flexibility was extremely appreciated. In addition, they find purpose in their work. I have a very specific task here and now as an employee of a health insurer: I want to be there for my customers, no matter where they are. Our service values to act 'reliable, proactive, transparent, and dependable' are becoming more important than ever. In addition, there is the strategic aspect, our vision of the future, that creates meaning and purpose at work: We want to be a health partner for our customers. We want to improve our communication, be more empathetic in approaching our customers. We want to care more and create an even stronger connection and customer benefit with the help of digital channels. By doing so our future is already being reshaped during the crisis.

Does purpose play a particularly important role now?

More and more people are asking the question of purpose at work. They want to live in a sustainable world. Finding meaning and purpose in your daily work helps to move forward courageously in this difficult situation. The employees notice how quickly we have put ourselves in a position to continue working and how we have not allowed any great fears to arise in the first place. In addition, we are now reaping what we have sown through communication over the last couple of years. Employees are now moving forward. Everyone has become aware of what we have expressed as our vision and mission: true customer focus, the values, our invest in the future of the company. They have developed the attitude and ambition to achieve this.

(continued)

How can companies become more resilient and harvest in a next crisis situation? What is your advice?

First, I recommend working very hard on the vision and mission of the company. Employees must always get the chance to understand how their work contributes to the company's vision and mission. This creates a sense of purpose. Employees need to know what the company stands for, what values guide their actions, where the company wants to go. It helps if you can always refer to these values at any time, in any situation.

The second point is communication. Staying in touch with the employees and investing in communication is important: Especially when it comes to the vision and mission of the company, where the creative and the innovative ideas emerge from, it is important to be very open and sensitive to new vibes in your company. It is about developing a good sense of where the organization is and what it needs. At the same time, in a crisis like now, it is important to be clear and coherent in your communication. Because this clarity creates trust and opens a new space for shaping the future.

It sounds like a tug-of-war between crisis management and focusing on the future....

That is it. We now need *double ambidexterity*, so to speak. Providing security in the crisis and protecting today's business is one side. In the 'today' we have the operational core business as well as the innovation projects of the digital transformation. *Both* must be managed and protected in the crisis. In the current situation, it is a matter of securing the *entire* business operations consisting of our core business *and* the digital innovation projects. In fact, the two worlds are moving closely together.

What is the second side?

Companies must not get stuck in protecting the 'Here and now'—just as the digital transformation must not get stuck in executing the old and proven. A new future after the Corona pandemic has to be envisioned and shaped right now. Again, we need to take care of both at the same time and lead ambidextrously.

This is a double transformation.

Yes, from the past into the new digital world and at the same time from the crisis into the future! And in this crisis, it becomes apparent whether you were successful before. The achievements of the digital transformation now also support companies in overcoming the Corona crisis. The complex effects of the current crisis require— now more than ever—leadership tools for complex systems including a new understanding of leadership and collaboration. At the same time, the crisis mode supports our way of working: We have become more flexible, less bureaucratic, we take responsibility and act in solidarity. The digital transformation is accelerated, barriers are overcome.

(continued)

What risks do you see for the company's management?

The risk is obvious. Companies must not lose themselves too much in defining crisis scenarios while others are shaping the future. Scenarios must be defined quickly; the effects must be described and conclusions must be drawn. If necessary, a reprioritization is needed and financial resources must be reallocated. Yet, any reprioritization should not be based purely on business management or hard financial criteria. It must, above all, take the future into account. We need ambidexterity at this point too!

What opportunities do you see?

I see a great opportunity in reshaping the company's vision of the future *in parallel* with establishing the crisis scenarios: What do I expect as a company after this exceptional situation? What will remain? What will be different? I have to check whether the business drivers known today will still exist in the future. There might be completely new customer expectations. Are there any regulatory changes? Will megatrends alter? Corona forces us to rethink the future once again and to correct our previous picture if necessary. We have to redefine values and possibly go in a different direction. At this point of time the world is at a standstill, everyone is slowed down. This opens up the opportunity to catch up with the market in certain areas and to extend one's lead in others. And it is precisely for this that we need an idea of the future in order to decide which opportunities to seize now at this time.

Thank you very much Wiltrud Pekarek!

Protect Your Business

The "double ambidexterity" outlined by Wiltrud Pekarek is shown in Table 6.2. Ensuring security in the crisis and protecting the world of today is *one* side and the first important step of the crisis management. In addition to day-to-day operations, the "today" in most companies already includes numerous future activities of the digital transformation.

Table 6.2 Double ambidexterity in the crisis

Today (exploitation)		New future (exploration)	
Protecting business operations and innovation projects during the crisis. This includes		Building the new vision of the company after the crisis, deriving new objectives for the company. This includes	
(a) the core business, the business operations (exploitation)	(b) the innovation projects launched, the ongoing digital transformation activities (exploration)	(a) describing visible trends and future scenarios based on existing experiences	(b) Thinking ahead and creating a new picture of tomorrow based on latest experiences of the crisis
Ambidexterity: Leading both in "safeguard mode"		Ambidexterity: Designing the vision for a post-crisis future	
Double Ambidexterity: Tackling both at the same time in a crisis			

Table 6.2 shows on the left the corresponding "immediate actions" of firefighting to safeguard today's business operations.

Reshaping the Picture of the Future
But simply continuing on this path to the future is not enough, in Pekarek's view. Those who get stuck in putting out fires now will miss out on the new future after the pandemic. The future after the crisis will be different. On top and in parallel to safeguarding business operations, this must be actively shaped and translated into a new vision for the organization.

The corresponding strategy must be rethought and rebuilt by companies, see right column Table 6.2.

6.4   Interview 3: Thomas Fischer, MANN+HUMMEL

In mid-April 2020, *Ambidextrous Leadership* meets Thomas Fischer, Chairman of the Supervisory Board of MANN+HUMMEL, a global leader in filtration technology. Headquartered in Ludwigsburg, Germany, with over 80 locations worldwide, the company offers filtration solutions in two segments: transportation and life sciences & environment. The product portfolio includes filtration solutions for automotive and industrial applications, clean indoor and outdoor air, and the sustainable use of water [11].

Thomas Fischer explains why the values of the family-owned company are particularly important now and how crucial it is to have empathetic leaders who take care of and who empower people in times of crisis.

"It's All About Empowering People"
Interview with Thomas Fischer, Chairman of the Supervisory Board of MANN +HUMMEL, on the role of leadership during and after the crisis.

Thomas Fischer, we currently experience an unprecedented health, economic and financial crisis. How are you dealing with it inside your company?

In this exceptional situation, we are striving to go back to the normal wherever possible, to continue in a targeted manner and to build trust among the workforce. Unfortunately, I can't meet with the leadership team face to face now to discuss all the issues. But I find time for my managers every evening. Those who work on site drop by for a quick exchange, we stand together and talk about the difficulties and topics of the day. The quick chat, even controversial exchange, the relaxing joke— we try to restore normality.

Is it always easy?

I know it from other crises in the past. When the pressure gets too heavy, people need an outlet for their emotions. You have to offer a protected area that allows

(continued)

people to come together and exchange ideas about the situation and their challenges. Arguing, having different opinions, letting out the pressure in an 'unfiltered' way—if that is possible, things go much better the next day, some things are easier then.

How do you lead your company through the crisis?

Our leadership team has a global visibility and presence. They care deeply about their employees. Our CEO is currently 'trapped' in the US and cannot travel. He therefore controls and orchestrates our world from Michigan. Another of our top executives works in Singapore. It is fortunate that we are well positioned globally. In Asia, Europe and the Americas, we have executives who are close to the local employees.

And here in Germany?

I have visited every site in Germany in the last 2 weeks. I talk to the leadership team and the workers' council. I just walk through so that the local employees can literally see that we care. Those who continue to come to the company were very worried at first, full of fear. However, they have noticed that the company is paying attention to appropriate actions to protect them. At the same time, we have intensified internal communications on all channels. Managers organize online conferences or publish video messages about the latest developments.

How serious will the effects be?

We are preparing ourselves for a sharp drop in sales and a negative impact on earnings, which will entail drastic cost-cutting measures. Nevertheless, the team is doing great, also because we communicate a lot and well. What currently helps in our communication is something like the Liverpool FC's football anthem 'You'll Never Walk Alone'. Every football fan knows it. It's all about solidarity and people sticking together in difficult times. It is exactly this feeling of solidarity that we try to convey on our internal communication platforms such as "Mann+Hummel Connect".

How do you master the balancing act between crisis management and preparing for the future?

What currently stresses people in the company is to ensure the ramp-up of our value chain despite short-time working. We have the supply chains well under control—at the moment, not knowing what the situation will be like tomorrow. This brings us to the topic of agility. You can manage this quite well in a small firm, where you can act flexibly on demand. If, on the other hand, you work across several locations and with thousands of employees, that is challenging. And on top, not losing sight of our future innovation projects makes it exhausting. To be available and to offer support from the top management of the company is extremely important now.

How do you achieve solidarity in your team? What motivates people now?

First, we achieve it through high consistency and self-discipline. This works because the senior leaders get along very well with each other and they speak with

(continued)

one voice: It is one team, and one message. People in the company understand why we are taking certain actions. They know that it is about their future, our customers' future, and the company's future. But more importantly, our company has recently launched some great projects, e.g. in medical technology. We are producing new types of filters that reduce air pollution in indoor spaces—now in quantities that we have never seen before. Together with partners, we work on respirators with air filter units. These are all 'manageable innovations'. And they will not save us in terms of sales or earnings. But the people in the company are proud that they can make a contribution. As we take these meaningful actions, we can better cope with the drastic cost-cutting measures that we need to survive in the long run. We are in a comfortable position here: filtration, clean water, clean air, clean mobility—these issues are particularly important to people at the moment. In addition, we have another element of cohesion: people feel, now more than ever, that they are members of a family. The values of the family-owned business are more unifying than usual. We take care to act fairly. E.g., we demand lower financial contributions due to the crisis from our employees on short-time work than from the top management. Top management must now commit, and we strictly act on this.

How can managers handle current situation? What do you recommend?

It is important to talk to people in the company, including one-on-ones. Our managers at all levels know this and are encouraged to communicate a lot with their teams. This is not to control whether work is being done in the home office. It is to offer support and help.

Does that always work out?

We have trained leadership and communication a lot. However, we have never paid sufficient attention to it. In the current exceptional situation, we can no longer do without it. We now need entrepreneurial people who can communicate and lead. What we have known for a long time, but have never consistently enforced is: We need to take specialists and experts out of management positions and remove this burden from them. They should be able to work in their specialist field; this is where we need them in the company. However, the best experts are not necessarily the best leaders.

What do you mean by leading?

For us, leadership is first and foremost "listening". Listening to the employees, to the customers, to the market. When you consciously listen, you perceive the present moment, e.g. the present situation of your company. Then you are able to actively derive and shape a tangible process from it. Not everyone needs to be the great strategist. But you must be able to present your own area of responsibility so clearly and with credibility that a path and goal become visible and can be agreed upon. This commitment has become increasingly important to me over many years.

(continued)

Commitment requires courage, perseverance, resilience and the ability to communicate. For me, this is leadership. Not every employee needs to be enthusiastic about a company's strategy. Yet, he or she needs to be happy to run with it, most of the time at least. And finally, leadership is about empowerment. It is all about empowering people. Unfortunately, many of us indeed claim that they want their employees to work independently. Yet, these managers still take the final decisions. In this way, they do not lead, or not in the way in which I understand leadership.

What qualities and skills are important at the moment?

It is about being honest, reliable and consistent and not about avoiding conflict. To act in a social way does not mean that you avoid the conflict, but that you find a fair and acceptable solution. We need people in our leadership team who are able to do this—without hurting others. Who can deal with difficult issues in a transparent and credible way, and who can also say 'no'. Leaders who are also able to admit 'I don't know' and who care about people. Along with honesty and consistency, the empathetic side will need to become stronger. The ability to communicate and work together in and with different situations and cultures will become essential.

Leaders are supposed to be extremely clear and resolute and at the same time they have to be empathetic....

In a crisis you need to give precise and clear instructions. In a critical situation it is much more helpful for an organization to act and communicate very clearly. At the same time, we have to be passionate with people, get them involved, listen to them, and empower them. Between the poles, decisions can be discussed and also revised. It must be possible to correct quickly if a decision was wrong.

How do leaders achieve this ambidexterity?

By simply taking a step back and reflecting. By venturing into new worlds. Ambidexterity is about the chance to reflect, which few people take. We are always in a rush, our daily schedules are so filled, that this aspect is completely lost. This is what I have set out to do in the post-crisis period. I want my leaders at all levels to be able to take time for themselves and to reflect. When they have that time, new ideas and beliefs will come out. This will include discussion, exchange, sparring with others to shape and develop new knowledge and opinions.

Can you do that also now right in the middle of a crisis?

My leadership team is actually experiencing it right now. They take a lot more time to communicate, listen, and talk. And I do not mean the kind of meetings where endless discussions take place. This new way of communicating is more precise, direct and instant, combined with the chance to give people a hug in the figurative sense. We're learning every day how to better support people in their home offices. It is encouraging for me to discover how brilliant some people are at communicating during this time.

(continued)

What is the recipe for success now?
There is no one-size-fits-all recipe. Everyone has to find out for themselves, their company and their environment. We were never too optimistic in the current crisis. We have said from the beginning: 'It will take a long time' and we have supported this period intensively through communication. We are honest and credible at this point, as we are in our actions. We convey security and confidence, also because we openly share much more information with the employees. The leadership team is available at any time and the employees and middle managers dare to address the top management with their issues. Our leadership team has been shaping this open culture for a long time even before the crisis. Now we are benefiting from it and people are going with us.
Thomas Fischer, thank you very much for the interview.

In several steps, Thomas Fischer describes how his leadership team navigates the organization through the crisis in the first days and weeks of the corona pandemic. Ten essential insights are presented in Table 6.3.

Table 6.3 Ten essential insights for crisis management

1	Support for your leadership team	As management board, taking time for the executives, supporting leaders
2	Stress management	Getting together (also virtually), offering employees including managers times for an open exchange
3	Visibility	Showing up in the workforce, establishing as much contact and closeness as possible
4	Communication	Intensifying communication on all channels, intensifying personal communication
5	Consistency	Consistency, honesty, commitment and discipline in decision making and communication
6	Empathy	Listening and perceiving how the organization is doing
7	Support and help for the employees	Being available as a leadership team and providing assistance where possible
8	Purpose	'You'll Never Walk Alone!' Igniting a feeling of solidarity, communicating the values of the (family) company, initiating meaningful activities
9	Empowerment	Actively supporting people in the company and enabling them to act on their own responsibility
10	Reflection	Continuously reflecting on one's own actions

It is empathy and a sense of connectedness that form the common thread of crisis management at M+H. In the crisis, leadership is all about guiding people through the storm. Communication becomes the most important leadership tool. Leadership means proving decision-making abilities, discipline and consistency. It also means being empathetic and reactivating the company's purpose to provide stability to the employees.

And it is also the managers who need to get spaces and opportunities to relieve pressure and recharge their batteries. This is how they achieve the balance between crisis management and navigating to the future: "It's about the chance to reflect, which few people take now". When leaders take this time during crises, new ideas and convictions will emerge and they can bring purpose into the future (see also "Shift your Organization from Panic to Purpose" [12]).

6.5 Interview 4: Karin Pahl, Resilience Expert

The period of crisis, with its increasing external influences on organizations, demands a strong supply of leadership. Karin Pahl, who is resilience trainer and owner of PAHL Resilienz-Förderung in Bremen [13] as well as a lecturer at the University of Hanover, explains how leaders can navigate through stormy times with stability *and* flexibility at the same time. The interview took place at the end of April 2020.

In times of crisis, according to the expert, unexpected new possibilities can also arise if one uses previous experiences and activates one's own strengths, resources and mental strategies.

"Resilience Is Inherent in All of Us. It Can Be Trained"
Interview with resilience expert Karin Pahl about stability and flexibility in everyday management.

Karin Pahl, you have been working as a coach and trainer in companies for many years and have specialized in the field of resilience. Can you briefly explain the term?

The term resilience comes from the Latin (resilire) and stands for the mental or emotional ability to cope with a crisis. It is also known from physics and materials science: An external impact hits a material, let's take a rubber ball as an example or perhaps the sofa in your living room. After any external impact or deformation, the material is able to return to its original state. The quality of the material determines the resilience. Today, the term is also used to illustrate how organisms, economic and other systems are able to cope with considerable external pressure and how they assert and regulate themselves.

(continued)

And transferred to human beings...?

...resilience means that someone has numerous qualities within him-/herself so that he/she is able to cope with crises and get back quickly to the state before. Those who combine beneficial inner strengths, resources and mental strategies are able to return to their original mental state after external influences or disturbances. However, resilience is something very individual. Just as materials behave in completely different ways, so do people. Everyone has their own way of finding their way back to their personal original state. This means that an important step is to find out the individual strategy. For a resilient and healthy quality of life it is important to find ways to skillfully 'lead yourself'. People who train their inner stability and flexibility automatically ensure a high resilience.

What is the objective of resilience? What do we want to achieve by this?

Many people think resilience is about a difficult situation just 'bouncing off' you and *not* knocking you down. Resilience is therefore sometimes criticized. According to the motto: companies expect resilience from their employees so that they become even more efficient and, if possible, block out all stressful situations. This is exactly what is *not* meant by resilience. It is not about 'resistance', but about the ability to get through crises with a 'backpack full of resources, mental strategies and experience'. You go confident through stormy times—which is also the motto of one of my training series.

How exactly can we build confidence in stormy times?

Every person already has the abilities within him or her to be able to go through crises. It is important to allow oneself to be in crises and to learn from them. All the skills that you have acquired in stormy times can be put into a backpack, figuratively speaking, and taken out and used at the appropriate times. Crises happen. Everyone can develop individual strategies for dealing with them. In addition, if you do know what you stand for, what meaning, vision or mission you have in your life, then you have a good chance of building or expanding resilience.

Aren't there people who naturally find this easier than others?

It is true that there are people who are equipped with a more 'resilience-friendly' brain. However, those who do not use it will not benefit from it. It has been believed for a very long time that resilience is exclusively innate and not everyone has this ability. This is not true. Resilience is already inherent in each of us and can be trained. You have learned to walk as a child. You fell down again and again and then you noticed: 'I hurts, all right, I'll do it differently'. That is the first step.

So I am not just going through the stormy times....

... I also learn from it and take something with me that will enrich my future life. That is what resilience is all about. Thus, even unexpected new opportunities arise

(continued)

from stormy times, if you use everything that you continuously pack in your backpack.

I would like to get to resilience in companies.

The topic is addressed in many companies. But the word 'resilience' has almost become a buzz word. The real benefits often do not come into view. But some firms do not leave it at that. They look for new opportunities instead. Due to the digital transformation, they have realized that thinking and acting in old patterns no longer works. But they are still struggling to keep up. In today's VUCA world, it is very likely that something is going out of balance. Moreover, things are less predictable and more ambiguous. The need for action is obvious.

And now we have the current crisis on top of this....

The importance of resilience is becoming really clear now, because something is happening that no one could have imagined before. The global pandemic COVID-19 has reached the entire economy and all politics, health and social systems. It is about the resilience of all these sectors. For companies, it has enormous implications. The risk of a liquidity and existential crisis forces companies to act quickly and to take an incredible number of requirements into account. The greatest insight may be that the workforce and the topic of digitalization must be linked at maximum speed, which was previously hindered by theoretical thinking, long discussions and clinging to the tried and true. But in this crisis, the old approaches no longer work. Ways of exclusive thinking such as, 'We choose one way *or* the other' are beginning to falter. In this new world of work, uncertainty comes into play and this includes the ambidextrous ability to decide for '*both* one way *and* the other'—an important competence of resilience.

People in companies find themselves in a time of extreme tensions....

Different value systems now literally collide. On the one hand, there is a hierarchical system that provides a clear framework in which decisions are made at the upper management levels and responsibility is also taken there. In this system, employees expect to get clear announcements from the top. On the other hand, there is the flexible model of the agile working world. Here, the team organizes itself. It takes responsibility and makes decisions to the same extent. In the current situation, both sides have something in common: All are in the same state of emergency. Many people find themselves in the new home office environment. An environment that brings more challenges than expected. Ad hoc, the real interpersonal contacts are missing. In most companies, communication and core processes are being transferred to the digital virtual workplace, something that was unconceivable, e.g., for a field sales force where customer contact and emotions play an

(continued)

important role. Being able to rethink your core business and at the same time remain capable of acting are the key resilient competencies here.

Is resilience particularly important for leaders?

Yes, because many leaders are now facing a personal crisis as well. On the one hand, they have to provide clarity and, at the same time, pass on a great deal of responsibility to the teams in the home office. On the one hand, they must provide orientation and security, but on the other hand, they have been able to let go and trust. Managers are supposed to be role models. But how can they be that when their own fears of losing control and digital insecurity prevail? Another challenge is that teams can only be led at a distance. Many traditional managers are overwhelmed with the current situation. There are companies that are aware of this and that support them with coaches.

What is resilience about in this situation?

It is about maintaining inner stability and at the same time establishing flexibility in your thoughts and your actions, i.e. the ability to always be open to the unknown. This includes, for example, being able to switch between completely different leadership paradigms.

You have just mentioned two key aspects of ambidextrous leadership. Stability *and* flexibility in one's own thinking and actions—isn't that a contradiction?

No. That is precisely the exciting thing about resilience. If managers are able to think, act and react flexibly and still maintain an inner stability, then a company has already gained a lot in times of change.

What is stable and what is flexible—what is meant by this?

In my workshops, I like to use a little figure that sits on a large round belly. The figure cannot be knocked over, it always moves back to the original position. My point is to illustrate: If your 'belly' is filled with resources and mental strategies, then you have a certain stability, and at the same time you are still flexible in your reaction to external influences. There is also a physical exercise for this: One person acts as a rock in the surf and remains rigid with his body. The other person is flexible in body movements, like an elastic material. Both training participants receive a disturbing influence from the outside, which is supposed to cause the persons to tilt. Interestingly, the rigid rock quickly falters and tilts. The person whose body is elastic, who reacts flexibly to the external influences, who absorbs them and tries to redirect them, does not fall over.

(continued)

Figuratively speaking, through an inner elasticity....

...people achieve the highest level of stability. That is the amazing thing and the core of my resilience concept. Stability only comes about through one's own flexibility. In other words, you are stable because you are flexible!

Karin Pahl, thank you very much for the interview!

Ambidexterity Supports Resilience

While ambidextrous organizations often struggle with the tension of the two opposing worlds, the traditional hierarchical world and the flexible agile working world, in the weeks of the Corona crisis both worlds are moving closely together. *Both* worlds are in a state of emergency. Elements from *both* worlds are needed at the same time, to the same extent.

Top-Down, Formal and Centralized

On the one hand, the employees in the company expect clear guidance from above, a fast, direct communication controlled from a central point at the top and answers to their questions. They expect a well-functioning hierarchy and decision-making system (see Sect. 4.2.1). Processes and responsibilities must be clearly defined from the outset. The company management or the appointed crisis management team have decision-making authority and can make decisions quickly. Communication is highly formal, planned and it runs according to the linear sender-receiver model: information is distributed quickly and efficiently from top to bottom in a controlled manner (see Sect. 4.2.2). Thanks to hierarchy and centralized authority, the organization is mobilized to act in the shortest possible time [14].

Letting Go, Giving Responsibility, Enabling Self-Organization

But almost simultaneously with the start of the Corona crisis and within a few days, almost 100% of the business operations were shifted to the new home office environment. An environment that, according to Karin Pahl, brings more challenges than expected. All of a sudden the real interpersonal contacts, familiar tools and procedures are missing. Teams are forced to react quickly and organize themselves, and they are confronted with a significant increase in responsibility in the home office. Formal authority quickly shifts to the personal responsibility of the individual employee and completely new structures emerge [14]. Those who have invested in the growth of self-organizing dynamic teams before the crisis will benefit and observe how flexible and resilient such structures respond.

▶ **Resilience** "The capacity of a system to absorb disturbance and still retain its basic function and structure" [14]. A resilient system continues to function regardless of how badly it is shaken by external influences. Ideally, it even becomes stronger as a result. Julian Birkinshaw, London Business School Professor of Strategy and Entrepreneurship, distinguishes between three types of resilience [14]:

1. **Behavioral resilience:** the ability of employees and managers to cope with difficult circumstances over long periods of time.
2. **Operational resilience:** an organization's ability to keep its core processes going (e.g., the supply chain).
3. **Strategic resilience:** the ability of an organization to perceive and react to changes in its environment and to remain relevant to its customers. ◄

Ambidexterity as Key Competency of Personal Resilience
According to Karin Pahl, it is a key competency of resilient leaders during the Corona crisis to switch back and forth between the worlds, to be able to rethink one's actions while at the same time remaining stable and capable of acting. The next interview delves into the field of resilience at the corporate level.

6.6   Interview 5: Frank Riemensperger, ACCENTURE

Companies around the world are struggling with existential questions about the future in the first weeks of COVID-19: Are they resilient enough to survive the global economic and health crisis? Are they robust enough to survive global competition? And are they flexible and innovative enough for the radical leap into the post-pandemic digital world?

While the resilience concept described in Sect. 6.5 refers to the behavioral resilience of individuals in the company and builds on people's individual mental strategies, the next interview focuses on operational resilience at the company level.

A company is truly resilient [15] when the *entire* supply chain and the entire value network are resilient, explains Frank Riemensperger. He is chairman of the management board of the management and strategy consultancy Accenture for the country group Germany, Austria and Switzerland [16]. He is senate member of the German Academy of Science and Engineering acatech and member of the senate of the IT industry association Bitkom.

"Reboot into the New, Changed World"
Interview with Frank Riemensperger, Chairman of the Management Board of Accenture DACH
Frank Riemensperger, we are currently going through a global health crisis that also has serious impacts on processes within companies. How is Accenture adapting to this?
We are a company that provides services. Only a small part of our actual production is office-bound. That is why the switch to remote work from home was

(continued)

comparatively easy for us. We have already established the digital infrastructure for this years ago. We already work in a very distributed manner and communicate virtually. We were able to implement remote work for 98% of our employees within 1 week.

How are your customers doing?

They went through several phases. In the first 2 weeks, the customers quickly reconfigured the new workplace and the new ways of working. For us, this period initially brought more work: Collaboration, virtual working, remote working—these are things that we implemented not only for ourselves, but also for our customers. After the phase of reconfiguring the sorting started, the moment of 'settling into the crisis'. In this second phase, we have seen completely different behavioral patterns across industries. The automotive industry stopped production, the mechanical engineering industry did too. Pharmaceutical companies were carrying on. You did not notice anything in energy supply either. The healthcare industry continued. Food retailing as well. Many small and medium-sized businesses, restaurants or the travel/holiday sector were brutally affected. Then major disasters showed up like in aviation where entire airlines were grounded. Many others, however, were just pulling through. There is no 'one size fits all'.

Do you also see common patterns of behavior?

One thing is true for all companies: They have to build new forms of collaboration. What we have experienced in terms of innovation within 4 weeks is incredible. What was not possible before, e.g. according to the motto 'a bank has to work in the bank', can now be done from home in virtual teams. Project decisions are being made within days—unthinkable before. What are the decision paths? How are teams configured? How quickly are decisions implemented? How much lead time is needed? In addition to the serious financial damage to some—though not all—industries, this crisis is also one of the biggest triggers and drivers of a new way of organizing work. Innovations have emerged within a very short time. They will remain.

What exactly will remain?

The agility, the speed of decision-making will remain. The distributed form of working will remain. The more 'physical' it becomes, e. g. in the production line, the more you are naturally bound to a specific location. But even there, agility, the speed of making and implementing decisions, can have a positive impact. All of a sudden you notice that Germany can be fast in many respects. That was unusual for our country!

At many companies, home office and short-time work hinder the upcoming ramp-up. What do you observe?

Specifically with the restart, we are seeing that it is focused on the network nodes in enterprises. It is the program and interface managers that have to master a huge

(continued)

amount of work now. We are experiencing it ourselves right now. We sent 10,000 people in the DACH region to the home office. Now how do we get 10,000 people back from the home office starting May 4? It is a huge achievement just in terms of communication to reach out to all of them. This is now done by about 50–100 people who form the network nodes. This puts an immense burden on them—even without the additional challenge of short-time work.

What is important to you in leadership and communication now?

It is important for me to communicate a lot myself. I am very transparent, open and also talk about options that we still need to decide upon. Communication that is clear, authentic and honest and that shows options before decisions are made builds trust. After all, we are in a crisis where no one knows the end, where 3 weeks ago we didn't know exactly how bad it would get. I decided to openly share this uncertainty with the team, as well as our thoughts on how to respond. We also shared the insight that there is no right way to handle this: We just do not know how it is going to play out. That is why you have to start navigating in an agile way, working in hypotheses and scenarios. This approach has received positive feedback. People know what we think and are not surprised by measures.

What comes after the crisis?

What we will avoid is a 'back to normal'. There will be none of that. We have two major headings to this: First: 'Emerge stronger'. As a company—and this is not just for Accenture—we have to see the crisis as a challenge and ask ourselves, 'How do we come out of this stronger?' The second heading is: 'Reboot into the new'. It is important to develop a vision for the new and to *reboot* after the crisis, not to pick up the old but to carry the new vision. Like an operating system. But we reboot into the new, changed world.

What do you advise companies to do now? What must the new vision contain?

First, and this comes from mechanical engineering: We need to be much more digital. It is not the networked Industry 4.0, not the manufacturing, that is not working right now. It is digital sales. This is where only a few companies have invested. But now it shows: sales is the bigger problem. Many have stopped production, not because production and parts have been lacking, but because they have not sold anything digitally. Second, we need to become more resilient. It is about being able to handle fluctuations. And third, we need to significantly shorten our decision cycles. We don't have time to make slow decisions at all in this crisis. I ask myself: If companies can make quick decisions under pressure in a crisis, why can't they do so in day-to-day business? Even after the crisis, we need to lead in a much more agile way instead of reverting to institutional slowness.

(continued)

What we experience now is very extreme. Is there a middle path?

Of course, there is something in between. But companies *can* go to the extreme. Currently, many of them have proven that they are able to make good decisions much faster. Why have they been so slow so far? That is precious time that the competition is taking away from them in terms of market penetration and growth. You must have this discussion about ambidexterity now. Ambidextrous means, 'We've learned and practiced the old, and now we've experienced the new under pressure. How do we connect the two?' It's definitely not 'back to normal'.

Many companies were in the middle of digital transformation before COVID-19. Do you already see the next stage of transformation?

It will be about how companies become more resilient and how they learn to deal with major changes. The first answer to this is clear: We need more digital solutions. The second is to think more in ecosystems. Who are my alliance partners now? Many manufacturing companies now look at their supplier structures and evaluate the risk. Do they fail? Are they accessible at all? Are they reliable? Do they communicate properly? Resilience throughout the supply chain will become a big issue for companies.

Resilience experts say that individuals achieve stability through flexibility and agility. Can this also be applied to companies?

Yes! But you cannot be flexible and agile as a single company. Resilience means bringing the entire value network to the same digital level—with consistent and fast decision-making paths. You need to be resilient as an ecosystem. After all, it does not help you as an individual to have the confidence now when everyone else around you is burying their heads in the sand. Companies have to create a working culture for their individual ecosystem, i.e. their own employees as well as partners outside the company, that guarantees a similar level of performance for different participants in this system. And in Germany we are not familiar with this at all. We hardly ever look beyond the boundaries of the company.

Partnerships are gaining in importance?

I think so, especially for product-service systems. If we want to sell products physically, operate them digitally and continuously complement them with services, we can no longer do this alone. Companies need partners for that. And these partners must have a similar level of performance. Only then will the entire system be resilient.

New forms of collaboration, resilience, working in partnerships: What skills will be important for leaders in the future?

As before, leaders will need their individual performance capabilities. But trying to succeed on their own is simply no longer in vogue. The systems that we build now are so complex and interdependent that they only will grow with the help of people who really want to collaborate, who encourage collaboration, and who are willing to

(continued)

share their success. Especially now in the crisis, we can see that companies that focus on collaboration and shared success are doing much better than those in which everyone tries to optimize themselves. This may work within a static system. But in a fast-moving dynamic system, it leads to very poor performance. It is like traffic jams: everyone has their reaction time, and it adds up until everything finally stops. A company with the wrong culture can never be resilient. We need to strengthen collaboration and shared success.

Thank you very much, Frank. Riemensperger!

Ambidexterity Means: No Way Back to Old Patterns!
Ambidexterity demands great efforts from employees and management. It can lead to great overload of the organization, says the expert from Accenture in his book "Titelverteidiger" [17].

In this exceptional situation, ambidexterity also means taking advantage of the opportunities that are currently available and further developing the proven ability to change and make decisions. Companies have learned and practiced the old way for a very long time. Now they have experienced the new way under pressure. How can they combine the two?

In Riemensperger's view, there is no way back to normal (see Table 6.4). The crisis has changed companies and this new state has to remain. It is a matter of digitizing all areas of the company, of shortening decision-making cycles not only during the crisis, of consistently relying on collaboration and partnerships, and of ensuring operational resilience throughout the entire ecosystem—not just in one's own company (see also [18]).

Only those who now face up to these new conditions, who develop a new vision and continue to pursue the agility that was tested during the crisis will be able to defend their position in the global economy. They might emerge from this much stronger.

Table 6.4 Ambidexterity: Take the plunge—there is no way back!

Before Corona	After Corona
Digitization of selected business areas	End-to-end digitization of all areas of the company
Evolved decision-making structures	Dramatically shortened decision cycles
Strong focus on own company	Think consistently beyond the boundaries of the company, act in ecosystems, ensure operational resilience throughout the value network
Promote individual success	Focus on joint success, promote and demand cooperation
Use proven routines and methods, pursue existing vision	No back to normal! New ways of working, new vision to pursue!

6.7   Interview 6: Gregor Pillen, IBM

Gregor Pillen has been CEO of IBM Germany and General Manager for Germany, Austria and Switzerland since January 2020. The American IT group has over 350,000 employees worldwide and a turnover (2019) of over 77 billion dollars [19].

A few weeks after taking office, crisis management begins for Gregor Pillen in the DACH region. In mid-May, as the easing of Germany's first lockdown begins, he shares his latest experiences with *Ambidextrous Leadership*.

"It Is Peaceful Coexistence"

Interview with Gregor Pillen, Chairman of the Management Board of IBM Deutschland GmbH + General Manager IBM DACH

Mr. Pillen, you have been in office since January 2020 and are starting your first year with a global health, economic and financial crisis. How is your company adjusting to the situation?

After all, an economic and financial crisis is nothing new. What is being added now is the combination with health fears and the lack of clarity about how to deal with the pandemic and whether it can be overcome. Because of our philosophy and technology, we have always focused on the sovereignty and personal responsibility of our employees. They are equipped to work from any location. In that respect, we—like many similar companies—have been able to switch very quickly. Ninety-five percent of our total value is currently created from home. This includes not only the people here in Germany, but also the teams at the centers in Romania, India and China. They all work from home.

What role does communication play in the current crisis?

If you have severe changes where you cannot predict what will happen tomorrow or the day after tomorrow, you have to significantly improve your communication frequency. It was important for me to get the employees involved right at the beginning of the lockdown and to find out together what the crisis means for us and what happens next. There were two goals: First, to overcome the current crisis and second, to develop a common understanding of what our working world would look like afterwards. Looking forward helps us to see the light at the end of the tunnel. We worked with Slack stormboards and idea jams to do this and get everybody involved. This has been very well received by our employees and is now being done on a global level as well.

You directly involved the employees in the foresight process?

Yes! At IBM, we have a mantra: Only through engaged employees do we achieve the customer experience that ultimately creates value for the customer and our shareholders. And across these three dimensions—our employees, our clients, IBM—we built a 3-day facilitated 'Slackstorm' to think together: What does the

(continued)

crisis mean for us? What is changing right now with the rise in remote work? How do the needs of our client change? How do we want to be perceived as IBM in 4–5 years when the crisis is over? This joint effort enabled us to connect with the IBMers. We have implemented their ideas directly, e.g. the "Webex for Kids" campaign. We offer this campaign in schools with our partner Cisco. Our employees help as coaches to use the technology. We also very quickly had set up a team that built a chatbot with the IBM Watson Assistant. This is now being used, among other things, when you dial the patient hotline 116 117. We have made great efforts to get the staff involved. Firstly, to find out how they feel and what we need to do to address them properly. Then, to take up their ideas and implement them. For the good of the customers, for the good of the company, but also to show the employees that it has added value for them as well. That brought a huge boost.

Can you give another example for how you communicated during the crisis?

Shortly after Easter, we added something tangible to the virtual workplace by sending all employees a small gift by postal mail: a classic IBM poster and a card with greetings. Signed by my leadership team as a little 'Thank You'. People noticed that we connect all worlds. And we wanted to send them a signal that we very much appreciate the fact that they stay connected with our customers from the home office. You are not prepared for something like that. Now, when our customers get in touch with our employees, they all have an IBM poster in the background and you notice, 'ah, that's IBM'.

How exactly did the Slackstorm go?

For the Slackstorm we had asked: 'If you look at IBM as a company in Germany with its impact on its employees, with its added value for customers and its branding, how can you describe that in three words? What do we look like in 2020? How do we look in 2022, how do we look in 2025?' This mental framework encouraged participants to think about where we actually want to go and how we want to be perceived in the future. This process is not finished. But I notice that the thinking, 'We care about today, we care about tomorrow, we care about the future, and we invite you to participate in iterations' is something important right now. In a crisis, you have to take short-term actions where the work council's co-determination also has to be incredibly flexible. This balance and dialogue have brought us further and closer together.

You are the chairman of a local market organization of a global group. How do the different levels—global, European and DACH—relate to each other?

IBM makes great efforts to create a framework for all challenges that can then be adapted in the markets. When the lockdown started, it was more of a bottom-up process. Each local company implemented the appropriate lockdown measures at individual speed. Now, when you start easing the restrictions, we want to balance between IBM's philosophy and what each country region dictates. We built the

(continued)

framework for that globally. The local experience we have gained in crisis management has been brought together at headquarters in a framework that we now share
with policymakers and our clients. According to this global IBM framework, we are
moving forward. However, it is up to the local markets to decide which location
should move first from what is known as Phase 0 to the next phase. Here, we are
moving at the pace that our customers and the respective market demand of us.

What was also important to you personally in the last few weeks?

Personally, it was important to me to ensure an open and empathetic communication. The people I addressed should notice that I was just as affected. When I started
in my current position in January, I did classic roadshows, visited subsidiaries, and
was in Switzerland and Austria. The lockdown brought a certain asymmetry. Some
employees already had the opportunity to meet the management in person and others
did not. At the end of March, we therefore introduced the video series 'A conversation with...', which is published twice a week. In this series, I always conduct a video
interview on different topics and meet with different people from the company. Right
at the beginning, for example, I interviewed our company doctor about Corona. The
series has an amazingly high number of clicks and a very good response. Above all,
this is because I really try to address the employee really personally.

You are doing this from your home office?

Yes, this is broadcast from my home office. It may also be fun now and then. Once
someone recognized a bottle of cognac in the background. After that, I picked up on
it and showed the kitchen or where I live with my family. The viewers always
discover something private. They comment on it and make it into what everyone
feels: You can no longer completely separate the private from the professional. You
have to find a way here. Sometimes you have to ask people to simply turn off the
camera—I do that too. Or also keep saying, 'Remember, you need something in your
environment to support you.' In my case, it is the espresso machine or the ergometer I
put in my apartment so I can exercise in between. Employees notice things like that
and they realize: 'Actually, he has the same challenge to overcome as we do.'

What do you recommend to your managers in the current situation?

What I strongly recommend is to keep in touch. We call it 'stay connected'. You
have to communicate with people more often. In this, it is important for leaders to
also show emotions and to schedule times for the interpersonal exchange: e.g. to
organize a video meeting once in a while, which is not about business, but about the
small talk that you would have in the cafeteria. I recommend these breaks because it
gives back what is missing, when you are always rushing from one video conference
call to another. And very importantly, leaders need to be clear about leading by
example. That means talking more about solutions, keeping a positive mindset and
not lamenting. In short: that you remain human on the one hand and show emotions,

(continued)

but at the same time think about how you can convey a certain power and motivation in the conversation. And finally, this also applies to me: we are all not TV stars. That means you also have to show a certain modesty, you can't be perfect. That's what makes it authentic.

How do you support your customers in the current exceptional situation?

One example: IBM was forced to redesign the big annual THINK conference in San Francisco into a digital event—the biggest digital event in our history. It worked out wonderfully. Here in Germany, Austria, Switzerland, we also converted a traditional format, where our top customers meet twice a year, into an online event. There was an exchange of experiences, impulse lectures and surveys. We used all available technical options for this. The participants' view of the current situation was interesting: the switch to remote was a problem for very few of them. However, the companies were much more concerned with the question of how to further develop their culture based on the current experiences. The rapid adoption of digital tools has shown that we are technically equipped to collaborate. But what does it mean culturally? If we spark this dialogue as IBM, we can provide input and discuss it together. In doing so, our clients win and so do we, because we want to find a sustainable basis for culture and collaboration. This can be a hybrid model—i.e. not completely back to the office. This hybrid approach can significantly increase the robustness and flexibility of organizations as a whole and bring new ideas. Our customers also want to keep working on this. Because if there is another pandemic, we need to be more resilient.

How does IBM master the tension between crisis management and preparing the company for the time after the crisis?

You call it a tension, which would be an extreme stretch. I do not feel that. In fact, I am convinced that it is precisely the coexistence of both that is incredibly necessary in order to maintain the balance: On the one hand, we have to react to changes in the market that cannot be predicted at this point of time. We ask ourselves everyday: Are we on the right track? On the other hand, we strategically move forward. After all, that's what people need. If you feel you are only reacting, then you miss the creative part. But if you only rave in the distance, you have nothing to take care off in the here and now. For me, the two sides go together. As IBM we always engage in changing the world which you can see e.g. in the way our research and development works. We already have it in our genes to optimize the here and now while building innovations and visions for tomorrow. This is peaceful coexistence of both paradigms.

Gregor Pillen, thank you very much for the interview!

Looking ahead helps to see the light at the end of the tunnel—this is a core element of leadership in the crisis at IBM. Gregor Pillen and his leadership team achieve this by acting in *unison*: they react to the here and now and *at the same time,* together with employees and clients, they look to the future after the crisis. In this balance and in this dialogue, when everyone is already working on the new picture of the future, Pillen sees the key to being able to make crisis management and decision-making faster and more effective, while at the same time allowing a new working world to emerge.

For this coexistence, the continuous work with *both* worlds, IBM exploits a variety of communicative options and shows that even in an almost completely virtual collaboration with 95% value creation from the home office, the physical and haptic world plays a role. In the home office, e.g., the virtual and physical worlds merge, supported by posters in the background of the video conferences. At the same time, the boundaries between the professional and private worlds are gradually dissolving. It is the conscious handling of these circumstances that helps to draw boundaries nevertheless. It is important to support employees in establishing a healthy balance.

What ultimately drives IBM and its clients is the question of what a new corporate culture can look like after the crisis, one that brings more resilience and flexibility to organizations. It seems to be best to keep to a hybrid model of coexisting worlds!

Peaceful Coexistence! Building an Ambidextrous Culture
1. **Merging the virtual and physical worlds of work**
   → Consciously work with virtual and physical/haptic elements in communication, play with both worlds.
   ✓ Establish and maintain a connection with employees and support them in virtual communication in the home office.
2. **Boundaries between private and professional life become blurred**
   → Consciously address this circumstance, support employees in finding the balance and creating spaces for both
   ✓ Thus increase the robustness of all
3. **Navigating in the here and now and building the future at the same time**
   → Conscious integration of both aspects in the daily work routine
   ✓ By looking ahead, necessary measures are better accepted in the here and now, preparations for the future after the crisis start immediately, robustness for future crises grows ◄

6.8   Conclusion: Fearless Through the Crisis, Ready for the Leap

Does the virus really eat up good leadership? Or does good leadership empower firms to emerge stronger from the crisis? In six interviews with experts and top managers from the German corporate landscape this chapter documented the exceptional situation of the first Corona Lockdown in Germany in 2020. In the conversations, the insight prevailed: Those who lead ambidextrously, hold the key to a resilient, adaptable organization that flexibly finds ever new solutions and thus stands stable in times of crisis (Fig. 6.2).

Fig. 6.2 With ambidexterity through the crisis!

In the Crisis: Leading Ambidextrously in Areas of Tension

During the first days of an acute crisis, trenches quickly open up for leaders: Do I immerse myself in problem solving? Or do I pay close attention to people's concerns? Do I communicate clearly and top-down the next steps or do I address the many questions of the teams? How do I create a sense of purpose and belonging in the face of simultaneous cost-cutting measures and short-time work? How do I keep the business running when it is completely unclear what will happen next? In the midst of all these areas of tension, leadership itself quickly finds itself in crisis. Unless, as the interviews concluded, one picks up on the contradictions and *consciously* works with them in an *ambidextrous approach*.

The Backpack of Experience

In addition, ambidexterity means consistently using the new insights and experiences *after the crisis*. Now it is time to take up the changes among employees, customers and partners and build a new future. The direction is now clearly forward, the backpack is bulging with new experiences. In fact, there is no single recipe for the new future of companies. Yet, the following ingredients were repeatedly recommended by the interview partners and by experts from science and practice against the background of the COVID 19 crisis:

Seven Impulses for the Time After the Crisis
1. **People**
   Empathy, cohesion, sense of purpose: In times of crisis, employees seek support from leaders [12]. The central recommendation of all interviews is to consciously maintain connections with employees in a state of emergency—and more so than before in the environment of digital channels and platforms. Creating opportunities for communication and interaction becomes a key leadership competency in everyday life, combined with a focus von people and purpose. While in the acute crisis situation it is important to redirect people from panic to meaningful action [12], e.g. by focusing on the values of a family business or initiating aid projects or innovation projects, the shift from profit to purpose is also seen as a strong driver of entrepreneurial action in the long term. According to Julian Birkinshaw [14], it will be "purpose" and social issues that will keep organizations running in the future. A vision that is aligned with this will help companies to get better through the next crisis.

2. **Digitization**
   End-to-end digitalization + digital ecosystems: The Corona crisis has been a catalyst for the digitization of business processes of organizations. It also made visible which areas of value creation have been neglected in the digitization efforts of the recent months and years. Digital value creation and the management of data flows are becoming ever more important in the face of a global, networked virtual economic world.
   In addition, the crisis is making digital ecosystems leap in importance, explains London Business School Professor of Innovation Management Michael Jacobides [20]. Companies whose value proposition focuses on creating connections and networking will emerge from crises significantly stronger: "These firms who have created the web of relationships will have an even stronger hold" [20]. The way we connect in the future—with work, with health services, with government, etc. will be determined by digital platforms. Now more than ever, we need to engage and connect with platforms that are changing the world.

3. **Decision-Making**
   Short decision cycles, high agility: During the crisis, company managements and decision-makers have proved that they can make quick, pragmatic decisions and set the organization in motion in the shortest possible time. Clarity, consistency, speed and commitment are the qualities in demand here. However, the dramatically shortened decision-making cycles are not only needed during the crisis, but also urgently *afterwards in* the global and increasingly fierce competition. Agility and speed must remain an integral part of the organization, management and processes (see Sect. 6.6).

(continued)

4. **Dual Operating System**

   Balancing top-down and bottom-up structures: During the weeks of the first lockdown the balance of power has shifted and has changed the way how organizations work together. Hierarchies and top-down communication were the means of choice for quickly establishing safe working conditions, for moving the workforce to the home office, securing business operations, and distributing company-wide information on a daily basis. According to Julian Birkinshaw, hierarchies play a crucial role in mobilizing an organization in the shortest possible time. Only a central authority can achieve the level of joint action required in an emergency [14].

   At the same time, the teams were forced to react quickly and organize themselves bottom-up from the very beginning. They were confronted with a significant increase in responsibility in the home office. What could be observed here was a shift from formal authority to the personal responsibility of the individual and the emergence of completely new structures.

   Birkinshaw emphasizes: Crisis management means achieving the right balance between the two (see also Sect. 6.5). An organization that pursues only one side will have problems [14]. A coexistence of the operating systems *hierarchy and network* (see Sect. 5.1), on the other hand, has proven its worth.

5. **Cooperation**

   Virtual, self-organized team-work: Just a few days after of the first lockdown in Germany, the world's largest internet hub in Frankfurt reported a new record data throughput and a 120% increase in video conference traffic [21]. The lockdown has fueled trends towards an agile working world. Digital tools, virtual jam sessions, online workshops across company boundaries—the technical prerequisites for virtual collaboration have been met and have quickly established themselves in everyday working life.

   Whether it is orchestrating interactions, managing attention, or dealing with technology: Even if digital tools had already been in use before Corona, collaboration that has moved completely to the internet now requires new technical and social skills from leaders [22]. It also means redefining roles and responsibilities and supporting teams in self-organization. For it was precisely the increase in responsibility in the teams during the lockdown that led to rapid progress and, in many places, new ideas for projects and ways of working.

   Collaboration and teamwork are the key here: Success is achieved by those who collaborate in a team and in a network. This approach—strengthening cooperation where possible and pursuing joint success, in short: "ecosystem before ego system"—will also be relevant for the competitive advantage in the future.

(continued)

6. **Partnering**

   Cross-company cooperation: Reliable cooperation across company boundaries has emerged as a competitive advantage during the crisis. Anyone who only looks at their own company in the crisis and in the future will be left behind in a globally networked world of digital platforms. At the latest, this will happen in the next pandemic. However, if you as an individual company keep an eye on the stability of your entire value creation network and ensure that all partners in the network remain efficient, you will be much better prepared for the global competition as well as for crisis situations [23].

7. **Vision**

   New vision of the future / new value proposition: Will we go back to normal after all? Certainly not. Organizations will adapt to further, perhaps more frequent and also more severe disruptive influences. The strategic resilience described by Julian Birkinshaw [14] will be achieved by firms who work with the experiences from the crisis. When they rebuild their company vision into one of a resilient organization of the future they will remain relevant to their stakeholders in the long term (see Sect. 5.3.3.1). Against the background of the 2-month lockdown and the knowledge that people's habits change after an average of 66 days [24], we should carefully analyze the new expectations of stakeholders and the changed behavior of our competitors. How will they think, act, consume? The experiences of the interviewees show that it is important to stay in touch with your employees, customers and partners as a company management. Despite the hardships and losses of the global COVID-19 pandemic, new opportunities (or necessities) for value propositions will emerge. Perhaps we will even find new types of network organizations, as a result of the changing stakeholder behavior. People will be more open to accepting new approaches. In the best case, our systems will become even stronger as a result of the experience of the crisis [14]. ◀

Conclusion: With Ambidexterity Through the Crisis

The seven impulses are a recommendation for action to take the leap into the future. What we have learned for the moment of the exceptional situation is: We have to play *two* games. That of the present and that of the future. Just like the interviewees in this chapter, London Business School professor Michael Jacobides concludes about crisis management in the COVID-19 crisis, "What we have to do is balance—playing two games." It is about "survival" *and* about "rebirth" [20]. It is about the light in the tunnel and at the same time about sowing the green meadow after the tunnel (see motif of the interviews on the crisis Sects. 6.3 and 6.7). So let us tackle *both* activities with **double ambidexterity** in order to successfully build a resilient future organization (Table 6.5).

Table 6.5 "Playing two games"

1. With ambidexterity through the crisis	2. Preparing the leap into the future
Building behavioral and operational resilience	**Building strategic resilience**
= Light in the tunnel	= Green meadow after the tunnel
– Providing security, fulfilling duty of care – Leading confidently through areas of tension – Securing today's business operations and innovation projects – Making quick decisions – Communicating transparently, creating proximity – Listening, leading empathically – Supporting people in the home office – Conveying purpose + cohesion – Discussing the future together	– Identifying new needs/behaviors of customers, partners, employees, competitors – Building a vision of the future with new fields of action based on the experience of the crisis and new stakeholder needs (cf. 7 impulses) – Embedding the vision of the future in digital ecosystems and platforms – Anchoring the new path in vision, mission, strategy (reposition and invest) and communicating the new path
Resilient organization through double ambidexterity	

References

1. "Der Erreger, der die ganze Welt trifft". Sonderseite von ZEIT Online zum Coronavirus SARS-COV-2. Online: https://www.zeit.de/thema/coronavirus [Accessed: 10.05.2020].
2. "Showdown zum Lockdown". ZEIT Online, April 15, 2020. Online: https://www.zeit.de/wissen/gesundheit/2020-04/ausgangsbeschraenkungen-coronavirus-lockdown-schulen-betriebe-bildungseinrichtungen-oeffnung-deutschland [Accessed: 10.05.2020].
3. "Lockdown in Deutschland. Die Langzeitfolgen für die Wirtschaft". ZDF Frontal 21, April 14, 2020. Online: https://www.zdf.de/politik/frontal-21/lockdown-und-die-wirtschaftlichen-langzeitfolgen-100.html [Accessed: 10.05.2020].
4. "Virus frisst Grundrechte", Süddeutsche Zeitung vom 28.03.2020. Online: https://www.sueddeutsche.de/politik/eingriffe-virus-frisst-grundrechte-1.4859550 [Accessed: 09.05.2020].
5. "Grundrechte in Corona Zeiten". ZDF heute, April 20, 2020. Online: https://www.zdf.de/nachrichten/politik/coronavirus-grundrechte-infektionsschutzgesetz-100.html   [Accessed 17.05.2020].
6. "Corona-Krisenmanagement von Unternehmen ist ausbaufähig", Springer Professional, April 3, 2020. Online: https://www.springerprofessional.de/fuehrungsqualitaet/corona-krise/corona-krisenmanagement-von-unternehmen-ist-ausbaufaehig/17859222 [Accessed: 10.05.2020].
7. Das Krisen-Management ist ausbaufähig. Reaktion auf Corona. FAZ, March 27, 2020. Online: https://www.faz.net/aktuell/karriere-hochschule/buero-co/arbeitgeber-reaktion-auf-corona-nur-bedingt-zufriedenstellend-16699506.html [Accessed: 10.05.2020].
8. Holzwarth, Constanze (2020): https://www.constanzeholzwarth.com and https://twitter.com/drholzwarth [Accessed: 16.05.2020].
9. Knight, Rebecca (2020): "How to Handle the Pressure of Being a Manager Right Now". Harvard Business Review vom April 30, 2020. Online: https://hbr.org/2020/04/how-to-handle-the-pressure-of-being-a-manager-right-now? [Accessed: 22.05.2020].

10. HALLESCHE (2020): Geschäftsbericht 2019. Online: https://www.alte-leipziger.de/-/media/ dokumente/berichte/geschaeftsberichte/hallesche/geschaeftsbericht_hallesche_2019.pdf? la=de&hash=B648F3FEB9243CCDEEE47ED89F0F6050814EE8F2 [Accessed: 03.05.2020].
11. MANN+HUMMEL (2019): Geschäftsbericht 2018. Online: https://www.mann-hummel.com/ fileadmin/corporate/04_Unternehmen/1_Wir%20%C3%9Cber%20Uns/5_Unternehmensdaten/ Gesch%C3%A4ftsberichte/M_H_GB2018.pdf [Accessed: 03.05.2020].
12. Goodson, S.; Demos, A.; Dhanaraj, C. (2020): "Shift your Organization from Panic to Purpose". Harvard Business Review, April 27, 2020. Online: https://hbr.org/2020/04/shift-your-organiza tion-from-panic-to-purpose [Accessed: 22.05.2020].
13. Pahl, Karin (2020): http://www.karinpahl.de [Accessed: 16.05.2020].
14. Birkinshaw, Julian (2020): "Coping with a pandemic: from strategic agility to resilience". London Business School Pandemic Webinars. Online: https://www.london.edu/campaigns/executive- education/pandemic-webinars#previouswebinars [Accessed: 22.05.2020].
15. Accenture (2020): Resilienz: Was Ihre Mitarbeiter jetzt brauchen. Online https://www.accenture. com/de-de/about/company/leadership-during-coronavirus [Accessed: 17.05.2020].
16. Über Accenture Deutschland. Online: https://www.accenture.com/de-de/about/company/about- germany. [Accessed: 09.05.2020].
17. Riemensperger, Frank; Falk, Svenja (2019): Titelverteidiger. Wie die deutsche Industrie ihre Spitzenposition auch im digitalen Zeitalter sichert. München: Redline. Online: https://www. accenture.com/de-de/about/events/titelverteidiger-buch [Accessed: 16.05.2020].
18. Accenture (2020): COVID-19: Mit den Folgen für Mensch und Unternehmen umgehen. Online: https://www.accenture.com/de-de/about/company/coronavirus-business-economic-impact [Accessed: 17.05.2020].
19. IBM (2019): IBM Annual Report. Online: https://www.ibm.com/annualreport/assets/downloads/ IBM_Annual_Report_2019.pdf [Accessed: 10.05.2020].
20. Jacobides, Michael (2020): "Surviving past survival mode: learning from successful turnarounds and what this new crisis may bring". London Business School Pandemic Webinars. Online: https://www.london.edu/campaigns/executive-education/pandemic-webinars#previouswebinars [Accessed: 09.04.2020].
21. DE-CIX (2020): "We are all online: Internet in the times of Corona". Pressemitteilung vom 21. April 2020. Online: https://www.de-cix.net/en/about-de-cix/news/we-are-all-online-internet-in- the-times-of-corona [Accessed: 22.05.2020].
22. Raffoni, Melissa (2020): "5 Questions That (Newly) Virtual Leaders Should Ask Themselves". Harvard Business Review vom 01.05.2020. Online https://hbr.org/2020/05/5-questions-that- newly-virtual-leaders-should-ask-themselves [Accessed: 22.05.2020].
23. Gallien, Jeremy (2020): "Supply chain resiliency: a path to corporate wisdom". London Business School Pandemic Webinars. Online https://www.london.edu/campaigns/executive-education/ pandemic-webinars#previouswebinars [Accessed: 22.05.2020].
24. Lally, van Jaarsveld, Potts, Wardle (2009): How are habits formed: Modelling habit formation in the real world. In: European Journal of Social Psychology 40. S. 998-1009. Online: http:// repositorio.ispa.pt/bitstream/10400.12/3364/1/IJSP_998-1009.pdf [Accessed: 22.05.2020].

How to Take Action

7

Abstract

How can leaders drive the digital transformation? How do you lead through a crisis? Which methods are best suited to make the leap into the digital future? There are numerous studies and projects that have comprehensively explored the period of change of the digital transformation. The approach presented in this book differs from previous publications by starting at a critical point in everyday work life: the daily communication of leaders. Communication creates corporate culture. It drives innovation. And it can change the mindset of an entire organization. This chapter summarizes how leaders can use their communicative actions to make innovation happen in the midst of today's core business. In this final section of the book, the individual chapters and their respective findings are linked to form an overall picture of ambidextrous leadership.

7.1 Communication Is the Most Important Leadership Tool

Evolution or revolution? *Both is* required of organizations in times of digitalization. Operating in opposite worlds at the same time is a balancing act that demands a great deal of flexibility and adaptability from people in organizations. Corporate success today requires that leaders master *both*: that they can navigate the evolution *and* the revolution. In the period of digital transformation, leadership means orchestrating both, the present and the future.

The approach presented in this book differs from numerous other studies and findings in that it starts at a critical point of companies: the daily communication of their leaders. Communication creates corporate culture. It drives innovation and can change the mindset of an entire company.

© Springer-Verlag GmbH Germany, part of Springer Nature 2022
J. Duwe, *Ambidextrous Leadership*,
https://doi.org/10.1007/978-3-662-64032-6_7

If you have arrived at the "two-world" space at the end of this book, it is best to stay right there. Whether artificial intelligence, cloud computing, blockchain technology, machine learning as a service or API economy... in the upcoming years and decades, the leaps in technology and the brand new digital business models that are possible as a result will multiply or *X-fold*. At the same time, the behavior of users and the forms of collaboration in companies will change and evolve dramatically—also fueled by drastic events such as the COVID-19 crisis. Our journey will thus continue and head toward an **X-world space....**

Customer Obsession

"Mass personalization", "hyperpersonalization" and "business to user" are the buzzwords that companies are confronted with today and in the future. Through networking and digitalization, companies move closer together in their value creation with the aim of satisfying ever more individual customer demands [1]. Amazon CEO Jeff Bezos sees "customer obsession", the "obsessive customer focus" as the *only* way for large organizations to remain successful in the long term [2]. Offering highly personalized customer experiences will fundamentally change the way companies innovate: "It is not pure technology innovations that will secure the company's competitive advantage, but rather new value propositions that put the customer's individual benefits first" [1].

Achieving customer benefits, requires a more open approach to business models that are designed not only for a single company but for a *network of partners in an ecosystem*. The idea of cross-company collaboration between companies must therefore be put to the center, because in the world of business ecosystems, company boundaries play a subordinate role from the user's point of view. In order to provide common interfaces and solution spaces for the customer, companies will increasingly focus on collaboration and "follow a common vision to provide value for the customer. In doing so, a ... keystone or shaper of the ecosystem sets the direction and provides the platforms and tools and utilities necessary to realize the value" [1].

The COVID 19 crisis (see Chap. 6) has also shown: companies get more resilient when they invest in their partnerships and pay increased attention to the orchestration of the performance in their ecosystem. Our current understanding of leadership and collaboration will completely reinvent itself for the digital, data-driven world and for unpredictable events such as the global Corona pandemic. Even in an environment of crisis, it is important to open up and think and act beyond corporate boundaries.

As a key player in the market, you will increasingly lead and influence other market participants that are *outside of your* direct influence. In this environment, cross-company network and ecosystem management will become a key leadership competency. Orchestrating new customer demands, digital technologies and business models as well as a new way of collaboration in the "X-world" space will become your very personal day-to-day business.

Communication Is the Most Important Leadership Tool

In a world of digital ecosystems and partnerships you will need a spirit of experimentation, a willingness to take risks, and the courage to try out new things. What helps is a culture of entrepreneurship, as underlined by the concluding interview in this book. According to Ronald Gleich, Professor of Management Practice & Control at the Frankfurt School of Finance & Management in Frankfurt am Main, the most important means for leading in this volatile environment is *communication*.

"A culture of entrepreneurship is more important than ever".

Interview with Prof. Dr. Ronald Gleich, Professor of Management Practice & Control at the Frankfurt School of Finance & Management in Frankfurt/ Main, Germany.

What do you think is the essence of ambidextrous leadership?

In the digital transformation, a culture of entrepreneurship is more important than ever. If you want to make radical innovation happen, you need visionary people who are willing to experiment and who take risks despite their company's focus on short- and medium-term profits. You need people who have the courage to break new ground and who are able to reset and start from scratch. Companies today are forced to manage this balancing act between their core business and a rapidly growing digital ecosystem business. This is only possible with a leadership team that acts and thinks in both directions.

How can we act in both directions?

Whereas the continuous improvement of an existing product portfolio requires a strategy-induced and top-down management approach, radical innovations require completely different, much more decentralized bottom-up approaches that drive creativity and solution-finding processes. Integrating both worlds at the same time in everyday life only becomes possible through a leadership and communication style that pays attention to the specific innovation context.

Why is communication suitable for this?

The most important leadership instrument in everyday life is, after all, communication. The way leaders communicate with each other and with employees has a strong influence on the motivation, ways of thinking, behavior, mutual understanding, trust, and thus also on the success and performance of innovation teams.

How is communication related to innovation?

Through the way leaders communicate and interact, they significantly shape the innovation practice and the respective culture. They can help and support teams to develop new ideas by means of a moderating, network-oriented communication style. Or they can push them toward a fast and efficient implementation of tasks by

(continued)

means of clear, top-down instructions. Depending on the innovation context, top-down leadership can coexist naturally with decentral communication structures.

How does this balancing act work?

When the senior management team openly protects and promotes both strategic directions a company can more easily cope with this tension. To achieve this balance, it is necessary to communicate a powerful vision that attracts and connects efforts and teams from both worlds. It is really important to keep focusing on the exchange between exploration and exploitation and the creation of synergies—which is above all a top management responsibility. If leaders want to successfully drive radical and incremental innovation, they must clearly communicate the necessity of both and emphasize the 'raison d'être' for both strategic fields of action.

Professor Gleich, thank you very much!

7.2   The Six Essences of Ambidextrous Leadership

To give you a comprehensive picture of ambidextrous leadership, this book takes three different perspectives: a theoretical perspective (1), a training and learning perspective (2), and finally a practical perspective (3). In the second edition of Ambidextrous *Leadership, a* chapter on leadership and crisis management has been added.

The approach of the book is based on scientific research on organizational ambidexterity. It provides a comprehensive insight into the current concepts of sequential, structural and contextual ambidexterity. The communication-centered approach presented against this background is based on a research study on the communication behavior of senior managers in the high technology sector of Germany's Industry 4.0. *Ambidextrous leadership* is furthermore based on the leadership training developed in addition to the book. For the practical perspective, expert interviews have been conducted exclusively for this book with managers from various industries and organizations.

By focusing on the everyday activities of managers in companies, *Ambidextrous Leadership* offers you concrete starting points that you can begin with tomorrow. The essences of the individual chapters are summarized below.

The Essences of Chaps. 1–6:
1. In the digital transformation, ambidexterity is a central leadership competence.
2. Leaders achieve ambidexterity through their communication. There are two natures of communication, a mediating nature and a reality-creating nature.
3. Communication-based ecosystem management enables leaders to tap into the blue ocean of new digital solutions (exploration).

(continued)

> **The Essences of Chaps. 1–6:** (continued)
> 4. Formal, centrally controlled top-down communication in the organizational pyramid helps leaders to efficiently navigate the exploitation environment.
> 5. Ambidextrous leadership requires four additional steps: communicating an ambidextrous vision (1), communicating a dual strategy (2), integrating both worlds through communication (3), and reconfiguring and reconnecting resources from both worlds (4).
> 6. In a crisis, "double ambidexterity" increases the resilience of companies.

Chapter 1: The Trade-Off

In Chap. 1, we looked at examples of dual organizations that navigate through two worlds at this very moment. We looked at car manufacturers that transform into providers of digital mobility services. We were able to observe mechanical engineering companies that become partners for networked, intelligent automation solutions for Industry 4.0. How are these companies making the leap into the digital future, even though today's business still requires their full attention?

In his research on the "Innovator's Dilemma" Harvard professor Clayton Christensen explained the danger of successful companies that, while making profits with today's business, miss the moment to jump into the future. It is precisely when companies are in the black and sales are flourishing that they need to invest in new technologies—and *especially then,* when these new solutions disrupt current products and technologies [3]. In order to avoid falling into the innovator's dilemma, it is necessary to orchestrate both worlds equally well: the present and the future.

However, this effort to transform must first and foremost begin at the top of companies. Whether globalization, commoditization, digitization, shorter product life cycles, price wars or disruptive technologies—in a dynamic market and technology environment, board members, managing directors and senior managers must be prepared for the various external influences. They must efficiently drive the existing business and anticipate future business opportunities. All of this weighs heavily on leaders: they could oversleep digitalization or even slow down the transformation process altogether. So, what can we do to counteract this danger?

If leaders transform themselves into software and IT experts as quickly as possible, companies will still not make the leap into the digital future. Digital competence will also not emerge even if successful companies throw their familiar structures and processes overboard, dispense with hierarchies and fully embrace a start-up culture. Rather, companies will successfully master the digital transformation when their leaders are able to navigate today's world as well as the world of the digital future. When they involve and value the people in today's organization and at the same time lead them purposefully and courageously into a still uncertain future. When they celebrate the present and welcome the future at the same time.

▶ **Essence 1**
   In the digital transformation with its highly dynamic market and technology environment, ambidexterity is a key leadership competence. Leaders drive today's world and pave the way for the digital future at the same time. Ambidexterity must start at the executive level.

Chapter 2: Success Through Ambidextrous Communication

Chapter 2 has presented the central communication-based approach against this background. We first looked at what exactly happens in companies during the period of digitalization. To do this, we dived into the scientific concept of organizational ambidexterity and examined why ambidexterity is the only viable thought model for the period of digital transformation. In manufacturing companies, this period is defined by the simultaneous optimization of the existing hardware-oriented core business and the development of new digital solution spaces.

The nature of transformation and the period of ambidexterity have been explained in Fig. 2.1 as the overlap of two technology S-curves describing the degree of maturity. The replacement of an existing technology by its substitute technology is a transformation process that can last for many years and decades: In this period of change current solutions must carry us into the future until future solutions are ready to become a company's new cash cow. For this reason, an intensive examination of the transition period is necessary.

The concept of ambidexterity offers an excellent approach to transition—it can be used as a theoretical model as well as a practical guideline for everyday leadership. It supports leaders to navigate the exploration/exploitation trade-off during digital transformation and to facilitate a symbiotic coexistence of both. The balancing act will succeed if leaders follow *contextual* ambidexterity in offering appropriate strategies for communication depending on the situation.

For the transformation period, the phase of ambidexterity, leaders need specific patterns of action that create a balance between existing and new business areas. At the very top of the company, an identity and vision for the organization must be developed that is based on a dual strategy. The tensions that are caused by this must be balanced, and the tensions at all levels—technology, business model and organization—need to be actively dissolved.

In the digital transformation, it becomes obvious that leadership is different from a formal position and legitimate power. Leadership is independent from a positional authority granted by the company. It arises flexibly and dynamically from the interaction of the team members and it is based on leadership and orchestration skills rather than on formal positions. Communication and interaction between individuals and teams is moving to the center of decision-making processes. Leadership means to orchestrate the interaction processes through communicative actions. In a communication-centered understanding of leadership, however, leaders will have to distance themselves from a predefined role of the manager who is supposed to have the deepest expertise. Instead of one person knowing it all, knowledge unfolds in the communicative interaction within the team and a leader knows how to activate this mechanism.

Basically, leaders can work with the two natures of communication: On the one hand, communication serves the transmission of information and, on the other hand, it empowers the construction of reality (innovation). The first nature assumes that the information regarding a decision is already available and only needs to be distributed. The second nature of communication comes into play when you want new ideas to emerge and to be negotiated through communication. Especially for innovation processes it is important to know about both natures of communication, since there is an innovation-creating character of communication that reaches far beyond the mere transmission of information. As leaders we can use the knowledge of the two natures of communication in a targeted manner: for existing and as well as for new businesses.

Depending on the innovation context—exploitation or exploration—we have to act differently. Even in the midst of a hierarchical top-down culture of a traditional core business, we can establish internal ecosystems and decentral networks for innovation and new business. This is a use case for ambidextrous communication. Ambidexterity here goes far beyond combining patterns of action for exploration and exploitation. In addition, the whole picture with regard to existing and new business fields must be communicated to the employees of an organization through specific, balancing action.

▶ **Essence 2**

Leaders can apply ambidexterity by using different types of communication. There are two natures of communicative action: the transmission of information and the generation of knowledge through communicative interactions. We can use the two natures of communication "tailor-made" for radical and for incremental innovation and thus drive and balance both.

Chapter 3: Breaking New Ground

Chapter 3 deals with the topic of exploration. When it comes to building innovative new businesses, technologies and markets, the researchers Chan W. Kim and Reneé Mauborgne divide the global markets into a "blue and a red ocean" [4]. Red oceans are characterized by saturated markets, commoditization, and price wars. Companies in the blue ocean do not focus on the competitor but on the user experience. In contrast to the conventional idea of a trade-off between the lowest possible costs for the company and the greatest possible benefit for the customer, companies tap into the blue ocean when they both improve their cost structure and achieve added value for the customer. This is where digitalization comes into play; digital technologies can improve cost structure *and* customer value.

However, the decision for a Blue Ocean strategy leads to massive changes within organizations and their processes. Only a paradigm shift in core processes and routines will empower companies to enter radically new solution spaces that lead to a blue ocean of digital solutions. Yet, far too little attention is paid to the mechanisms of networks and ecosystems in companies. Innovation processes are still tailor-made for today's world. But how can companies play a major role in dynamic global business ecosystems if they do not think and act in adequate structures and processes themselves?

Instead of managing departments or divisions in the organizational pyramid, leaders are required to orchestrate value creation networks across divisions and disciplines. They have to build self-organizing cooperative value creation systems that generate customer benefit across the company and far beyond its boundaries.

Ecosystem management as a leadership skill is based on thinking and acting in communication and network structures. The leadership approach presented in this book is also referred to as *Ecosystem Thinking*. It describes a communication-centered approach to leadership in highly networked global markets, digital data- and service-oriented businesses, and individualized customer value.

If we want to create a culture of collaborative innovation, commercialization and marketing of digital innovations in ecosystems, leadership is responsible for connecting the dots. And communication must be the method of choice because ecosystem management *equals* communication management.

Communication-based frameworks such as design thinking or agile project management can additionally help you install an operating system that puts people and teams in companies in the driver's seat of digital transformation. While leaders say goodbye to the old "know-it-all"-management, they start using a structuring, facilitating approach so that innovative solutions and ecosystems can emerge and grow like a movement across the enterprise and beyond.

▶ **Essence 3**
   Ecosystem management and the implementation of an agile operating system helps
   leaders to tap into the blue ocean of new digital solutions (exploration). Ecosystem
   management is communication management. It is based on thinking and acting in
   communication and network structures.

Chapter 4: Improving Your Current Business
Chapter 4 gets back to the present and looks at the world of exploitation. In most cases, when companies talk about digital transformation, they tend to glorify the digital future. But shaping transitions also means leveraging the best of the known world and strengthening and advancing the existing successful organization. Despite the need to digitally transform your company, the world continues to revolve around your core business, around profitability, price competition, efficiency and cost reduction. Stanford professor and organizational theorist James March, who coined the term of the "exploration/exploitation trade-off" in the early 90s, explains: Exploitation creates value based on existing skills, knowledge, resources etc. It drives continuous improvement, efficiency, and speed [5]. In a formal, hierarchical organizational structure for exploitation, a rather authoritarian top-down management style often prevails. Margin and productivity are important metrics of strategy- and revenue-driven management control. Tight planning,

efficient decision-making processes, targeted implementation of strategic measures and a policy of stability and continuity are at the heart of corporate management for exploitation [6].

Although we are familiar with the world of the red ocean, we make far too little use of the opportunities that strictly organized communication offers. Communication is often a tool that can run *alongside* in everyday management. But in dynamic markets with price wars and competition, communication should be the *first* management tool to improve your intraorganizational efficiency. Whether you choose articles on the intranet, videos, podcasts or town hall event—in order to implement a strategy in the organization, centralized communication is an efficient means. Communication serves to transfer strategic information, clarity is achieved, and it leads people in the organization to take action. It is important to use communication tools consciously and effectively in order to lead the organization to a common understanding in the shortest possible time.

However, a precondition for centralized top-down communication is that managers *know the answer* and the right approach. Top-down management requires a high level of expertise on the side of the leaders, because in order to give clear instructions for action, they must know the right path. This tends to be the case in a rather stable environment of continuous development, where you build upon existing knowledge and resources. Top-down communication is most likely to succeed when the answers to problems are already available and it is *just a* matter of rolling out strategic measures.

Once this is met, you can start planning and organizing communication. Communication should firstly occur as a top-down distribution of information. Secondly, it should be formally and officially planned, and thirdly, control and coordination should be centralized. In this way information can be distributed quickly and efficiently through the hierarchical levels according to Shannon and Weaver's linear model of communication. Suitable means of communication for distributing official information are, for example, town-hall meetings, intranet articles, videos or notes, classic print media articles in employee magazines, podcasts, posts or blog contributions in social media up to official reporting in steering committee meetings with minutes taken. Always think of your communication activities as a campaign. As in an election campaign, it is important to repeat your messages over a certain period of time.

▶ **Essence 4**

Formal, centralized top-down communication in the "organizational pyramid" helps leaders navigate the exploitation environment. When it is clear what needs to be done and when it is only a matter of getting things done quickly and efficiently, you communicate the strategy top-down. This will bring power and speed to your team in the shortest possible time and establish a common understanding: One company, one voice.

Chapter 5: Connecting the Two Worlds

Chapter 5 leads us into the world of contextual ambidexterity when it comes to balancing exploitation and exploration. How does this trade-off turn into an elegant balancing act (see Sect. 6.7)? How can leaders successfully introduce new ways of thinking and innovating to a company and at the same time prioritize the existing business?

Whether it is incubators or innovation hubs—in large companies, separate organizational units for innovation outside of existing structures and processes have emerged in recent years. However, these spin-offs do not drive large companies into the future. More often than not it can be observed how large companies' collaboration efforts with their innovations units fail. The existing processes, the traditional culture, the slower pace are not made for the agile operating systems. At the same time, the existing structures are far too strong for people to dare to shake the foundations. But this is precisely where ambidextrous leadership begins. The two worlds do not connect by themselves. A clear commitment and the courage to transform must come from the top.

The reality of everyday corporate life also shows that senior managers in particular operate in an ambidextrous context. The more far-reaching a manager's influence, the more likely it is that multiple innovation approaches will be pursued in his or her division. Even if you have established *separate* worlds within your organization, such as separate business units for the existing business and the future business, you need to orchestrate both at the top level. At the very top, in the place where you oversee the present and the future, ambidexterity is *always* contextual in nature. That is, you are confronted with both *every single day.*

Ambidextrous leadership now demands far more from you than the ability to safely navigate one environment and the other. What is required of senior leaders is to bring both worlds together: You need a connecting and balancing approach to the "two-world space". For you as a leader, the context in which you operate can change every moment. You are expected to move between the worlds as the context changes. And this is a stressful field of action for leaders as they need to have a high level of behavioral (and also cognitive) ambidexterity. To solve this constant tension, four core elements can support ambidextrous behavior:

1. Ambidextrous leaders communicate a strong and inclusive vision of the future.
2. They continuously communicate a dual strategy that addresses both worlds.
3. They bring both worlds together through communication.
4. And they create profitable new organizational connections through communication.

The exercise of literally writing with both hands gave a first idea of what it means for organizations to change from the dominant hand to the non-dominant hand. This exercise was to better understand how people in organizations will feel when they go through the process of digital transformation. The experiences range from frustration to curiosity, from denial to confidence and optimism. And the full range is what you will deal with as a leader in an ambidextrous organization.

▶   **Essence 5**

Ambidexterity is more than the ability to navigate through exploitation and exploration. Ambidextrous leadership requires four additional steps: communicating a powerful "two-world" vision (1), communicating a dual strategy (2), connecting both worlds through communication (3), and reconfiguring and reconnecting the resources through communication (4).

Chapter 6: Ambidextrous Leadership in Times of Crisis

The Corona pandemic has challenged the robustness and resilience of leaders and organizations more than other crises before. How can leaders safely navigate their organizations through crises? What makes companies resilient in the long term? How does a new changed vision emerge that creates meaning in crisis and keeps organizations moving forward? The interview study in Chap. 6 takes us right into the middle of the COVID-19 crisis. In six interviews with persons from the German corporate landscape, the chapter documents the exceptional situation of the first months in 2020 in Germany. Between March and May, the experts shared their leadership experiences and insights into successful crisis management. They explained how ambidexterity helped them to develop resilience.

Interview 1: Ambidexterity = Navigating the Tensions

Constanze Holzwarth, psychologist and management consultant, describes different areas of tension in which organizations and people find themselves in cases of emergency. She explains the importance for leaders to quickly become aware of the conflicts that emerge from the exceptional circumstances (i.e. in the first 72 h of the first lockdown): Keeping contact to the teams *despite* reducing contact and organizing home office for the employees, being empathetic *despite* making rational decisions, making top-down announcements *and* offering time and space for questions and emotions. Simply identifying these extremes helps leaders to move more easily between the different modes and to reduce stress (see Sect. 6.2).

Interview 2: Ambidexterity = Start Rebuilding the Vision of Your Company as Soon as Possible

Wiltrud Pekarek, member of the board of HALLESCHE Krankenversicherung, explains why it is important to pay attention to the time after the crisis as soon as possible *after* having fulfilled one's duty of care and safeguarding business operations (core business + ongoing future projects). Those who leave it at managing the crisis will not catch up with the "New Normal" afterwards. To be prepared for the future companies have to rethink and rebuild their vision around the new normal as soon as possible (see Sect. 6.3).

Interview 3: Ambidexterity = Consistency Combined with Empathy, Purpose and Cohesion

In Interview 3, **Thomas Fischer** from MANN+HUMMEL emphasizes the importance of purpose and values of the family-owned business in the crisis. While you have to be clear and consistent in managing the crisis, empathetic leadership becomes just as crucial. The robustness of your company increases with growing cohesion—cohesion of the leadership team, cohesion of all employees. In order to successfully balance rational action and crisis management and empathic leadership, it is essential for leaders to take a step back during the crisis and to take moments to reflect (see Sect. 6.4).

Interview 4: Ambidexterity = Flexibility Is the Key to Stability

The expert for personal resilience **Karin Pahl** explores the stress test of the Corona pandemic for individual managers more deeply. As hardly seen before, the two corporate worlds collide in this crisis: the hierarchical world of top-down management and the world of agile working in virtual spaces. Both worlds are in a state of emergency. Both worlds are challenged to the utmost. And elements from both worlds are needed for managing the exceptional situation. Being able to switch back and forth flexibly and at the same time remain stable and capable of acting are the key resilient competencies of leaders at the moment of the Corona crisis. They achieve individual resilience by quickly becoming aware of their inner strengths during a crisis. Those who activate beneficial resources and mental strategies within themselves are able to always return to their original mental state after extreme external influences (Sect. 6.5).

Interview 5: Ambidexterity = No Way Back to Old Patterns. Take the Leap Now!

Frank Riemensperger from Accenture takes resilience to the organizational level. Companies will only be resilient in their day-to-day operations when the *entire* supply chain and the *entire* value network are resilient. In addition, ambidexterity against the background of a crisis means: There is no way back to old patterns! The crisis has changed companies. And this new, more resilient state must remain. Only those who now face up to the new conditions and develop a new vision for their company will stay competitive in the global economy. We need to keep the agility that helped us navigate the crisis and continue to work with these newly gained experiences (Sect. 6.6).

Interview 6: Ambidexterity = Both Worlds Belong Together

Gregor Pillen, IBM, finally resolves the tension of ambidexterity and transforms the balancing act into a harmonious play. During the crisis, Pillen designs an ambidextrous culture in which different worlds are allowed to merge: e.g., the conscious use of virtual *and* haptic elements of communication supports the rapid move of the employees to the home offices during the lockdown. At the same time, the new form of collaboration paves the way for a hybrid model in the future in which parts of the newly experienced working world can continue. In the ambidextrous culture, Pillen is also concerned with a *conscious* approach to the blurring boundaries: e.g. the seamless transition between professional and private spheres at home requires a conscious design and balance of the working conditions. Another element of the ambidextrous culture is the harmony between managing the present situation and rebuilding the vision for the future. Through a company-wide joint foresight in iterative steps, necessary measures as part of the crisis management are accepted more easily by the employees, because at the same time they are involved in preparing the time after the crisis. In this way, strategic resilience for future crises grows.

▶ **Essence 6**
  In a crisis, "double ambidexterity" increases the resilience of companies. In order to build a robust, resilient organization, leaders firstly need a high degree of flexibility in dealing with contradictions and tensions in the here and now. Secondly, they strengthen the resilience of their organization by starting to build a new vision of the company early on in the crisis and leading the organization towards this new vision.

And not only now—in the midst of the digital transformation and in times of crisis like the COVID 19 pandemic—companies need an ambidextrous understanding of leadership. On the technology, business model, culture and user side, there will be evolutionary advancements as well as radical disruptions in the coming months and years. At the same time, we need to prepare for other, yet unknown, health, financial, and economic crises that will require companies to be highly resilient.

So welcome to the "**X-world"-space**. You will find yourself permanently in a hybrid state. Because what comes after the digital transformation? What follows the current crisis? The next wave (or S-curve), the next global state of emergency is already waiting. Somewhere out there. And we will constantly need all hands and keep switching between proven routines and a beginner's mind....

7.3 Epilogue: Training the Beginner's Mind

In many successful organizations there is this very special spirit: The founding and entrepreneurial spirit of the early days. With this vitality and enthusiasm everything once began.

More than 20 years after founding of Internet company Amazon [7], CEO Jeff Bezos faces the question, "How do you keep the vitality of Day 1, even inside a large organization?" [2]. How can you stay in the mindset of new beginnings and not be tempted to let Day 2 of 'stagnation' and 'decline' set in? Maintaining the vitality and energy of day one "requires you to experiment patiently, accept failures, plant seeds, protect saplings, and double down when you see customer delight," [8] Bezos explains in one of his annual letters to the company's shareholders. Because if "Day 2" dawns, companies become slow. They then make excellent decisions, but too slowly. They focus on improving internal processes instead of customer value. But only true customer obsession, the obsessive focus on customer value, is what can best protect companies from the dawn of Day 2 [8].

That, on the other hand, the lightness of being a beginner again can lead to the greatest creativity (and that the success of large companies can become a burden) was also reported by Apple co-founder Steve Jobs. In his speech to graduates of Stanford University in June 2005, he described the time after he left Apple in 1985 as the most creative period in his life: "The heaviness of being successful was replaced by the lightness of being a beginner again, less sure about everything. It freed me to enter one of the most creative periods of my life" [9].

So, the goal must be to keep the mind of the beginner for many years. As soon as we know too much about something and know the answer too well, we make a different outcome or a new path impossible: "In the beginner's mind there are many possibilities, in the expert's mind there are only a few," explained Japanese Zen master Shunryu Suzuki in his teachings on the beginner's mind [10].

Perhaps this beginner's spirit is only quietly blowing through the corridors of your company at the moment. But if you reactivate it as a leader, if you always face company life anew as a beginner—especially in times of crisis—the spirit of the first day can blow through meeting rooms, cafeterias, offices and boardrooms again soon. It will rush through production halls and development labs and ensure that new ideas also find space in digital, virtual, global calls and meetups.

Wherever the spirit of the first day appears, it raises dust—even virtual dust—and brings back the energy of departure and the enthusiasm that we feel, when we design and build the future.

It helps leaders and teams through the unpredictable present and at the same time leads us into a new and different future. "We can have the scope and capabilities of a large company and the spirit and heart of a small one. But we have to choose it" [2], Jeff Bezos explains the secret of Amazon's success. So let us recapture the spirit of the early days and get started.

References

1. Bauer, Wilhelm; Leistner, Phlipp; Schenke-Layland, Katja; Oehr, Christian; Bauernhansel, Thomas; Morszeck, Thomas H. (2016): Mass Personalization. Mit personalisierten Produkten zum "Business to User" (B2U). Stuttgart: Fraunhofer Gesellschaft. Online: https://www.stuttgart.fraunhofer.de/de/studie_b2u.html [Accessed: 24.05.2020].

2. Bezos, Jeff (2017): 2016 Letter to Shareholders. Online: https://www.amazon.com/p/feature/z6o9g6sysxur57t [Accessed: 24.05.2020].

3. Christensen, C.M. (2011): The Innovator's Dilemma: Warum etablierte Unternehmen den Wettbewerb um bahnbrechende Innovationen verlieren. 2nd rev. edition. München: Franz Vahlen.

4. Kim, W. Chan; Mauborgne, Renée (2016): Der Blaue Ozean als Strategie. Wie man neue Märkte schafft, wo es keine Konkurrenz gibt. 2. aktualisierte und erweiterte Aufl. München: Carl Hanser. Online: https://www.blueoceanstrategy.com/tools/red-ocean-vs-blue-ocean-strategy/ [Accessed: 17.05.2020].

5. March, J.G. (1991): Exploration and Exploitation in Organizational Learning. Organization Science, 2 (1), p. 71–87.

6. O'Reilly, Charles A.; Tushman, Michael L. (2004): The Ambidextrous Organization. In: Harvard Business Review 82 (4), p. 74–81.

7. Amazon (2020): Annual Reports, Proxies and Shareholder Letters. Online: https://ir.aboutamazon.com/annual-reports-proxies-and-shareholder-letters/default.aspx [Accessed: 23.05.2020].

8. Bezos, Jeff (2017): "Tag 2 ist Stillstand. Gefolgt vom Tod." Jeff Bezos' Management Tipps – übersetzt. In: Handelsblatt vom 13.04.2017. Online: http://www.handelsblatt.com/unternehmen/management/jeff-bezos-management-tipps-uebersetzt-tag-2-ist-stillstand-gefolgt-vom-tod-/19669374.html [Accessed: 24.05.2020].

9. Jobs, Steve (2005): 'You've got to find what you love,' Jobs says. Commencement Address delivered by Steve Jobs on June 12, 2005 at Stanford University. Online: http://news.stanford.edu/2005/06/14/jobs-061505/ [Accessed: 24.05.2020].

10. Suzuki, Shunryu (2012): Zen-Geist, Anfänger-Geist. Unterweisungen in Zen-Meditation. 3. Aufl. Freiburg, Basel, Wien: Herder.

Printed in Great Britain
by Amazon

43959512R00139